WYE COLLEGE

(University of London)

SCHOOL OF RURAL ECONOMICS

FARM BUSINESS UNIT

Farm Management Pocketbook

by

JOHN NIX

(National Westminster Bank Professor of Farm Business Management)

with Paul Hill

FIFTEENTH EDITION

(1985)

SEPTEMBER 1984

Copies of this booklet may be obtained from Publications, School of Rural Economics, Wye College, near Ashford, Kent, TN25 5AH.

PRICE £3.50 (post free UK)
(12 to 49 copies: £3.25 post free UK)
(50 and over copies: £3.00 post free UK)
SBN 0 86266 009 2

FOREWORD TO THE FIRST EDITION

This booklet is intended for farmers, advisers, students and everyone else who, frequently or infrequently, find themselves hunting for data relating to farm management—whether it is for blunt pencil calculations on the back of an envelope or for feeding into a computer. The material contained is based upon the sort of information which the author finds himself frequently having to look up in his twin roles as adviser and teacher in farm management. There are several excellent handbooks already in existence, but this pocketbook endeavours to cover a wider field and thus to be substantially more comprehensive. It is intended that most of the data herein contained will have a national application, although there is inevitably some bias towards conditions in the south-eastern half of the country.

The development of farm planning techniques in recent years has outstripped the quality and quantity of data available. It is hoped that this booklet will go a little further in supplying the type of information required. It cannot, however, claim to be the ultimate in this respect. For example, there are many variations in labour requirements according to farm conditions and sizes and types of machine used and there are many more variations in sheep and beef systems than are dealt with here. More detailed data on these lines are gradually becoming available from various sources. It is hoped further to refine the material in this booklet and to keep it up to date in subsequent editions, as the information becomes available. As a help towards this end, any comments or criticisms will be gratefully received.

The author wishes to thank his many friends and colleagues who have given him so much time and help in compiling this information.

John Nix
October, 1966

First published October 1966
Fifteenth Edition   September 1984

iii

FOREWORD TO FIFTEENTH EDITION

Most of the figures in this edition have been revised compared with the fourteenth edition, produced last year. A few items have been left as they were, either because of lack of information or time. Many figures are given in imperial (in brackets), as well as in metric.

Several sections have been supplemented, *e.g.* grazing livestock units, interest rates, and the list of addresses included for the first time last year. More importantly, two new sections have been added: on forestry and "other crops". "Minority" crops and livestock are not normally included in this book, in order to keep down the length and cost. However, so much interest is currently being shown in these crops, as a result of the "threat" to cereals, etc., that it has been decided to include a few notes and figures on several of them, despite the limited evidence in most cases of likely results on commercial farms.

Most of the figures are predicted forward one year, *i.e.* to 1985. Thus the crops data relate to the 1985 harvest, *i.e.* the 1985/86 marketing year (N.B. not just, in the case of product prices, those prevailing at or just after harvest time). The livestock data relate either to the 1985 calendar year (*e.g.* for milk production) or to 1985/86 (*e.g.* for winter fattened beef), as appropriate. The estimates were made during the first half of the summer of 1984. In a few cases current (*i.e.* mid-1984) figures are given, where it seemed particularly difficult to try to forecast ahead. The year to which the figures relate is normally stated.

Most users of this book will hardly need telling that forecasting some of the prices has been far more difficult this year than for some years past—since the days when inflation was exceeding 20 per cent a year. Can milk prices possibly fall lower, in real terms, than they are now in mid-1984? How much effect on cereal prices will the high and increasing level of EEC production (especially of feed wheat) have, and to what extent will the "threats" (as far as arable farmers are concerned) of the politicians and EEC spokesmen be carried out, as regards reductions in intervention prices and the raising of intervention standards? Not easy to forecast!

The figures for yields and prices assume a "normal", or average, season, based on trends, *e.g.* for potatoes, looking 18-24 months ahead to 1985/86, no one can predict what the *actual* average yield and price for that particular year will be. Similarly with pig production: no attempt is made to predict the *actual* position of the pig cycle during 1985—only what the average trend figure is likely to be, in neither an "up" or "down" stage, given estimated changes in the relevant indices.

The data in this book should always be used with caution. *The figures should be adjusted as appropriate according to circumstances and price and cost differences.* As far as possible the assumptions in the tables are set out so as to enable this to be done fairly readily.

The authors wish to thank all those who assisted with this edition, and also those people who have been kind enough to write in with suggestions for desirable alterations. Such suggestions are always welcome.

John Nix
July, 1984

CONTENTS

I. GROSS MARGIN DATA

1. GENERAL NOTES

Definition. The Gross Margin of an enterprise is its enterprise output less its variable costs. Enterprise output includes the market value of production retained on the farm. The variable costs must (a) be specific to the enterprise and (b) vary in proportion to the size of the enterprise, i.e. number of hectares or head of stock. The main items of variable costs are: Crops: fertilizer, seed, sprays, casual labour and contract work specific to the crop. Non-Grazing Livestock: concentrate feed, vet. and med., marketing expenses. Grazing Livestock: as for non-grazing livestock, plus forage crop variable costs.

Points to Note about the concept are as follows:

1. The gross margin is in no sense a profit figure. The so-called "fixed costs" (rent, labour, machinery, general overheads—see pages 106-107) have to be covered by the total farm gross margin before arriving at a profit.

2. The gross margin of an enterprise will differ from season to season, partly because of yield and price differences affecting output and partly because variable costs may vary, e.g. the number and type of sprays required. Different soils and other natural factors, as well as level of management, will also cause differences between farms.

3. Items of variable cost may vary from farm to farm, e.g. some farmers use casual labour (a variable cost) to plant and pick their potatoes, others use only regular labour (a fixed cost); some farmers employ a contractor to combine their cereals (a variable cost), others employ their own equipment (a fixed cost); some employ a contractor to cart their sugar beet to the factory (a variable cost), others have their own lorry (a fixed cost). These differences must be borne in mind in making inter-farm comparisons.

4. Provided points 2 and 3 are borne in mind, comparison of gross margins (particularly averages over several seasons) with standards can be a useful check on technical efficiency.

5. The other main usefulness of gross margins lies in farm planning. This is not simply a matter of substituting high gross margin enterprises for low gross margin enterprises. The gross margin is only one relevant feature of an enterprise, although an important one. It says nothing about the call the enterprise makes on the basic farm resources—labour at different times of the year, machinery, buildings, working capital requirements, etc. All these factors and more have to be taken into account in the planning process.

1

6. This is not to argue that these other costs should be allocated. Complete allocation of many farm expenses is only possible on an arbitrary basis, since they are shared by two or more, possibly all, farm enterprises. Allocation can therefore be completely misleading when making planning decisions. The same is true even when regular labour and machinery are employed specifically on certain enterprises, if such costs are calculated on a per hectare or per head basis. This is because when enterprises are substituted, expanded, contracted or deleted the variable costs for each enterprise will vary roughly in proportion to the size of that enterprise, but other costs will not, except possibly for fuel and some repair costs. Most "fixed" costs may stay the same, others will change—but not smoothly in small amounts at a time. Either the same regular labour force will cope with a revised plan or a smaller or larger number of men will be needed. The same is true of tractors, other machines and buildings. Such cost changes must of course be taken into account, but allocating these costs on a per hectare or per head basis will not aid, and may positively confuse, planning decisions. The only point of making such calculations is for efficiency comparisons, e.g. labour costs per cow.

7. Allocating fixed costs at a flat rate (e.g. per hectare) for all enterprises, deducting this from the gross margin and hence calculating a "net profit" from each enterprise can also be misleading. It ignores the whole problem of enterprise inter-relationships, differences between enterprises in total and seasonal requirements for labour, machinery and capital, and other factors such as different quality land on the same farm.

8. Changes in the scale of an enterprise may well affect its gross margin per unit, e.g. increasing the area of winter wheat from 20 per cent to 40 per cent on a farm will mean some wheat being taken after wheat, and a smaller proportion of the crop being drilled under the best conditions; hence yields will in all probability fall. Even if yields remain the same, variable costs (e.g. fertilizer use) will probably increase.

9. Gross margins used for planning future changes should also take account of possible changes in price, and the effect of changes in production techniques.

Low, Average and High Levels

The three performance and production levels given for most crop and livestock enterprises are meant for the most part to indicate differences in natural factors, soil productivity, and/or managerial skill, *given the level of variable cost inputs*. They refer, at each level, to *an average over several years*.

2. CASH CROPS
WINTER WHEAT

Production level	Low	Average	High
Yield: tonnes per hectare (cwt. per acre) ...	4·9(39)	6·3(50)	7·7(61·5)
	£	£	£
OUTPUT: Feed Wheat	540(218)	695(281)	845(343)
Milling Wheat	590(238)	755(306)	925(374)

Variable Costs:			
Seed		40(16)	
Fertilizei		90(36·5)	
Sprays		70(28·5)	

TOTAL VARIABLE COSTS per hectare (acre)		200(81)	

GROSS MARGIN per hectare (acre)			
Feed Wheat	340(137)	495(200)	645(262)
Milling Wheat	390(157)	555(225)	725(293)

Notes

1. *Prices.* The price assumed in the above tables (for the 1985 harvest crop, averaged throughout the 1985/86 season) is £110 per tonne for feed wheat and £120 for milling wheat. In 1983/84 the differential between feed and milling wheat was very much higher than usual (£15 to £20 per tonne, compared with the more common £5 or so per tonne); this could continue. The intervention price for feed wheat increases from £113·05 per tonne in August 1984 to £127·36 in May 1985, a monthly increase of £1·59 per tonne. The intervention prices for bread wheat increase at the same rate from £121·72 in August 1984 to £136·03 in May 1985. It has been assumed in the above table that the yields of feed and milling wheat are the same. However, better quality varieties normally yield less than strictly feeding quality varieties, given the same conditions, treatment, etc.

2. *Straw* is not included above. Average yield is 2½ tonnes per hectare; value £10 to £30 per tonne according to region and season; variable costs (twine) approx. £4·00 per tonne.

3. *Sprays.* Costs exclude high cost specialized sprays, e.g. against wild oats and chemicals used prior to direct drilling.

4. If a *Contractor* is employed, extra variable costs (£ per hectare) will be approximately as follows:
   - Spraying: £12·50 (material included above)
   - Combine Drilling: £24
   - Combining: £63 (excluding carting)
     £78 (including carting)
   - Drying: £35 to £70 (according to yield and moisture content; transport one way is included; it is assumed that ⅔ of the crop needs to be dried)
   - Baling Straw: £30 (including twine).

5. *Fuel and Repairs* (per hectare): grain £47, straw £18.

6. *Specialized Equipment Prices:* see pages 89-91.

7. Yields: effect of break crop. The evidence concerning the effect of different types and lengths of rotational breaks on subsequent cereal yields is variable. As a rough guide, where no better evidence is available, it is suggested that first crop wheat yields might be 0·25 tonne (2 cwt.) above those quoted, and second and subsequent wheat crops might yield 0·25 tonne (2 cwt.) less than those given.

8. *Labour:* see page 68.

N.B.—Approximately 50% of home-grown wheat is used for animal feed and 42% for milling.

SPRING WHEAT

Production level	Low	Average	High
Yield: tonnes per hectare (cwt. per acre)	3·5(28)	4·4(35)	5·3(42)

	£	£	£
OUTPUT: Feed Wheat	385(156)	485(196)	585(236)
Milling Wheat	420(170)	530(214)	635(257)

Variable Costs:

Seed		50(20)	
Fertilizer		70(29)	
Sprays		40(16)	

TOTAL VARIABLE COSTS per hectare (acre)		160(65)	

GROSS MARGIN per hectare (acre)

	Low	Average	High
Feed Wheat	225(91)	325(131)	425(171)
Milling Wheat	260(105)	370(149)	475(192)

Notes

1. *Prices:* See Winter Wheat.

2. *Straw.* See Winter Wheat.

3. If a *Contractor* is employed, extra variable costs (£ per hectare) will be as shown for Winter Wheat (p. 3, note 4).

4. *Fuel and Repairs* (per hectare): grain £47, straw £18.

5. *Specialized Equipment Prices:* see pages 89-91.

6. *Labour:* see page 70.

N.B.—Only some 2% of the wheat in England and Wales is now spring-sown, and the proportion is still declining.

SPRING BARLEY

Production level	Low	Average	High
Yield: tonnes per hectare (cwt. per acre)	3·5 (28)	4·4 (35)	5·3 (42)
	£	£	£
OUTPUT: Feed Barley	375 (152)	475 (191)	570 (231)
Malting Barley	420 (170)	530 (214)	635 (257)
Variable Costs:			
Seed		40 (16)	
Fertilizer		60 (25)	
Sprays		30 (12)	
TOTAL VARIABLE COSTS		130 (53)	
GROSS MARGIN per hectare (acre)			
Feed Barley	245 (99)	345 (138)	440 (178)
Malting Barley	290 (117)	400 (161)	505 (204)

Notes
1. *Prices.* The price assumed in the above table (for the 1985 harvest crop, averaged throughout the 1985/86 season) is £107·50 per tonne for feed barley and £120 for malting barley. The malting premium was abnormally high in 1983/84; it is usually very high for the best malting barleys, especially early in the season, particularly Maris Otter samples with a low nitrogen content. Intervention prices for feed barley are as for feed wheat (p. 3). It has been assumed in the above table that the yields of feed and malting barley are the same. However, varieties intended definitely for malting normally yield less than strictly feeding varieties, given the same conditions, treatment, etc.
2. *Straw* is not included above. Average yield is 2 tonnes per hectare; value £10 to £30 per tonne according to region and season; variable cost (twine) approx. £3·30 per tonne.
3. *Fertiliser.* Costs on continuous barley will be approximately £14 higher.
4. If a *Contractor* is employed, extra variable costs will be as shown for Winter Wheat (p. 3, note 4).
5. *Fuel and Repairs* (per hectare): grain £47, straw £18.
6. *Specialized Equipment Prices:* see pages 89-91.
7. *Labour:* see pages 69-70.

WINTER BARLEY

Production level	Low	Average	High
Yield: tonnes per hectare (cwt. per acre)	4·1 (32·5)	5·3 (42)	6·5 (52)
	£	£	£
OUTPUT: Feed Barley	440 (178)	570 (231)	700 (283)
Malting Barley	490 (199)	635 (257)	780 (316)
Variable Costs:			
Seed		35 (14)	
Fertilizer		80 (33)	
Sprays		55 (22)	
TOTAL VARIABLE COSTS		170 (69)	
GROSS MARGIN per hectare (acre)			
Feed Barley	270 (109)	400 (162)	530 (214)
Malting Barley	320 (130)	465 (188)	610 (247)

Notes
As for Spring Barley above.

N.B.—The proportion of barley that is autumn-sown has been rapidly increasing in recent years. The Home-Grown Cereals Authority estimate that 62% was autumn-sown in 1983, compared with 52% in 1982. Just under 70% of home-grown barley is used for animal feed and approximately 25% for malting and distilling. On average about 25% of spring-sown barley is of malting quality; more than 40% of the UK production of malting barley is now likely to be exported.

SPRING OATS

Production level	Low	Average	High
Yield: tonnes per hectare (cwt. per acre):	3·5 (2·8)	4·4 (35)	5·3 (42)

		£	£	£
OUTPUT:	Feed Oats	365 (149)	460 (187)	555 (225)
	Milling Oats	405 (163)	505 (205)	610 (247)

Variable Costs:

Seed	45 (18)
Fertilizer	60 (25)
Sprays	20 (8)
TOTAL VARIABLE COSTS	125 (51)

GROSS MARGIN per hectare (acre):

	Low	Average	High
Feed Oats	240 (98)	335 (136)	430 (174)
Milling Oats	280 (112)	380 (154)	485 (196)

Notes

1. The (1984/85) price assumed in the above table is £105 per tonne for feed, £115 for milling.

2. *Straw* is not included above. Average yield is 2½ tonnes per hectare; value £10 to £30 per tonne according to region and season; variable costs (twine) approx. £3·30 per tonne.

3. If a *Contractor* is employed, extra variable costs will be as shown for Winter Wheat (p. 3, note 4).

4. *Fuel and Repairs* (per hectare): grain £47, straw £18.

5. *Labour:* see page 70.

WINTER OATS

Production level	Low	Average	High
Yield: tonnes per hectare (cwt. per acre):	4·0 (32)	5·0 (40)	60 (48)

		£	£	£
OUTPUT:	Feed Oats	420 (170)	525 (212)	630 (255)
	Milling Oats	460 (186)	575 (233)	690 (279)

Variable Costs:

Seed	45 (18)
Fertilizer	65 (27)
Sprays	25 (10)
TOTAL VARIABLE COSTS	135 (55)

GROSS MARGIN per hectare (acre):

	Low	Average	High
Feed Oats	285 (115)	390 (157)	495 (200)
Milling Oats	325 (131)	440 (178)	555 (224)

Notes

As for spring oats above.

N.B.—Probably about half the oats grown in the U.K. are spring and half winter; the proportion of the latter increases from north to south and probably exceeds 80% in the south of England.

MAINCROP POTATOES

Production level	Low	Average	High
Yield: tonnes per hectare (tons per acre) ...	25(10)	35(14)	45(18)
	£	£	£
OUTPUT	1650(670)	2310(935)	2975(1205)
Variable Costs:			
Seed		375(152)	
Fertilizer		225 (91)	
Sprays ,,, ...		125 (50)	
Casual Labour for picking		250(101)	
Sundries (P.M.B. levy, bags, etc.) ...	165 (66)	200 (81)	235 (96)
TOTAL VARIABLE COSTS	1140(460)	1175(475)	1210(490)
GROSS MARGIN per hectare (acre) ...	510(210)	1135(460)	1765(715)

Notes
1. *Prices.* The (1985/86) price assumed above is £70 per tonne for ware and £17·50 for chats (assumed to be 7½ per cent). Prices in 1983/84 were well above this level owing to a low average yield caused by a wet spring and therefore late planting. The "guaranteed" price for the 1984 harvest crop remains at only £43·94 per tonne.

   As a guide to the seasonal increase in prices needed to compensate storage costs and wastage, in 1982/83 growers had the chance to contract 15% or more of their crop to the Potato Marketing Board at the following prices (maincrops): mid-Oct.-Dec., £46 a tonne; Jan.-March, £50; April, £52; May/June, £54.

2. *Physical Inputs.* Seed: 80% planted with certified seed: 2·75 tonnes per hectare at £150 per tonne; 20% with once-grown seed: 2·25 tonnes per hectare at £100 per tonne. Sprays: herbicide, blight control, and haulm destruction.

3. *Casual Labour.* It has been assumed that casual labour is employed for picking behind a spinner or elevator-digger. Other jobs for which casual labour may be employed are.

Planting:	£50 per hectare
Picking on harvester:	£105 per hectare
Riddling:	£200 per hectare (£5·70 per tonne).

4. *P.M.B. levy* (1984). In addition to a levy of £37·60 per hectare a further £188·60 per hectare is charged for potatoes grown in excess of quota.

5. *Chitting.* Additional annual cost of chitting is approximately £26 per tonne of seed, or £70 per hectare, including depreciation and interest on the chitting house.

6. *Fuel and Repairs* (per hectare): £95.

7. *Specialized Equipment Prices:* see page 91.

8. *Potato Store Costs:* see page 119.

9. *Labour:* see page 72.

EARLY POTATOES

Production level	Low	Average	High
	£	£	£
OUTPUT per hectare (acre)	1750 (700)	2250 (900)	3000 (1200)
Variable Costs:			
Seed		475 (190)	
Fertilizer		200 (80)	
Sprays		50 (20)	
Casual labour (picking only)		200 (80)	
Sundries		175 (70)	
TOTAL VARIABLE COSTS		1100 (440)	
GROSS MARGIN per hectare (acre) ...	650 (260)	1150 (460)	1900 (760)

Notes

1. *Prices and Yields.* The average yield of first earlies in England and Wales is 15 to 18 tonnes per hectare. However, no yields or prices per tonne are quoted, since yields increase and prices fall as the season progresses. Thus both depend on the date of lifting, e.g. late May to early June, 7 to 12 tonnes per hectare; July, 20 to 30 tonnes per hectare. Prices in late May to mid June are typically three times those in July; the earliest crops (mid May) usually fetch between £500 and £700 per tonne. The average output of £2250 given above could be obtained from 10 tonnes at £225 per tonne, 15 at £150, 20 at £112·50 or 25 at £90.

2. *Casual labour* for planting: £55 per hectare.

3. *P.M.B. levy* (1984). £18·80 per hectare on crops harvested by 9th July. The excess levy is £188·60 per hectare

4. *Chitting.* See Maincrop Potatoes.

5. *Fuel and Repairs* (£ per hectare): £85.

6. *Labour:* see page 74.

SECOND EARLY POTATOES

Output (average): 32·5 tonnes/ha (13 tons/acre) @ £60/tonne = £1950 (790) (lifting July to early September).

Variable Costs: Seed £400 (161), fertilizer £225 (91), sprays £65 (26), miscellaneous £190 (77); total £880 (355).

Gross Margin: £1070 (435).

Labour: see page 73.

SUGAR BEET

Production level	Low	Average	High
Yield: tonnes per hectare (tons per acre) ...	28 (11·25)	37 (14·75)	46 (18·25)
	£	£	£
OUTPUT	905 (365)	1195 (485)	1490 (600)
Variable Costs:			
Seed		45 (18)	
Fertilizer		150 (61)	
Sprays		120 (49)	
Transport (Contract)	105 (42)	140 (57)	175 (72)
TOTAL VARIABLE COSTS	420 (170)	455 (185)	490 (200)
GROSS MARGIN per hectare (acre) ...	485 (195)	740 (300)	1000 (400)

Notes

1. *Prices.* The figures above are based on an estimated price (for 1985) of £29·50 per tonne, for roots of 16·4 per cent sugar content (*i.e.*, the approximate national average), plus transport allowance averaging £2·85. (The agreed 1984 price for 'A' and 'B' quota was £27·72 per tonne at 16% sugar content).

   The price is varied by 0·9 per cent (1 per cent below 15 per cent sugar content) of the contract price for each 0·1 per cent difference in sugar content.

   In addition, early and late delivery allowances are paid, as follows for 1984/85. Early delivery: additional 1% of the U.K. minimum price per day, starting on 10th October, back to the opening date of each factory; (*e.g.*, delivery on 1st October means an extra 10% on the price per tonne). Late delivery. 26th Dec.-7th Jan.: 0·8% of U.K. minimum price; therafter, the rate rises by 0·2% per day to a maximum of 5%.

2. *Effect of Harvesting Date.* As the season progresses, changes occur in the crop before lifting, approximately as follows, on average:

	early Sept. to early Oct.	early Oct. to early Nov.	early Nov. to early Dec.	early Dec. to early Jan.
Yield (tonnes of washed beet per hectare) ...	up 3·75	up 1·9	up 1·25	up 1·25
Sugar Content (%) ...	up 1%	up $\frac{1}{4}$%	down $\frac{1}{4}$%	down $\frac{3}{4}$%
Yield of Sugar (kg per hectare)	up 1000	up 375	up 190	down 60

3. *Casual Labour* (spring hoeing). Nothing has been included under variable costs for casual labour for spring hoeing, although this is still employed on some farms. However, on such farms the cost of sprays (for chemical weed control) is probably less than assumed above.

4. *Contract.* Contract mechanical harvesting costs £140 to £185 per hectare (excluding carting).

5. *Transport.* Contract haulage charges vary widely according to distance from the factory. The figure assumed above is £3·30 per tonne of unwashed beet including cleaner-loader hire (dirt and top tare assumed at 14%).

6. *Fuel and Repairs* (per hectare): £85.

7. *Specialized Equipment Prices:* see page 91.

8. *Labour:* see page 75.

9

VINING PEAS

Production level (1)				Low £	Average £	High £
OUTPUT per hectare (per acre) (2), (3)			...	650(263)	800(324)	950(384)
Variable Costs:						
Seed (4)	...	...	...	...		90(37)	
Fertilizer (5)	...	...	...	...		20 (8)	
Sprays (6)	...	...	...	...		45 (18)	
TOTAL VARIABLE COSTS	...	...	...		155(63)	
GROSS MARGIN per hectare (per acre)		...	495(200)	645(261)	795(321)

Notes

1. The categories "low", "average" and "high" are related to the actual growers of vining peas, not to farmers and farm land in general. As the factories will normally only place contracts with the better growers the "average" figure above virtually refers to "premium" farmers on good land. If all farmers had the opportunity of producing this crop the average output would probably be no higher than the "low" figure above, even at present prices.

2. £800 average output equals 4·6 tonnes/ha (36·65 cwt./acre) @ £172·50 per tonne (1985 est.). This is an average over the whole crop where it goes for freezing. Where the peas are for canning yields are likely to be heavier and prices lower.

3. The above price excludes payment for harvesting (approx. £55 per tonne) and transport (average £20 per tonne). Some firms work on a delivered factory price basis. Most of the harvesting is now done by pea-pod pickers, costing approx. £125,000. (All estimates for 1985.)

4. *Seed:* this is a "subsidised" price in the sense that the grower pays below the market price for seed but receives a lower price for his product than he otherwise would. Average seed cost on a market price basis is approx. £185 per ha.

5. *Fertilizer:* many growers use no fertilizer; it is more often used on light land.

6. *Sprays:* both herbicide and aphicides. There are large seasonal variations according to weather conditions and the need for midge control.

7. *Labour:* see page 76.

DRIED PEAS

Production level	Low	Average	High
Yield: tonnes per hectare (cwt. per acre) ...	2·5 (20)	3·2 (25·5)	3·9 (31)
	£	£	£
OUTPUT	500 (200)	640 (260)	780 (315)
Variable Costs:			
Seed		105 (43)	
Fertilizer		20 (8)	
Sprays		60 (24)	
TOTAL VARIABLE COSTS		185 (75)	
GROSS MARGIN per hectare (acre) ...	315 (125)	455 (185)	595 (240)

Notes

1. These peas are combine harvested. They include peas (especially marrowfats) for human consumption (after processing) and protein peas, for animal feed.

2. *Price.* The (1985) price assumed is £200 per tonne (allowing for E.E.C. subsidy to compounders). The contract price for *peas for processing* is normally higher (averaging approx. £225 for 1984 harvest crops grown on contract) but varies according to the percentage of wastage. *Feeding peas,* sold on the open market, are subject to wide price variations, particularly as poor samples can fetch very low prices.

3. *Physical Inputs.* Seed: 250 kg @ 42p. Fertilizer: 250 kg of no nitrogen compound at £125 per tonne (£31 (13)), where applied, but many crops receive no fertilizer.

4. *Harvesting* can be a difficult operation. Most crops are direct combined, although there is a high risk of loss and poor quality, as well as heavy wear and tear on the combine. Drying and handling the crop can be very difficult, much care being needed. Sometimes the crop is desiccated before direct combining, using diquat, to avoid shedding. Cutting and windrowing the crop prior to combining is a safer method, and should help ensure a more even crop with less need for drying, but obviously these benefits are only gained at the cost of more labour and machinery.

5. *Labour:* see page 76.

FIELD BEANS

A. Spring Beans

Production level Yield: tonnes per hectare (cwt. per acre) ...	Low 2·2(17·5)	Average 2·9(23)	High 3·6(28·5)
	£	£	£
OUTPUT	395(160)	520(210)	650(260)
Variable Costs:			
Seed		55(22)	
Fertilizer		15 (6)	
Sprays		30(12)	
TOTAL VARIABLE COSTS		100(40)	
GROSS MARGIN per hectare (acre) ...	295(120)	420(170)	550(220)

Notes
1. *Price.* The (1985) price assumed is £180 per tonne (allowing for E.E.C. subsidy to compounders). As with dried peas the price can be very uncertain and the contract price is normally higher.

2. *Physical Input.* Seed: 225 kg per hectare @ 24p; average cost is approximately £10 less if own seed is sown in alternate years. Fertilizer: 200 kg of no (or low) nitrogen compound @ £125 per tonne (£25 (10)), where applied, but many crops receive no fertilizer. Sprays: weed control and against blackfly.

3. *Labour:* see page 78. The crop is normally direct combined.

B. Winter Beans

Production level ... ... Yield: tonnes per hectare (cwt. per acre) (2)	Low 2·4(19)	Average 3·1(24·5)	High 3·8(30)
	£	£	£
OUTPUT	420(170)	545(220)	665(270)
Variable Costs: (3)			
Seed		55(22)	
Fertilizer		10 (4)	
Sprays		40(16)	
TOTAL VARIABLE COSTS		105(42)	
GROSS MARGIN per hectare (acre) ...	315(128)	440(178)	560(228)

Notes
1. *Price.* The (1985) price assumed is £175 per tonne (allowing for E.E.C. subsidy to compounders).

N.B.—Nationally the proportion of winter beans grown is probably at least twice that of spring beans.

2. The yield of winter beans is generally assumed to be 0·5 to 0·6 tonnes per hectare above spring beans *provided* a full crop is obtained, that is, where there is no exceptional damage from frost and birds and, in particular, where there is no severe attack of chocolate spot. Because of these possibilities the crop is a riskier one than spring beans. Whether the average yield over a period of years is higher or lower than spring beans depends mainly upon the incidence of attacks of chocolate spot, which can write off the crop completely. In drier parts of the Eastern counties this may be only one year in six or eight but in South-eastern counties the frequency may be substantially higher.

3. Some Eastern counties farmers apply no fertilizer to the crop and may still hoe (usually twice) between the rows, thus obviating the need for chemical weed control. As blackfly spray is not usually necessary owing to the earlier flowering, variable crops may consist of seed alone.

For full details (yields, prices, variable costs) of *actual* average Cash Crop Gross Margins in Eastern England in recent years, see the following annual reports:

Report on Farming in The Eastern Counties of England, University of Cambridge, Agricultural Economics Unit, Department of Land Economy.

Farming in the East Midlands, University of Nottingham School of Agriculture, Department of Agriculture and Horticulture, Sutton Bonington.

OILSEED RAPE

A. Winter

Production level	Low	Average	High
Yield: tonnes per hectare (cwt. per acre) ...	2·2(17·5)	3·0(24)	3·8(30·25)
	£	£	£
OUTPUT	640(258)	870(352)	1100(446)
Variable Costs:			
Seed		22·5 (9)	
Fertilizer		130 (53)	
Sprays		67·5(27)	
TOTAL VARIABLE COSTS		220 (89)	
GROSS MARGIN per hectare (acre) ...	420(169)	650 (263)	880(357)

B. Spring-Sown

Production level	Low	Average	High
Yield: tonnes per hectare (cwt. per acre) ...	1·6(12·5)	2·1(16·5)	2·6(20·5)
	£	£	£
OUTPUT	455(185)	600(242)	740(300)
Variable Costs:			
Seed		22·5 (9)	
Fertilizer		130 (53)	
Sprays		67·5(27)	
TOTAL VARIABLE COSTS		220 (89)	
GROSS MARGIN per hectare (acre) ...	235(96)	380(153)	520(211)

Notes

1. Prices (1985) assumed are £285 per tonne for spring-sown rape (38 per cent oil content) and £290 per tonne for winter-sown rape (42 per cent oil content). The intervention prices for 1984/5 increase by £3·22 per month from £265·53 in July and August to £291·26 in April and May. Prices reached very high levels, up to £340 a tonne, during the 1983/4 season, when they will probably average between £305 and £310. It is not, however, expected that this will be sustained. Intervention prices for 1984/5 were cut by 2 per cent as compared with 1 per cent for cereals. In 1972-4 an average of 15,000 ha per annum were grown in the U.K.; in 1983 220,000 ha were grown.

2. *Physical Inputs.* Seed: 8 kg per hectare (11 kg may be used with 175 mm rows). Spraying is against both weeds and pests.

3. Winter crops are mainly sown between 10th August and 10th September (before the end of August if possible). Spring-sown crops are best sown between late March and mid-April. Winter crops are harvested between late July and mid-August, most of the crops either being windrowed and combined from the swath or desiccated by diquat and direct combined. Spring-sown crops are harvested in the first half of September.

4. *Labour:* see page 77.

N.B.—The proportion of spring-sown oilseed rape is almost certainly less than 5 per cent, and still declining.

HERBAGE SEEDS

Variable Costs

Seed. The following are the approximate seed costs per hectare per annum when sown. Seed rates (kg per hectare) are given in brackets, together with the most usual life of the crop. Italian ryegrass £35 to 50 (13 to 17, one year); perennial ryegrass £30 to 50 (11 to 13, two years), timothy £35 to 50 (7 to 9, four years plus); meadow fescue £30 to 50 (11 to 13, two or three years); cocksfoot £12·50 to 25 (4·5 to 7, two or three years); red clover £35 to 50 (11 to 13, one year); white clover £20 to 25 (3·5).

Fertilizer. Average costs per hectare are approximately as follows. Ryegrass £140, cocksfoot £130, other grass seeds £120, red clover £20 (often nil), white clover £40.

Output and Gross Margin per hectare (estimates for 1985 crop)

(N.B. Prices include E.E.C. subsidies)

	RvP Italian Ryegrass		S.24 Early Perennial Ryegrass		S.23 Late Perennial Ryegrass	
	Average	High	Average	High	Average	High
Yield (100 kg) ...	10·2	15·3	10·1	15·1	9·1	13·6
Price per 100 kg (£)	72·50		65·0		80·0	
OUTPUT (£)	740	1110	655	985	730	1090
Variable Costs (£) ...	210	225	210	225	210	225
GROSS MARGIN (£) ...	530	885	445	760	520	865

	S.352 Timothy		S.215 Meadow Fescue		S.26 Cocksfoot	
	Average	High	Average	High	Average	High
Yield (100 kg) ...	4·0	6·0	6·4	9·6	6·5	9·7
Price per 100 kg (£)	135		97·50		97·50	
OUTPUT (£)	540	810	625	935	635	950
Variable Costs (£) ...	190	205	190	205	170	185
GROSS MARGIN (£) ...	350	605	435	730	465	765

	Essex Broad Red Clover		Kent Wild White Clover and Kent Indigenous Perennial Ryegrass	
	Average	High	Average	High
Yield (100 kg) ...	3·0	4·5	0·8(WWC)+ 4·0(PR)	1·2(WWC)+ 6·0(PR)
Price per 100 kg (£)	120		625(WWC), 62·50(PR)	
OUTPUT (£)	360	540	750	1125
Variable Costs (£) ...	80	90	100	110
GROSS MARGIN (£) ...	280	450	650	1015

Notes

1. Average yields are the 6-year averages for cleaned seed except for Essex Broad Red Clover, Kent Wild White Clover and Kent Indigenous Perennial Ryegrass, which are estimated. The "high" levels are approximately 50 per cent greater. A considerable amount of skill is necessary to attain these "high" levels, but exceptional skill and experience and good soil can produce yields well above the "high" levels shown. Most grasses give their highest yield in their first harvest year, assuming good establishment.

2. *Prices* in the table are estimated 1985 prices for British certified seed of Aberystwyth varieties *including E.E.C. Subsidy* (other than for crops grown under individual contracts). The actual prices received in any one year are very uncertain.

3. No allowance has been made above for by-products. Some crops produce 4 to 5 tonnes of threshed hay, which is, however, of low feeding value. This could be worth £150 or more per hectare. Some grasses, especially spring-sown ryegrass, also provide substantial quantities of autumn and winter grazing. The clovers can be either grazed or cut for hay or silage and do not have to be "shut up" until mid or late May, or, in some cases and seasons, even early June. More grazing (until end of May) and better quality threshed hay is provided with a combination of ryegrass and white clover than with the specialist herbage seed grasses.

4. If the seed crop is to be undersown, specialist growers often reduce the seed rate for the cover crop by up to half and restrict nitrogen dressing: the cereal yield may thus be reduced by up to 0·6 tonnes per hectare. If this is not done the grass seed yield is usually lower in the first year compared with direct drilling, except for ryegrass.

5. *Labour:* see page 79.

Acknowledgement: Considerable help for this crop has been provided by K. B. Knappett, Seed Production Branch, N.I.A.B. and Mr. W. S. Holliwell, Holliwell Seed and Grain Co. Ltd., Wye.

HOPS

1. *Output per mature hectare*

	East Kent	Hants/ Surrey (1)	Other Areas in S.E. (2)	Hereford/ Worcs.	National
Yield (zentner (3)):					
Average (4)	40·1	31·7	33·3	35·9	35·1
High ...	50·0	39·5	41·5	45·0	44·0
Cash Return (£) (5):					
Average	6425	5825	4550	5300	5150
High ...	7825	7075	5475	6400	6225

(1) Hants/Surrey: virtually all seedless hops since 1976.

(2) Mid-Kent, Inner Weald; Outer Weald, Sussex.

(3) zentner = 50 kg.

(4) 5-year average per mature hectare , 1979-83. "High" figures = "average" plus approx. 25 per cent.

(5) Cash per mature hectare, including E.E.C. income aid: two-year average, 1982 and 1983.

2. *Variable Costs* per mature hectare (1983 crop (est.), materials only)

	£
Fertilizers and Manures	190
Washes and Powders	310
Herbicides	65
String	190
Pockets	55
Drying fuel	165
Total	975

3. *Average Direct Labour Costs per mature hectare* (1983 crop (est.))

	£
Growing	460
Picking	475
Drying	110
Maintenance	120
Total	1165

Acknowledgement: G. C. Hall, Production Manager, Hops Marketing Board.

FRUIT

(Estimates for **1985** : established crops : per hectare (per acre in brackets))

Note: The following data are based primarily on a small-scale survey carried out in Kent in early 1984 by Angela Edwards, supplemented where appropriate by national statistics and other data. The *wide range* of yields, prices and costs, both from farm to farm and season to season, has to be stressed. Thus these figures can only be considered to be very broad guidelines. Similarly, labour requirements, both regular and casual, vary enormously—as the range given (obtained from survey date) demonstrates. *Prices* are net of marketing, handling and transport and assume sales in the open market unless otherwise stated and exclude pick-your-own crops. *Yields* refer to *marketed* yields only. The figures relate to *average* levels; "high" outputs may be about 50 per cent above those shown; naturally the top producers will achieve still better results, especially in good years.

	Dessert Apples	Culinary Apples	Pears	Plums
Yield (tonnes)	17·5 (7)	22·5 (9)	17·5 (7)	10 (4)
Net Price (£/tonne)	300	240	210	320
	£	£	£	£
OUTPUT	5250 (2100)	5400 (2160)	3675 (1470)	3200 (1280)
Variable Costs: [1]				
Fertilizer	50 (20)	65 (25)	60 (24)	65 (25)
Sprays	250 (100)	285 (115)	160 (64)	75 (30)
Packaging	500 (200)	625 (250)	180 (72)	310 (125)
TOTAL VARIABLE COSTS[1]	800 (320)	975 (390)	400 (160)	450 (180)
GROSS MARGIN	4450 (1780)	4425 (1770)	3275 (1310)	2750 (1100)
Casual Labour (£/ha)	250-600	250-600	200-475	250-400
Regular Labour (hours/ha)	100-250	100-250	100-250	100-150

	Strawberries	Raspberries	Blackcurrants
Yield (tonnes)	9 (3·65)	6·25 (2·5)	6·25 (2·5)
Net Price (£/tonne)	950	1600	275
	£	£	£
OUTPUT	8550 (3460)	10000 (4000)	1725 (690)
Variable Costs: [1]			
Fertilizer	75 (30)	75 (30)	100 (40)
Sprays	275 (110)	225 (90)	225 (90)
Packaging	1350 (540)	1250 (500)	—
Other	100 (40)	125 (50)	125 (50)
TOTAL VARIABLE COSTS[1]	1800 (720)	1675 (670)	450 (180)
GROSS MARGIN	6750 (2740)	8325 (3330)	1275 (510)
Casual Labour (£/ha)	2000-3000	2500-4500	0-500
Regular Labour (hours/ha)	25-200	150-500	125-250

(1) Excluding casual labour, establishment and storage.

FIELD-SCALE VEGETABLES

(Estimates for 1985, per hectare (per acre in brackets))

Note: Same source and comments apply as to Fruit (p. 18)

	Carrots	Dry Bulb Onions	Dwarf Beans (for Processing) Sliced	Whole
Yield (tonnes)	30(12)	35(14)	8.25(3·3)	6·5(2·6)
Price (£/tonne)	90	85	122·5	160
	£	£	£	£
OUTPUT	2700 (1080)	2975(1190)	1010(410)	1040(420)
Variable Costs: [1]				
Seed	60(24)	125 (50)	185(76)	120(49·5)
Fertilizer	100(40)	150 (60)	145(59)	175(72)
Sprays	90(36)	275(110)	50(20)	45(18·5)
Packaging	150(60)	250(100)	—	—
Other	—	125 (50)	—	—
TOTAL VARIABLE COSTS [1]	400(160)	925(370)	380(155)	340(140)
GROSS MARGIN	2300(920)	2050(820)	630(255)	700(280)
Casual Labour (£/ha) ...	100-150	250-500	—	—
Regular Labour (hours/ha)	50-150	40-60	N.A.	N.A.

	Brussels Sprouts	Cabbage	Spring Greens
Yield (tonnes)	12(4·85)	25(10)	22·5 (9)
Price (£/tonne)	175	100	120
	£	£	£
OUTPUT	2100(850)	2500(1000)	2700(1080)
Variable Costs: [1]			
Seed	250(100)	175 (70)	40(15)
Fertilizer	160 (65)	140 (55)	125(50)
Sprays	175 (70)	175 (70)	110(45)
Packaging	100 (40)	160 (65)	140(55)
Other	—	40 (15)	100(40)
TOTAL VARIABLE COSTS [1]	685(275)	690(275)	515(205)
GROSS MARGIN	1415(575)	1810(725)	2185(875)
Casual Labour (£/ha) ...	750-850	£350-550	250-500
Regular Labour (hours/ha)	30-100		35-60

	Autumn Cauliflower	Winter Cauliflower	Lettuce Round	Crisp
Yield	1125 (450) (crates of 12)	875 (350) (crates of 12)	45 (18) ('000 head)	25 (10)
Price	£2·50/crate	£2·70/crate	11p/head	20p/head
	£	£	£	£
OUTPUT	2810 (1125)	2360 (945)	4950 (1980)	5000 (2000)
Variable Costs: [1]				
Seed/Plants	75 (30)	75 (30)	750 (305)	750 (300)
Fertilizer	125 (50)	150 (60)	150 (60)	150 (60)
Sprays	90 (35)	90 (35)	75 (30)	160 (65)
Packaging	450 (180)	350 (140)	625 (255)	750 (300)
Other	—	—	75 (30)	75 (30)
TOTAL VARIABLE COSTS[1]	740 (295)	665 (265)	1675 (680)	1885 (755)
GROSS MARGIN	2070 (830)	1695 (680)	3275 (1300)	3115 (1245)
Casual Labour (£/ha) ...	375-950	325-700	400-600	
Regular Labour (hours/ha)	40-75	40-75	100-150	

(1) Excluding casual labour.

OTHER CROPS

The following notes are presented for the information of those considering growing crops that are at present little grown in the U.K. but are attracting increasing interest in view of the current "threat" to cereals and concern over the longer-term future of oilseed rape. It has to be borne in mind that results on commercial farms are limited at present and research findings, etc., are not always a good guide to what may actually be achieved in practice. The material has been brought together by Angela Edwards. We are both extremely grateful to all those who were kind to supply information for these crops, although they are not entirely responsible for the following figures, some of which have been adjusted by the author. In particular we thank:

R. J. Alston and S. Hale, Writtle Agricultural College.

P. Dealtry, Seeds Director, Nickersons.

G. Doody, Seeds Manager, Central Seed Unit, Dalgety Agriculture Ltd.

L. Easson, Agricultural Research Institute of Northern Ireland, Hillsborough, Co. Down.

I. Lowe, Harlow Agricultural Merchants.

D. M. Miles, Guinness Barley Research Station.

M. Pertwee, Frank Pertwee and Sons Ltd.

M. J. Pugh, Evening Primrose Oil Co. Ltd.

1. DURUM WHEAT

Traditionally grown in North America and Mediterranean Basin. Varieties have been bred that will grow elsewhere. France already has an expanding area; so has West Germany: 1982, 300 ha; 1983, 1,000 ha; 1984, 5,000 ha (its pasta requirements equate to 100,000 ha).

The source of semolina and pasta; some used in breakfast cereals. Must be of high quality for semolina. Must be grown under contract.

Good price premium over other cereals for past six years (£30/tonne premium over intervention wheat expected in 1984), but market saturation could cause fall in future: one forecast is for a 25% drop in 1985. Export markets expected to dry up as all E.E.C. countries become self-sufficient. Cannot compete with Canadian, etc. crop on world markets and North American durums are needed to mix with U.K. crop.

Optimum drilling period: middle two weeks in October (March-April possible but yields reduced). Some question mark over winter hardiness: must not drill before October.

Harvest: usually one week before feed wheats drilled at same time. Critical operation: harvest as soon as reach 20% moisture content: crop liable to sprouting and quality for semolina reduced if harvest delayed. Must be dried to 15%.

21

Production level	Average	High
Yield: tonnes per ha (cwt. per acre) ...	5 (40)	6 (48)
	£	£
OUTPUT (1984: est. £175/tonne) ...	875 (355)	1050 (425)
Variable Costs:		
Seed	90 (36)	
Fertilizer	90 (36)	
Sprays	70 (28)	
TOTAL VARIABLE COSTS	250 (100)	
GROSS MARGIN per hectare (acre) ...	625 (255)	800 (325)

N.B. Extra drying costs estimated at £8 per tonne.

2. EVENING PRIMROSE

Rapidly increasing demand for the seed oil: its full value only recently discovered—said to be the richest source of essential fatty acids known, especially the rare GLA (gamma-linolenic acid), which has medicinal properties for many serious diseases and disorders. Thus several major companies have now invested heavily in research and development. Brand-named evening primrose oil capsules available in chemists and health food shops.

The companies are seeking growers—but not for large areas: 2 to 5 ha, possibly 8 maximum; farmers who have grown seed crops before preferred. Plant breeding programmes under way: new varieties expected shortly. Still much to learn re growing the crop. Wide range of soils suitable, but not acid, high pH, or fen land.

Some growers (especially if on sands) are planting it in March/April for harvesting early/mid-October, others (especially on stronger soils) before the end of July (*possibly* August), after another crop, for mid-September harvesting the following year—but winter kill is possible. Germination and establishment very difficult (the seeds are tiny); shallow drilling (½″) and seedbed consolidation important. Plants produced under glass in peat blocks are being tried—but expensive; irrigation highly desirable. Weed control a major problem until established. No significant pest or disease problems known at present. Relatively little fertiliser needed—lush vegetative growth unwanted.

Uneven ripening and pod setting a further problem. Crop has to be desiccated (perhaps twice) before combining, which needs to be slow to avoid shattering the pods; seed must be dried quickly, to 10-12%.

Yields: 0·25 to 0·85 tonnes/ha (2 to 7 cwt./acre): 0·5(4) a good crop at present. A high-risk crop.

Price: £1,600 a tonne offered for 1984 crop but at least one company offering £3,500 for the 1985 crop.

Possible variable costs, £ per ha (acre): seed 0 (provided by contracting company); fertiliser 25 (10); sprays 62·5 (25); desiccant 37·5 (15).

3. FLAX

Same species as linseed, but one variety used for fibre and one for seed.

In 1939-45 War, 50,000 ha grown in Northern Ireland (N.I.) and up to 4,000 ha in Scotland, near the Tay. But by 1960s N.I. entirely dependent on imports. There is a strong demand to mix with other, synthetic fibres: U.K. imports £8 to 9 millions worth a year, N.I. accounting for £6 to 7 millions.

In E.E.C., 100,000 ha grown in 1960, but down to 58,000 ha in 1982 (80% in France, the rest in Belgium and Holland). In Eastern Bloc countries, 1,500,000 ha grown (80% in U.S.S.R.).

The rapid decline in N.I./U.K. has been due to processing difficulty. The crop has to be "retted" (now possible by applying glyphosate), then "scutched". There is a new scutching mill in N.I. but none in Scotland, despite a good demand and a keen desire by some to develop the crop; some is at present sent to France for scutching (there is no mill in England or Wales), but this is uneconomic commercially.

With the mill, the area of flax in N.I. has developed in recent years: no. of ha = 1980: 0; 1981: 4; 1982: 8; 1983: 20; 1984: 267 (50 growers)—the first year of commercial production.

Can be grown on wide variety of soils, preferably medium-heavy. Can follow 2 or 3 cereal crops. Lodges readily: thus care needed, as with control of weeds, as certain of them can contaminate the fibres.

Sowing: April (March possible if no danger of sharp frost; the crop is not frost-resistant). Conventional narrow drill can be used.

Mid-July: spray with 4 litres/ha glyphosate + 1 litre/ha wetting agent. Leave for 4 weeks to desiccate and further 2 weeks to ret: continuously moist conditions needed at this stage.

Yield: tonnes per ha (cwt. per acre)	6 (48) of straw (1·25 (10) of fibre)
	£
Sales (£130/tonne straw)...	780 (315)
E.E.C. subsidy*	100 (40)
TOTAL OUTPUT	880 (355)
Variable Costs:	
Seed	85 (34)
Fertilizer	30 (12)
Sprays	35 (14)
Desiccant and Wetting Agent	60 (24)
Bale twine	15 (6)
Pulling and baling	125 (50)
TOTAL VARIABLE COSTS ...	350 (140)
GROSS MARGIN per hectare (acre)	430 (215)

Early September: crop is pulled (not cut) when moisture content below 16%. Baled in large round bales after 2 or 3 hours in swath, to dry the roots. The scutching mill provide the pullers (£22,000) and baler (£200 modification to standard model) and charges grower £125/ha. Grower carts bales from field and stores for short time and takes to mill when it requires. Contract with mill necessary to qualify for subsidy.

4. LINSEED

Produces both oil and meal. E.E.C. imported 660,000 tonnes in 1982. World price very variable. E.E.C. price support arrangements. U.K. area increasing (1980: 330 ha, 1984: 1200 ha) and further increase forecast.

Advantages: good break crop re pest immunity; normal cereals machinery adequate; can harvest late, as does not shed; spring-sown.

Drawbacks: small root system, so unsuited to soils prone to drought or waterlogging; competes poorly with weeds, hence careful herbicide treatment needed; as the seed flows easily, trailers, etc., need careful sealing.

Drilling: end March to mid-April; can sow later, but yield drops; susceptible to frost. Should not be grown more than 1 year in 5.

Harvesting: end of August-early September; (but possible to leave till October). Moisture content most likely 12-16%: must be dried to 9% for storage.

E.E.C. area subsidy based on guide price per tonne: £318 in 1982, £337 in 1983. Seed producers get additional subsidy.

Production level	Average	High
Yield: tonnes per ha (cwt. per acre) ...	1·85 (15)	2·5 (20)
	£	£
OUTPUT (£330/tonne* inc. subsidy) ...	610 (245)	825 (335)
Variable Costs:		
Seed		85 (33)
Fertilizer		70 (28)
Sprays		35 (14)
TOTAL VARIABLE COSTS		190 (75)
GROSS MARGIN per hectare (acre) ...	420 (170)	635 (260)

* Price some £55 per tonne higher for seed production.

5. LUPINS

"Farmers Gripped by Lupin Fever": headline in *The Guardian*, 9th August, 1984.

High protein content of 30% plus and 9% oil: hence a good substitute for soya beans. Approx. 50% more protein content than peas and beans. Hence E.E.C. subsidy to feed compounders introduced in 1984, with farmers' minimum price at £196·67 per tonne. Compounders can claim subsidy equal to 60% of difference between soya meal and the lupin activating price of £292·75 per tonne. In Europe, only France grows a commercial area: 8,000 ha. The crop is well established in U.S.S.R., Eastern Europe, Australia, New Zealand, South Africa, U.S.A.

Traditionally a light land crop. White-flowered varieties being grown at present. New varieties are being investigated, including ones which heavier soils will tolerate.

Advantages: not a cereal; nitrogen fixing; unmodified cereal machinery suitable; erect growth, resistant to lodging and shattering; spring-sown.

Drawbacks: harvested late; botrytis lowers yields, especially in a wet year: no certain control at present; late-germinating weeds can cause problems; fairly susceptible to frost damage; difficult to obtain seed, which is expensive, at present; possibly uneven ripening.

Drilling: end March-early April; (timing critical). Should not be grown more than 1 year in 4 or 5.

Harvesting: averages late September; (ranges from mid-September to early October).

Production level	Low	Average	High
Yield: tonnes per hectare (cwt. per acre)	2·0 (16)	2·5 (20)	3·0 (24)
	£	£	£
OUTPUT (£197/tonne inc. subsidy) ...	395 (160)	495 (200)	590 (240)
Variable Costs:			
Seed (300 kg @ £360/tonne) ...		110 (45)	
Fertilizer		25 (10)	
Sprays		50 (20)	
TOTAL VARIABLE COSTS		185 (75)	
GROSS MARGIN per hectare (acre) ...	210 (85)	310 (125)	405 (165)

N.B. However, one seedsman estimated in early July that 1984 yields (on about 150 U.K. ha) would only average 0·65 to 1·25 tonnes/ha (5 to 10 cwt./acre)—but the crop is new.

6. MAIZE FOR GRAIN

Included for "completeness", but there is little scope with present varieties because, as with Sunflowers (see below), our climate is not warm enough. Did reasonably well in good springs and summers for a while, in Southern England, some ten years ago, but results were very poor in late springs and cool summers and the harvesting in October/November grim in a wet autumn. Forage maize has been much more successful.

7. RYE

Better than barley and close to wheat in crude protein and energy value, but compounders have been slow to use owing to supposed palatability problems. Contracts are being offered for Ryvita, but the quality requirements are high. Ryvita currently use 30,000 tonnes a year, of which 20% has to be Canadian; it buys 12,500 tonnes a year from U.K. farmers and is prepared to raise this to 20,000, which is 4,000 ha. A U.K. increase to 8,000 ha is expected by some. (During 1945-50, 27,000-30,000 ha were grown in England and Wales; 1980-83: 6,250-6,500 ha).

Traditionally suited to light sandy soils, but now being suggested for heavier loamy sands. Very hardy: can withstand low temperatures and starts growing early in the spring. Has all-round good resistance to wheat and barley diseases and its vigour keeps weeds down.

But there are snags. It sprouts in a wet harvest. It grows very tall and lodges easily: hence high levels of nitrogen not possible (but growth regulator possibilities?). Its heavy straw crop means very slow combining (takes about twice as long per hectare as wheat and barley).

Drilling: 2nd and 3rd weeks September.

Harvesting: by mid-August (at relatively high moisture content, then dry to 14-15%).

Production level	Low	Average	High
Yield: tonnes per hectare (cwt. per acre)	3·5 (28·5)†	5·0 (40·5)	6·5 (52·5)*
	£	£	£
OUTPUT (£124/tonne)	435 (175)	620 (250)	805 (325)
Variable Costs:			
Seed	50 (20)	50 (20)	
Fertilizer	65 (27)	85 (34)	
Sprays	55 (23)	65 (26)	
TOTAL VARIABLE COSTS	170 (70)	200 (80)	
GROSS MARGIN per hectare (acre) ...	265 (105)	420 (170)	605 (245)

† As grown traditionally: on light sandy soils unsuited to other cereals.

* Possibly unrealistic.

8. SUNFLOWERS

Much interest being shown and some field trials in U.K., but all small-scale. No real development likely for 6 to 10 years. New varieties are required, together with better pest and disease control.

Problems: the crop needs a warm climate; in Southern England a "fair" crop might be grown 3 years in 5; susceptible to botrytis, difficult to control; possibly bird damage.

Rapidly increasing area (482,000 ha in 1984) being grown in France, from just north of the Loire southwards, in place of oilseed rape.

The E.E.C. average yield in the two harvest years 1983 and 1984 (the latter as forecast on 7th August) was 2·0 tonnes/ha (16 cwt./acre), compared with 2·5 (20) for oilseed rape.

9. TRITICALE

A "man-made" cross between rye and hard wheat. Breeding programme in U.K., following development of varieties in U.S.A. for developing countries. Combines the hardiness of rye and the market-ability of feed wheat.

Price is between feed wheat and feed barley at present. Its main scope is on thin, poorish, marginal cereal-growing, Grade 3 soils. Low levels of fungicide are sufficient, because of its good disease resistance. Shorter-stemmed varieties and better weed and disease control are being developed. 6,000 ha grown in 1984 in U.K.; some forecast a consider-able increase.

Production level	Low*	Average	High
Yield: tonnes per hectare (cwt. per acre)	5·0 (40)	6·25 (50)	7·5 (60)
	£	£	£
OUTPUT (Price £109/tonne)	545 (220)	680 (275)	815 (330)
Variable Costs:			
Seed		65 (26)	
Fertilizer		90 (36)	
Sprays		70 (28)	
TOTAL VARIABLE COSTS		225 (90)	
GROSS MARGIN per hectare (acre) ...	320 (130)	455 (185)	590 (240)

* Poor soils; the average and high levels may be optimistic.

10. REMEMBER OATS!

FORESTRY
(Estimated for 1985)

A. Establishment Costs (before grant)

1. *Trees for planting* (per 100)

   Conifers—Sitka Spruce, Norway Spruce, Lodgepole Pine   £75-85

   Broadleaves—Oak, Beach, Ash   £160-240

2. *Tree Protection*

   Fencing—supplied and erected (per m): rabbit, £1.80; stock, £1.95; deer, £3.15; split post and rail, £5-6.

   Tree guards and shelters (per 100): plastic spiral 600-750 mm, £16·00; plastic tubes, £80-90.

3. *Contract Service* (per ha)

   Planting at 2 m spacing, including trees: conifers, £550; broadleaves, £650.

   Weeding, including materials: hand weeding, £170; herbicide, £60-80.

   Brashing (removing dead side branches): complete brashing, £235; removing 60-70% of dead branches, £115-130.

4. *Establishment Cost for Conifers*

   Providing that the site does not require clearing or draining prior to planting, and employing contractors for all operations, the cost of establishing a 10 hectare (25 acre) wood would be in the region of £13,500, *i.e.*, £1,350 per hectare (£550 per acre). Savings in fencing costs and other economies of scale may reduce average costs per hectare by 10% to 20% where larger plantations are established; conversely costs for small woods may easily be 25% higher per hectare established. Constructing access roads will typically cost between £200 and £250 per hectare (£80 to £100 per acre).

B. Production and Prices

1. *Production*

   Production is usually measured in terms of cubic meteres (m^3) of marketable timber per hectare and will vary according to the quality of the site, species planted and thinnings policy. Sites in lowland Britain planted to conifers typically produce an average of 12 to 18 m^3 of timber per hectare per year over the rotation as a whole and would accordingly be assessed as falling in yield classes 12 to 18. Under traditional management systems thinning begins 20 to 25 years after planting and is repeated at intervals of approximately 5 years until the wood is clear felled at between 50 and 60 years. Approximately 40-45% of total production will be from thinnings. Broadleaves typically produce an average of between 4 and 8 m^3 of timber per hectare per year and fall in yield classes 4 to 8.

2. *Prices*

   Prices for standing timber are extremely variable, depending on tree size and quality, ease of extraction from site, geographical location (nearness to end user) and quantity being sold. The following prices are averages paid for standing coniferous timber sold by the Forestry Commission in the year to 30th September, 1983:

Average tree size (m³)				Price (£ per m³)	
				England	Wales
Up to 0·074	...	...	...	4·23	2·45
0·074-0·124	...	...	...	5·24	3·75
0·124-0·174	...	...	...	6·76	4·45
0·174-0·224	...	...	...	8·39	6·37
0·224-0·274	...	...	...	7·87	8·64
0·274-0·424	...	...	...	11·40	10·24
Over 0·424	...	...	...	16·53	16·62

C. Grants and Taxation

1. Grants

Under the Forestry Grant Scheme administered by the Forestry Commission, grants are available for approved plantings at the following rates:

Area of wood (ha)				Rate of Grant (£ per ha)	
				Conifers	Broadleaves
0·25-0·9	...	...	...	600	850
1·0-2·9	...	...	...	480	700
3·0-9·9	...	...	...	400	600
10·0 and over ...	...	...	...	230	450

80 per cent of the grant is paid on completion of planting and the remaining 20 per cent 5 years later, providing that the plantation has been properly maintained.

Grants towards the cost of areas of amenity woodland may be available from local authorities and the Countryside Commission. Grant aid may also be available towards the cost of establishing shelter belts under the Agriculture and Horticulture Grant Scheme and the Agriculture and Horticulture Development Scheme (see pages 145-6).

2. Taxation

Income from the occupation of commercially run woodlands is taxed under Schedule B for income tax purposes, unless an election is made for it to be taxed under Schedule D as a trade. Under Schedule B income tax is assessed each year on one-third of the woodland's "annual value". Annual value is the rent the land would yield if let in its natural, unimproved state and will normally be a very small amount. No account is taken of actual expenses, revenue or the value of the standing timber. Under Schedule D income tax is charged on the surplus of the proceeds from the sale of timber after deducting allowable expenses and capital allowances. If a loss is produced it can be set against other income. An election for Schedule D is irrevocable and assessment will only revert to Schedule B on a change of occupier.

3. GRAZING LIVESTOCK
DAIRY COWS
A. Friesians

Performance level (yield (1))			Low	Average	High	Very High
Milk Yield per Cow (litres) (2)	...	...	4500	5250	6000	6750
Milk Yield per Cow (gal.)	...	... ...	990	1155	1320	1485

			£	£	£	£
Milk Value per Cow (3)	...	... ...	652	761	870	979
Concentrate Costs per Cow (4)	...	...	216	269	336	410

Margin of Milk Value over Concentrates per						
Cow (5)	... ...	...	436	492	534	569
Value of Calves less Herd Depreciation (6)			(+)30	(+)30	(+)30	(+)30
Miscellaneous Variable Costs (7)	...	...	51	53	55	57

GROSS MARGIN per Cow before deducting						
Forage Variable Costs	...	... ...	415	469	509	542

Gross Margins per Cow and per Hectare (Acre) at 4 different stocking rates (8) are as follows:

Performance level	... ...	...	Low	Average	High	Very High
1. At 1·55 cows per forage hectare (low):						
(0·65 forage hectares (1·6 acres) per cow)						
Forage Variable Costs per Cow	...	...	61	61	61	61
GROSS MARGIN per Cow	...	... ...	354	408	448	481
GROSS MARGIN per Forage Hectare	...	549	632	694	746
GROSS MARGIN per Forage Acre	...	222	256	281	302

2. At 1·85 cows per forage hectare (average):						
(0·54 forage hectares (1·35 acres) per cow)						
Forage Variable Costs per Cow	...	...	**69**	**69**	**69**	**69**
GROSS MARGIN per Cow	...	... ...	**346**	**400**	**440**	**473**
GROSS MARGIN per Forage Hectare	...	**640**	**740**	**814**	**875**
GROSS MARGIN per Forage Acre	...	...	**259**	**300**	**329**	**354**

3. At 2·2 cows per forage hectare (high):						
(0·455 forage hectares (1·125 acres) per cow)						
Forage Variable Costs per Cow	...	...	73	73	73	73
GROSS MARGIN per Cow	...	... ...	342	396	436	469
GROSS MARGIN per Forage Hectare	...	752	871	959	1032
GROSS MARGIN per Forage Acre	...	...	304	353	388	418

4. At 2·5 cows per forage hectare (very high):						
(0·4 forage hectares (1 acre) per cow)						
Forage Variable Costs per Cow	...	...	83	83	83	83
GROSS MARGIN per Cow	...	... ...	332	386	426	459
GROSS MARGIN per Forage Hectare	...	830	965	1065	1148
GROSS MARGIN per Forage Acre	...	...	336	391	431	464

Notes
1. Performance level refers only to milk yield, although increases in this are usually (though not *necessarily*) associated with higher gross margins. As will be seen, increases in concentrate feeding are assumed as yield rises. Substantially higher levels of margin over concentrates than that included under "very high" performance are illustrated in Footnote 5 below.

2. *Yield.* The yield referred to is litres produced during a year divided by the average number of cows and calved heifers in the herd. Such has been the rate of increase in recent years that in this edition the forecast average yield for 1985 would have been raised to at least 5500 litres. However, it seems certain that the quotas imposed in 1984, together with severe cuts in the real price for milk, will cause farmers in general to reduce inputs, causing yield reductions. Some will of course react by reducing cow numbers. Many will do both.

3. *Milk Price.* This is assumed (as an average for the 1985 calendar year) to be 14·50p per litre, after deducting transport costs, capital contribution (0·046p per litre) and the co-responsibility levy (0·525p per litre in mid-1984).

The average price received is affected by seasonality of production and quality premiums. Receipts per cow are affected approximately as follows by each 0·25p per litre difference in price at each performance level:

Low	Average	High	Very High
±11	±13	±15	±17

Seasonal Prices Variations. New seasonal price adjustments began in April 1984, as follows (p/litre): March/April. −0·5; May/June, −2·5; July, 0; Aug./Sept., +1·2; Oct.-Feb., +0·8.

Compositional Quality Payments

A completely new pricing system was introduced on 1st April, 1984. Payments are now based on fat, protein and lactose instead of fat and solids-not-fat. The composition is measured by tests made in the month during which the milk being paid for has been produced: hence the term "contemporary payments".

The payment is currently (June 1984) as follows:

Fat: 1·851p per litre per 1 per cent.
Protein: 1·811p per litre per 1 per cent.
Lactose: 0·275p per litre per 1 per cent.

Average milk composition by breed is as follows:*

	Fat %	Protein %	Lactose %
Friesian/Holstein	3·78	3·26	4·52
Ayrshire	3·90	3·38	4·5 est.
Jersey	5·20	3·86	4·5 est.
Guernsey	4·64	3·63	4·5 est.
National Average...	3·9	3·3	4·6 †

* Source: National Milk Records.

† Plus 0·9% Minerals/vitamins = total solids 12·7%.

Hygienic Quality and Antibiotics. Deductions are made for milk failing prescribed tests.

4. *Concentrate Costs.*

Amounts: Performance level :	Low	Average	High	Very High
kg/litre :	·30	·32	·35	·38
(lb./gal. :	3·0	3·2	3·5	3·8)
tonnes/cow :	1·35	1·68	2·10	2·565

Price: taken (for 1985) as £160 per tonne, which is an average of home-mixed rations at £152·50 and purchased compounds at £167·50 (delivered) of varying nutritive value.

See also *Price of Concentrates,* page 32.

31

5. Margin over Concentrates and Concentrates per litre

The emphasis in the initial tables should be laid on the differences between the margin of milk value over concentrates per cow; the same large variation can occur with widely differing combinations of milk yield and quantity of concentrates fed.

In the following table, at each yield level figures are given for (a) margin of milk value over concentrates per cow (£) and (b) concentrates per litre (kg) at three levels of concentrate feeding.

Yield level Milk Yield per cow (litres)	Low 4,500		Average 5,250		High 6,000		Very High 6,750	
	(a)	(b)	(a)	(b)	(a)	(b)	(a)	(b)
	£	kg	£	kg	£	kg	£	kg
1·25 tonne (£200) concs. per cow	452	·28	561	·24	670	·21	—	—
1·75 tonne (£280) concs. per cow	372	·39	481	·33	590	·29	699	·26
2·25 tonne (£360) concs. per cow	292	·50	401	·43	510	·37	619	·33
2·75 tonne (£440) concs. per cow	—	—	321	·52	430	·46	539	·41

On the same assumptions re the other variable costs, etc. as in the tables on page 30 a very high *margin over concentrates of £650 per cow* would give a gross margin per cow before deducting forage variable costs of £623 and the following other results (£):

Stocking rate	Average	High	Very High
Gross Margin per Cow	554	550	540
Gross Margin per Forage Hectare	1025	1210	1350
Gross Margin per Forage Acre	415	490	546

Price of Concentrates. The calculations so far have been based on a price for concentrates of £160 per tonne. A difference of £10 per tonne has the following approximate effect on margin over concentrates and gross margin per cow, on the assumptions made regarding the quantity fed at each performance level:

Low	Average	High	Very High
±£13·5	±£17	±£21	±£26

Seasonality. At average feed levels, compared with a fairly even production of 48 per cent winter production and 52 per cent summer milk, a herd producing 56 per cent of its milk in winter will use approx. £25 more concentrates, and one producing only 42 per cent of its milk in winter approx. £25 less. This will of course be counterbalanced by differences in the value of milk produced (see further 9 below).

Typical Monthly Variation in Concentrate Feeding (kg per litre)

	Winter				Summer	
	Average	Premium			Average	Premium
October ...	0·38	0·28	April ...		0·33	0·19
November ...	0·38	0·33	May		0·20	0·09
December ...	0·38	0·33	June ...		0·15	0·04
January ...	0·38	0·33	July		0·25	0·14
February ...	0·38	0·33	August ...		0·30	0·17
March ...	0·38	0·28	September ...		0·33	0·19

Average winter: 0·38
Premium winter: 0·31

Average summer: 0·26
Premium summer: 0·14

Average whole year: 0·32
Premium whole year: 0·22

The actual distribution on any individual farm will obviously vary according to such factors as seasonality of calving, level of milk yield, grazing productivity during the summer, and the quantity and quality of bulk feeds in the winter. The March figure in particular will be affected by type of soil and seasonal rainfall.

6. *Net Annual Replacement Costs* (i.e. Herd Depreciation less Value of Calves). These have been estimated as follows (for 1985):

	£ per cow in herd
Cost of replacements: 22·5% of herd per year @ £600 ...	135
LESS Value of culls: 22·5% of herd per year @ £400 (allowing for casualties)	90
Herd Depreciation	45
LESS Annual Value of Calves*	75
Net Annual Replacement Gain	30

* Allowing for calving index of approx. 395 days and calf mortality; mixture of pure Friesian calves and beef crosses.

7. *Miscellaneous Variable Costs* (average)

	£
Bedding*	8
Vet. and Med.	15
A.I. and Recording Fees ...	15
Consumable dairy stores, etc. ...	15
Total	53

* *Straw* can vary from 0·4 to 1·5 tonne per cow and from £10 to £30 per tonne.

8. *Stocking Rate.* **The stocking rates given assume that all requirements of bulk foods—for both winter and summer—are obtained from the forage area,** i.e. none is bought in. On average about 55 per cent of the forage area (or production) is grazed and 45 per cent conserved. It will be observed that as the stocking density increases, gross margin *per cow* falls, but gross margin *per hectare* rises.

The levels of nitrogen are assumed to be as follows: 1·55 cows per forage hectare, 140 kg (112 units/acre); 1·85, 200 (160); 2·2, 260 (208); 2·5, 350 (280). An increase in potash application is also assumed. Seed costs clearly depend on the percentage of permanent pasture, if any, the length of leys, etc. **The following forage costs per hectare (fertiliser, seed and sprays) have been assumed:** 1·55 cows per forage hectare, £94 (£38/acre); 1·85, £128 (52); 2·2, £160 (65); 2·5, £208 (84). In using the same forage costs at all levels of margin over concentrates, the assumption is made that no part of these differences in margin over concentrates is obtained by substituting extra bulk fodder for concentrates.

An increase in stocking density can be obtained not only by intensifying grassland production, as above, but also by buying in winter bulk fodder (assuming the same level of concentrate feeding in both cases). This will cause the gross margin *per cow* to fall still further, but will usually result in a higher gross margin *per hectare* than where all forage is conserved on the farm—at any given level of grassland management.

In the table below four examples are given: two policies at two different stocking rates. (A) and (B) assume the land is used for grazing only, i.e. all winter bulk fodder is purchased. (C) and (D) assume the land provides grazing and half the winter bulk fodder, the other half being bought in. (A) and (C) assume a stocking rate equivalent to 1·85 cows per hectare where the land provides both grazing and all the winter bulk fodder, which is an average level of stocking. (B) and (D) assume the equivalent of 2·5 cows per hectare where all bulk food is provided both summer and winter, which is a very high level of stocking. It is assumed that the full winter fodder requirement is 2 tonnes of hay (or other equivalent foods), costing £100 per cow if it is all purchased. (Prices vary widely according to the season and part of the country.) Forage variable costs per hectare are £128 and £208 at the average and high levels of stocking respectively.

33

	Margin of Milk Value over Concentrates			
	Low	Average	High	Very High
	Gross Margin per Forage Hectare (Acre)			
	£	£	£	£
(A) All winter fodder purchased; average stocking rate	933	1144	1249	1360
	(378)	(451)	(505)	(550)
(B) All winter fodder purchased; very high stocking rate ...	1224	1469	1651	1801
	(495)	(594)	(668)	(729)
(C) ½ winter fodder purchased; average stocking rate	745	874	970	1049
	(301)	(354)	(393)	(425)
(D) ½ winter fodder purchased; very high stocking rate ...	969	1144	1273	1379
	(392)	(463)	(515)	(558)

It must obviously not be forgotten that "fixed" costs per hectare, e.g. labour and depreciation on buildings, will increase considerably as stocking density increases (unless a similar number of cows are kept on fewer hectares), at least when cow numbers outstrip the capacity of existing buildings and labour. Furthermore, husbandry problems such as poaching will multiply, unless zero-grazing is practised—with its further additions to fixed costs and management difficulties.

9. *Seasonality.* Price and concentrate feeding differences according to the seasonality of production have already been outlined in notes 3 and 5.

The following data are obtained from the M.M.B.'s F.M. Services, 1982-83 (from Rept. 39, An Analysis of Costed Farms 1982-83, Dec. 1983).

	Winter Milk	Summer Milk	Other Herds
Number of herds	239	56	754
Average herd size (no. of cows) ...	118	95	113
Average seasonality (per cent summer milk)*	42	65	52
Average yield (litres/cow)	5525	4657	5423
Milk price (p/litre)	14·70	14·26	14·47
Milk sales per cow (£)	812	664	785
Concentrates per cow (tonnes) ...	1·98	1·48	1·82
Concentrates per litre (kg)	0·36	0·32	0·34
Concentrates per cow (£)	277	211	256
Margin over Concentrates per cow (£)	535	453	529
Gross Margin per cow (£)	425	365	435
Stocking Rate (cows/hectare) ...	2·06	1·97	2·07
Gross Margin per hectare (£)	877	719	901
Gross Margin per acre (£)	355	291	365

* Winter milk herds: less than 46% production in the six summer months (April-Sept.). Summer milk herds: more than 60% in the six summer months.

It is frequently observed in making such comparisons that the summer milk producers tend to include a higher proportion of less efficient farmers. In theory the difference in yield per cow should not be so high and summer milk producers should use less concentrates compared with winter producers than survey results indicate; also, their stocking rate should be better than average survey figures compared with winter producers. In the above survey, the average gross margins of the top 10% of summer producers were 8% less per cow and 12% less per hectare than the top 10% of winter producers, compared with 14% and 18% less respectively in the average results given above.

10. *Labour:* see page 85.　　　　　　　11. *Building Costs:* see pages 116-7.

B. Channel Island Breeds

Performance level (yield)	Low	Average	High
Milk Yield per Cow (litres)	3250	3750	4250
	£	£	£
Milk Value per Cow	585	675	765
Concentrate Costs per Cow	193	235	280
Margin of Milk Value over Concentrates per Cow	392	440	485
Herd Depreciation less Value of Calves ...	12	12	12
Miscellaneous Variable Costs	51	53	55
GROSS MARGIN per Cow before deducting Forage Variable Costs	329	375	418
Forage Variable Costs	54	54	54
GROSS MARGIN per Cow	275	321	364
GROSS MARGIN per Forage Hectare (2·15 cows per hectare: 0·465 hectares/cow)	591	690	783
GROSS MARGIN per Forage Acre (1·15 acres/cow)	239	279	317

Notes

1. *Yield.* See Note 2 for Friesians (page 31). Guernseys average some 225 litres more than Jerseys but the latter should average a higher price of approx. 1·5p per litre.

2. *Milk Price.* This has been assumed to be 18p per litre, i.e. 3·5p above Friesian milk based on the difference in compositional quality plus the C.I. premium.

3. *Concentrate Costs.*

Amounts: Performance level:			Low	Average	High
kg/litre	...	...	·36	·38	·40
(lb./gal.	...	...	3·6	3·8	4·0)
tonnes/cow	...	...	1·17	1·425	1·7

Price: taken (for 1985) as £165 per tonne (half purchased compounds at £172·50, half home-mixed at £157·50).

The following table shows for each production level (a) the margin of milk value over concentrates per cow (£) and (b) concentrates per litre (kg) at three levels of concentrate feeding.

Performance level Milk Yield per Cow (litres)	Low 3250		Average 3750		High 4250	
	(a)	(b)	(a)	(b)	(a)	(b)
	£	kg	£	kg	£	kg
1·0 tonnes (£165) concs. per cow	420	0·31	510	0·27	600	0·24
1·5 tonnes (£248) concs. per cow	337	0·46	427	0·40	517	0·35
2·0 tonnes (£330) concs. per cow	255	0·62	345	0·53	435	0·47

35

4. *Net Annual Replacement Costs*. (i.e. Herd Depreciation less Value of Calves) were calculated as follows:

	£ per cow in herd
Cost of replacements: 22·5 per cent of herd per year @ £360 ...	81
LESS Value of culls: 22·5 per cent of herd per year @ £190 (allowing for casualties)*	43
Herd Depreciation	38
LESS Annual Value of Calves**	26
Net Annual Replacement Cost	12

* Cull cow prices for Guernseys are about £60 higher than for Jerseys.

** Allowing for calving index of 395 days and calf mortality; mixture of pure bred calves and beef crosses. Guernsey calves, especially crosses, fetch more than Jersey calves, averaging perhaps £10 more per head.

5. *Miscellaneous Variable Costs*. See Note 7 for Friesians.

6. *Stocking Rate*. See, in general, Note 8 for Friesians. The effect of varying the stocking rate on gross margin per forage hectare is as follows:

Cows per Forage Hectare	Forage Hectares (Acres) per Cow	GM/Cow before deducting Forage V.Cs.			Forage Var. Costs	
		Low £329	Average £375	High £418	p. Forage Hectare (Acre)	p. Cow
		Gross Margin per Forage Ha (Acre) (£)			£	£
1·8	0·56 (1·37)	504 (204)	590 (239)	668 (270)	85 (34)	47
2·15	**0·465 (1·15)**	**591 (239)**	**690 (279)**	**783 (317)**	**116 (47)**	**54**
2·5	0·40 (1·00)	680 (275)	795 (322)	902 (365)	142 (58)	57
2·85	0·35 (0·87)	754 (305)	883 (358)	1006 (407)	185 (75)	65

These figures assume that all forage requirements—in winter as well as summer—are provided by the farm forage area.

On average, Jerseys appear from limited evidence to utilise at least 0·05 hectares (0·125 acres) per head less than Guernseys, possibly as much as 0·075 ha (0·185 acres).

C. *Other Breeds* (including Ayrshires)

				Low	Average	High
Performance level (yield)	...	...	...	Low	Average	High
Milk Yield per Cow (litres)	...	...	...	3800	4400	5000
				£	£	£
Milk Value per Cow	...	...	...	560	649	737
Concentrate Costs per Cow	...	...	...	182	224	272
Margin of Milk Value over Concentrates per Cow	...	...	...	378	425	465
Herd Depreciation Value of Calves less			...	(+)3	(+)3	(+)3
Miscellaneous Variable Costs				51	53	55
GROSS MARGIN per Cow before deducting Forage Variable Costs	...	...	...	330	375	413
Forage Variable Costs	...	...	...	65	65	65
GROSS MARGIN per Cow	...	...		265	310	348
GROSS MARGIN per Forage Hectare (1·95 cows per hectare: 0·51 hectares/cow)			...	503	605	679
GROSS MARGIN per Forage Acre (1·25 acres/cow)	...	...		204	245	275

Notes

1. *Yield.* See Note 2 for Friesians.

2. *Milk Price.* See in general, note 3 for Friesians. The price assumed in the above table is 14·75p per litre. Ayrshires should in fact achieve a price approximately 0·5p per litre above Friesians/Holsteins.

3. *Concentrate Costs.* See notes 4 and 5 for Friesians. In the above table, the levels of feeding per kg (and tonnes per cow) are as follows: low ·30 (1·14 tonnes), average ·32 (1·4), high ·34 (1·7); price £160 per tonne.

   The following table shows, for each production level, (a) the margin of milk value over concentrates (£) and (b) concentrates per litre (kg) at three levels of concentrate feeding.

Performance level Milk Yield per Cow (litres)	Low 3800		Average 4400		High 5000	
	(a)	(b)	(a)	(b)	(a)	(b)
	£	kg	£	kg	£	kg
1·00 tonnes (£160) concs. per cow	400	0·26	489	0·23	577	0·20
1·50 tonnes (£240) concs. per cow	320	0·39	409	0·34	497	0·30
2·00 tonnes (£320) concs. per cow	240	0·53	329	0·45	417	0·40

4. *Net Replacement Costs.* (i.e. Herd Depreciation less Value of Calves) were calculated as follows (for Ayrshires):

	£ per cow in herd
Cost of replacements: 22·5 per cent of herd per year @ £450 ...	101
LESS Value of culls: 22·5 per cent of herd per year @ £295 (allowing for casualties)	66
Herd Depreciation	35
LESS Annual Value of Calves*	38
Net Annual Replacement Gain**	3

*Allowing for calving index of 395 days and calf mortality; mixture of pure bred calves and beef crosses.

**Higher cull and calf prices should be obtained for Shorthorns.

5. *Miscellaneous Variable Costs.* See Note 7 for Friesians (page 33).

6. *Stocking Rate.* See, in general, Note 8 for Friesians (page 33). The (average) stocking rate of 1·95 cows per forage hectare given above relates to Ayrshires (and compares with 1·85 for Friesians); Shorthorns would have as high a requirement as Friesians.

DAIRY FOLLOWERS *(per Heifer reared)*

A. *Friesians*

Performance Level	Low £	Average £	High £
Value of heifer (allowing for culls) (1)	570	570	570
LESS Value of calf (allowing for 7% mortality)	75	75	75
OUTPUT	495	495	495
Variable Costs:			
Concentrate Costs (2)	175	150	125
Miscellaneous Variable Costs (3) ...	33	33	33
TOTAL VARIABLE COSTS (excluding Forage)	208	183	158
GROSS MARGIN per Heifer, before deducting Forage Variable Costs ...	287	312	337
Forage Variable Costs (fert. and seed)	55	70	85
GROSS MARGIN per Heifer	232	242	252
Forage Hectares (Acres) per Heifer reared (4)	1·0(2·5)	0·85(2·1)	0·7(1·7)
GROSS MARGIN per Forage Hectare (5)	232	285	360
GROSS MARGIN per Forage Acre ...	94	115	146

B. *Channel Island Breeds*

Performance Level	Low £	Average £	High £
Value of heifer (allowing for culls) (1)	340	340	340
LESS Value of calf (allowing for 7% mortality)	15	15	15
OUTPUT	325	325	325
Variable Costs:			
Concentrate Costs (2)	145	125	105
Miscellaneous Variable Costs (3) ...	28	28	28
TOTAL VARIABLE COSTS	173	153	133
GROSS MARGIN per Heifer, before deducting Forage Variable Costs ...	152	172	192
Forage Variable Costs (fert. and seed)	48	58	68
GROSS MARGIN per Heifer	104	114	124
Forage Hectares (Acres) per Heifer reared (4)	0·8(2·0)	0·7(1·7)	0·55(1·35)
GROSS MARGIN per Forage Hectare (5)	130	163	225
GROSS MARGIN per Forage Acre ...	53	66	91

C. Ayrshires

Performance Level	Low £	Average £	High £
Value of heifer (allowing for culls) (1)	427·5	427·5	427·5
LESS Value of calf (allowing for 7% mortality)	27·5	27·5	27·5
OUTPUT	400	400	400
Variable Costs:			
Concentrates (2)	165	140	115
Miscellaneous Variable Costs (3)	33	33	33
TOTAL VARIABLE COSTS	198	173	148
GROSS MARGIN per Heifer, before deducting Forage Variable Costs	202	227	252
Forage Variable Costs (fert. and seed)	52	66	80
GROSS MARGIN per Heifer	150	161	172
Forage Hectares (Acres) per Heifer reared (4)	0·95 (2·35)	0·8 (2·0)	0·65 (1·6)
GROSS MARGIN per Forage Hectare (5)	158	201	265
GROSS MARGIN per Forage Acre	64	81	107

Notes

1. The heifer values are based on the purchase price of down-calving heifers, allowing for culls. Most heifers are home-reared. If heifers are reared for sale, the price of whole batches are likely to be lower than the values given in the tables, by perhaps 10 or 15 per cent. On the other hand the purchaser will often take the batch a few months before the average expected calving date, thus reducing feed and area requirements for the rearer.

2. The lower levels of concentrate costs are the combined result of more economical feeding and a lower average calving age. (Other things being equal, however, including the overall level of management, a lower calving age requires higher levels of feeding.)

3. Miscellaneous variable costs exclude straw. Straw requirements average approx. 1 tonne per heifer reared, but are variable, depending on time of year and age when calved, as well as system of housing and extent of outwintering.

4. The lower levels of area per heifer reared are the combined result of a higher stocking density and a lower average calving age.
   With an average calving age of 2½ years, a "replacement unit" (i.e. calf + yearling + heifer) equals about 1·4 livestock units, and the three stocking rates given above would be equivalent to 0·7, 0·6 and 0·5 forage hectares (1·7, 1·5, 1·25 acres) respectively per Friesian cow.

5. Much higher gross margin figures per hectare can be combined by intensive grazing methods, particularly if combined with winter feeding systems which involve little dependence on home-produced hay or silage (cf. Note 8, p. 25, last three paragraphs).

6. *Contract Rearing:* see pages 153-4.

7. *Labour:* see page 78.

Self-Contained Dairy Herd: Cows and Followers

At average annual replacement rates (22·5 per cent of the milking herd), just over one-quarter of a replacement unit is required for each cow in the herd, i.e. roughly one calf, yearling and heifer for every four cows (including calved heifers)—with a few extra calves reared to allow for culling. At average stocking rates for both this means approximately 1 hectare devoted to followers for every 3 hectares for cows. Since surplus youngstock are often reared and frequently the stocking rate is less intensive the ratio is often 1:2·5 or even 1:2 in practice. 1:3·5 is about the minimum where all replacement heifers are reared, unless their winter feeding is based largely on straw and purchased supplements, or unless there is a combination of long average herd life and early calving.

Gross Margin per Forage Hectare (Acre) (£) for the Whole Herd (i.e., Cows and Followers Combined); (at four levels of performance, including four commensurate levels of stocking rate, for the dairy cows; and three levels of performance, including different stocking rates, for the followers) are as follows, *assuming a 3:1 land use ratio* (dairy cow area: followers area); (Friesians only):

		G.M. per Forage Hectare (Acre) Dairy Cows			
		£ Low	£ Average	£ High	£ Very High
		549 (222)	740 (300)	959 (388)	1148 (464)
G.M. per Forage	Low	232 (94)	470 (190)	613 (248)	777 (315)	919 (372)
Hectare (Acre),	Average	285 (114)	483 (195)	626 (253)	790 (320)	932 (377)
Followers	High	360 (146)	502 (203)	645 (261)	809 (327)	951 (385)

As an example, the above table indicates that at the average level of performance and stocking rate for both cows and followers, the whole dairy gross margin per hectare (acre) figure falls to £626 (253) compared with £740 (300) for the dairy cows alone.

BEEF

Fat cattle prices were mainly 5 to 10p per live kg below target price levels in the second half of 1983 and 12 to 18p below in the first half of 1984. Approximate monthly target prices for the 1984/5 marketing year are given below (pence per kg liveweight). The average for the year is approximately 107p. The maximum rate of variable premium payable will be 8·74p per kg.

April 1984	...	...	... 111·2	October 1984	...	...	... 102·2
May	...	...	... 110·6	November	...	...	... 102·5
June	...	...	... 109·3	December	...	...	... 104·3
July	...	...	... 107·3	January 1985	...	...	... 106·7
August	...	...	... 104·9	February	...	...	... 110·0
September	...	...	... 102·9	March	...	...	... 111·2

The prices assumed in subsequent tables relate either to *the 1985 calendar year or 1985/6*, as appropriate (*e.g.* the latter is used for winter fattened beef). The spring price is taken to be 111p and the autumn price 102·5p. This assumes that market prices, together with any variable premiums paid, will be approximately at target levels and that these will be approximately the same as those for 1984/5. If average market prices fall more than 8·74p below target prices outputs (£) per head will be lower (assuming the same maximum variable premium). Only if market prices exceed target prices will they be higher.

Calf prices are highly variable. It is the balance between three (or four) factors: calf (or store) prices, fat cattle prices and feedingstuff prices (and in some cases stocking rate), that will mainly determine the levels of the gross margin and profit for the different beef systems included in the following pages. Small differences in each factor can cause large differences in the margins.

1. Early Weaning—Bucket Rearing (per calf)

										£
Value of Calf (6 months)			...	...	...	...	...	...	...	250
LESS Calf (1)		...	...	...	...	...	...	...	...	100
OUTPUT	...	...	...	...	...	...	...	...	...	150
Variable Costs:										
Concentrates (2)		...	...	...	...	...	...	...	...	75
Miscellaneous Variable Costs (including 5 forage)				...	...	...			10
TOTAL VARIABLE COSTS			...	...	...	...	...	...	...	85
GROSS MARGIN per Calf reared				...	...	...	...	...	...	65

Notes

1. £95 per calf (strong Friesian steers, 1 week old); 6 per cent mortality assumed, mainly in first 3 weeks.

2. Concentrates equal approximately £9·50 (12·5 kg @ £760/tonne) for milk substitute (to 5 weeks), plus 400 kg purchased concentrates (125 weaner pellets @ £185/tonne; 275 rearer nuts @ £165/tonne); £6 might be saved by home-mixing (£3 deducted above). Approximately 200 kg of hay and 200 kg bedding straw are also required.

3. Calves fed less well, i.e. with lower concentrate costs, will fetch proportionally lower market prices, probably resulting in a lower gross margin.

   To 12 weeks only: milk substitute plus concentrates (160 kg) approx. £38 a head. Calf value approx. £180. Gross margin approx. £37·50.

   Contract rearing charge (both 0 to 12 weeks and 0 to 26 weeks): £6·25 per week. Direct labour cost: approx. £16·50 per head to 6 months.

   Labour requirements (all beef systems): see page 86.

42

BEEF

2. Single Suckling (per Cow)

System	Late Winter/ Spring Calving		Autumn/Early Winter Calving		Upland
Performance Level (1)	Average	High	Average	High	Average
	£	£	£	£	£
Value of Calf (2)	250	265	285	315	245
Subsidies (3)	25	25	25	25	69
Less Cow and Bull Depreciation and Calf Purchases (4)	43	43	43	43	43
Output	232	247	267	297	271
Variable Costs:					
Concentrate Costs	35	45	45	60	35
Miscellaneous Variable Costs (5)	16	16	18	18	16
Total Variable Costs (excluding forage)	51	61	63	78	51
Gross Margin per Cow, before deducting Forage Variable Costs	181	186	204	219	220
Forage Variable Costs	45	50	48	54	50
Gross Margin per Cow	136	136	156	165	170
Forage Hectares (Acres) per Cow (6)	0·6	0·5	0·65	0·525	0·85 (7)
	(1·5)	(1·25)	(1·6)	(1·3)	(2·1)
Gross Margin per Forage Hectare	227	272	240	314	200
Gross Margin per Forage Acre ...	92	110	97	127	81

Notes

1. Performance level relates to variations in two factors: weaner calf weight and stocking rate. Improvement in the former is assumed to require extra concentrate feeding and in the latter extra fertilizer. "High" refers to the average levels likely to be achieved by the better fifty per cent of producers. It is clearly possible to set still higher "targets".

2. 94 per cent calving assumed (92 per cent upland). The figure is the estimated sale price less 6 per cent.
   Weight of calves: late winter/spring calving: average 230-250 kg, high 250-270 kg; autumn/early winter calving: average 260-290 kg, high 290-320 kg; upland 220-250 kg.

3. Suckler herd subsidy of £24.74 per cow; (note, milk producers and part-time farmers are ineligible). Hill Compensatory Allowance £44·50 per cow.

4. Assumptions: 6-year herd life of cows (purchase price £600, average cull value £410); 5 per cent calf mortality.

5. Straw is not included. Where yarded in winter, requirements average 0·5-0·75 tonne per cow for spring calvers and 0·75 tonne for autumn calvers.

6. The higher stocking density implies better use of grassland. Higher stocking rates can also be achieved by buying in some or all of the winter bulk fodder requirements, or by winter feeding largely on arable by-products, including straw. Purchased bulk fodder and/or straw balancer concentrates will reduce gross margin per cow but per hectare figures will be higher.

7. Forage Hectares (Acres) per cow and Gross Margin per Forage Hectare (Acre) relate to "in-bye equivalent" (3 hectares rough grazing are taken as being equal to 1 hectare of in-bye land).

BEEF

3. Double and Multiple Suckling (per Cow)

	Double Suckling	Multiple Suckling		
	Output level (1)			
No. of calves per cow	2	4	5·5	7
	£	£	£	£
Value of Calves (6 months old)	475	930	1255	1565
Subsidy (2)	25	25	25	25
Less { Calf Costs (including Replacement Calves) (3)	115	330	500	670
{ Cow Depreciation	38	40	42	44
OUTPUT (3)	347	585	738	876
Variable Costs:				
Concentrates	112	226	289	353
Miscellaneous Variable Costs (4) ...	25	35	42	50
TOTAL VARIABLE COSTS (excluding forage)	137	261	331	403
GROSS MARGIN per Cow, before deducting Forage Variable Costs	210	324	407	473
Forage Variable Costs	52	60	68	76
GROSS MARGIN per Cow	158	264	339	397
Forage Hectares (Acres) per Cow	0·65	0·7	0·75	0·8
	(1·6)	(1·7)	(1·85)	(2)
GROSS MARGIN per Forage Hectare ...	243	377	452	496
GROSS MARGIN per Forage Acre	98	153	183	201

Notes

1. The different levels of output refer only to different numbers of calves reared per cow. The standards are averages at each level of output. There are wide variations in prices obtained and paid per calf and in concentrate costs: together they can make a very large difference to the gross margin.

2. Beef cow subsidy (see note 3, p. 43).

3. Calf cost assumed: £100 (average steers and heifers, 1 week old). Calf mortality assumed: 7 per cent (double suckling) to 12 per cent (7 calves per cow).

4. Miscellaneous variable costs exclude straw: approx. 1 tonne per cow.

BEEF

4. Fattening Strong Store Cattle (per head) (1)

	Summer Fattening £	Winter Fattening £
Sales	533(2)	555(3)
LESS Purchased Store	444(4)	430(5)
OUTPUT	89	125
Variable Costs:		
Concentrates	5	67(6)
Miscellaneous Variable Costs	12	14(7)
TOTAL VARIABLE COSTS (excluding Forage)	17	81
GROSS MARGIN per Head before deducting Forage		
Variable Costs	72	44
Forage Variable Costs	21	11
GROSS MARGIN per Head	51	33
Forage Hectares (Acres) per Head	0·3(·75)	0·15(·37)
GROSS MARGIN per Forage Hectare	170	220
GROSS MARGIN per Forage Acre	69	89

Notes

1. The financial results of this enterprise are highly dependent on the market margin, i.e. the difference between the price per kg paid for the store and the price per kg obtained for the fat animal. Other important factors are the stocking rate and the degree of dependence on cash-crop by-products and the quality of conserved grass (and hence the quantity of concentrates required in relation to the liveweight gain) in the case of winter fattening.
2. 520 kg @ 102·5p.
3. 500 kg @ 111p.
4. 400 kg @ 111p.
5. 420 kg @ 102·5p.
6. 450 kg @ £150/tonne.
7. Excluding straw: average 0·75 tonne per head.

BEEF

5. Barley Beef (per Head)

									£
Sales (1)	...	...	...	...	...	...	...	...	447
LESS Calf (2)		...	...	...	...	...	...	...	102
OUTPUT	...	...	...	...	...	...	...	...	345
Variable Costs:									
Concentrates (3)		...	...	...	...	...	...	...	257
Miscellaneous (4)		...	...	...	...	...	...	...	10
Hay (5)	...	...	...	...	...	...	...	...	5
TOTAL VARIABLE COSTS	...	...	...	...	...	...	...	272
GROSS MARGIN per Head	...	...	...	...	...	...	...	73

Notes

1. 405 kg assumed, with killing out percentage of 52·5 per cent, i.e. 213 kg deadweight. Sale price assumed equals £2·10 per kg D.W. (=110p per kg L.W.), including premium over "guarantee" level. All year round production is assumed.

2. £95 per bull calf (1 week old) + 7 per cent mortality.

3. £38 calf rearing (to 12 weeks: see p.42) + £213 fattening ration + £6 food to losses. Fattening Ration: 17 parts barley @ £107·50 per tonne, 3 parts concentrate supplement @ £200 per tonne; plus milling and mixing. Total, £127·50 per tonne.
   Quantity: 1·67 tonne. This represents a conversion ratio of 5·6:1 from 107 kg to 405 kg. Each difference of 0·2:1 in the conversion ratio means a difference of £7·65 in food costs (60 kg).
   A difference of £5 per tonne in the cost of barley changes the feed cost by approximately £7 per head.
   Excellent performance would be: conversion ratio 5:1 (from 113 kg (12 weeks) to 405 kg)=fattening ration, 1·46 tonnes; gross margin:additional £27.
   Average daily liveweight gain: 0 to 12 weeks, 0·75 kg; 12 weeks to slaughter (at about 50 weeks old), 1·12 kg.

4. Excluding bedding.

5. Hay: 100 kg, assumed purchased.

BEEF

6. Fattening Single-suckled Calves and Wintering Single-suckled Calves for Sale as Stores (per Head)

SYSTEM (1)	A	B	C	D	E	F
	£	£	£	£	£	£
Sales (2)	472	444	436	500	538	333
LESS Suckled Calf	315	280	260	260	260	245
OUTPUT	157	164	176	240	278	88
Variable Costs:						
Concentrates	69	93	35	53	27	35
Miscellaneous (3)	9	9	12	18	21	8
TOTAL VARIABLE COSTS (excluding forage)	78	102	47	71	48	43
GROSS MARGIN per Head before deducting Forage Variable Costs	79	62	129	169	230	45
Forage Variable Costs	12	12	32	48	72	10
GROSS MARGIN per Head	67	50	97	121	158	35
Forage Hectares (Acres) per Head (4) ...	·15	·15	·4	·6	·9	·15
	(·37)	(·37)	(1)	(1·5)	(2·2)	(·37)
GROSS MARGIN per Forage Hectare ...	447	333	243	202	176	233
GROSS MARGIN per Forage Acre ...	181	135	98	82	71	94

Notes

1. A October and November born calves sold fat in spring at 16 to 18 months.
   B Spring-born calves sold fat in spring at 12 to 14 months.
   C Spring-born calves sold fat in late summer and autumn at 18 to 20 months.
   D Spring-born calves sold fat in late winter and early spring at 21 to 24 months.
   E Spring-born calves sold fat in summer and autumn at 27 to 30 months.
   F Spring-born calves sold as stores in spring at approximately 12 months.

   All systems assume half steer and half heifer calves, bought (or transferred to the fattening or store enterprise) in the autumn. The more intensive the system the more dependent is its profitability on the purchase price of the calf and the quality of the bulk winter fodder (whether hay or silage), which largely determines the quantity of concentrates needed and/or the rate of gain achieved.

2. Weights and Prices assumed:
   A 425 kg @ 111p.
   B 400 kg @ 111p.
   C 425 kg @ 102·5p.
   D 450 kg @ 111p.
   E 525 kg @ 102·5p.
   F 300 kg @ 111p.

3. Straw extra: 0·5 to 0·75 tonne per head.

4. Small variations in forage area per head have a large effect on gross margin per hectare (acre) in systems A, B and F, particularly A. For example, the gross margin per hectare (acre) for A is reduced from £447 (181) to £268 (108) at ·25 ha (·6 acre) per head.

BEEF

7. 18 Month Beef from Bucket Reared Calves (per Head)

	Autumn-born calf £	Spring-born calf £
Sales (1)	527	466
Less Calf (2)	127	117
Output	400	349
Variable Costs:		
Concentrates (3)	165	147
Miscellaneous (4)	21	19
Total Variable Costs (excluding Forage)	186	166
Gross Margin per Head before deducting Forage		
Variable Costs	214	183
Forage Variable Costs	35	35
Gross Margin per Head	179	148
Forage Hectares (Acres) per Head (5)	0·35(·85)	0·35(·85)
Gross Margin per Forage Hectare	511	423
Gross Margin per Forage Acre	207	171

Notes

1. Sale weights and prices. Autumn-born: 475 kg @ 111p, Spring-born: 455 kg @ 102·5p. Heifer calves normally fatten at lighter weights, with a smaller feed intake. Friesian steers usually fatten at heavier weights, with either more concentrates fed or at 21-24 months of age.

2. Calf (beef-cross bull calf, 1 week old). £120 for autumn-born calf, £110 for spring-born, plus 6 per cent mortality, mainly in first 3 weeks.

3. Concentrates. Variable, especially according to quality of winter fodder. Average, after 6 months old (£75: see page 42): autumn-born calf, 600 kg @ £150 per tonne; spring-born calf, 500 kg @ £145 per tonne (half purchased compounds, half home-mixed); plus allowance for losses.

4. Straw extra: average 0·5 tonne per head.

5. The area per head can be substantially lowered especially for autumn-born calves (to 0·3 hectare (0·75 acre), or even less), by intensive grazing on fresh leys. Given a 25% increase in forage variable costs per head, and assuming returns and all other costs remained the same, a reduction to 0·3 ha per head would increase the gross margin per hectare (acre) to £567 (229) for autumn-born calves and £463 (188) for spring-born calves.

6. In both cases there is a possibility that some calves will not finish in 18 months, i.e. that some autumn-born calves will have to be fattened off grass in their second summer, and that some spring-born calves will have to be finished during their second winter. The gross margin per hectare would then tend to fall.

BEEF
8. 24 Month Beef from Bucket Reared Calves (per Head)

	Autumn-born calf £	Spring-born calf £
Sales (1)	533	577
Less Calf (2)	127	117
OUTPUT	406	460
Variable Costs:		
Concentrates	150	190
Miscellaneous	23	26
Forage	55	47
TOTAL VARIABLE COSTS	228	263
GROSS MARGIN per Head	178	197
Forage Hectares (Acres) per Head	0·65 (1·6)	0·55 (1·35)
GROSS MARGIN per Forage Hectare	274	358
GROSS MARGIN per Forage Acre	111	145

Notes
1. 520 kg. Autumn-born: 102·5p per kg; spring-born: 111p.
2. See note 2, p. 48.

VEAL

	£
Sale value (1)	294
Less Calf (2)	101
OUTPUT	193
Variable Costs:	
Concentrates (3)	146
Miscellaneous	7
TOTAL VARIABLE COSTS	153
GROSS MARGIN per Head (4)	40

Notes
1. Sold at 170 kg liveweight (bought at 45 kg), average 102 kg dressed carcase weight, 15 weeks old. Killing out percentage, 60 per cent. Price assumed: £2·88 per kg d.c.w., which is the price required on the assumptions made to leave a £40 gross margin.
2. £95 per calf (strong Friesian bull calf, 1 week old); 6 per cent mortality assumed, mainly in first three weeks. Cheaper calves, of different breeds, can be purchased, but the fattening period could then be longer and the food conversion rate poorer. In recent years loose-housing in groups has gained considerably in popularity compared with the individual crate system assumed in the figures given here.
3. Feed: £760 per tonne. A conversion rate of 1·5 kg of food per kg liveweight gain is assumed (plus an allowance for losses) = approx. 192 kg total.
4. The gross margin is obviously highly dependent on calf price, the market price of veal, and feed efficiency.

SHEEP
A. Lowland Fat Lamb Production (per Ewe)

Performance level	Low	Average	High
Lambs reared per ewe (1)	1·2	1·35	1·6
Average price per lamb (£) (2)	35·75	35·25	34·75
	£	£	£
Lamb sales	42·9	47·6	55·6
Ewe Premium (3)	5·0	5·0	5·0
Wool (4)	3·2	3·2	3·2
Cull ewes and rams	6·3	6·3	6·3
Sub-total	57·4	62·1	70·1
LESS Ewe and ram replacements	16·3	16·3	16·3
OUTPUT	41·1	45·8	53·8
Variable Costs:			
Concentrates (50 kg)		7·5	
Vet. and Med.		2·5	
Miscellaneous and Transport		1·7	
TOTAL VARIABLE COSTS (excluding Forage)		11·7	
GROSS MARGIN per Ewe before deducting Forage Variable Costs	29·4	34·1	42·1
Forage Variable Costs (fertilizer and seed)	5·7	7·2	7·5
GROSS MARGIN per Ewe	23·7	26·9	34·6
Stocking Rate (Ewes, with lambs, per forage hectare (acre))	7·5(3·05)	9(3·65)	12(4·85)
GROSS MARGIN per Forage Hectare	178	242	415
GROSS MARGIN per Forage Acre	72	98	168

Notes
1. *Lambs reared per ewe* (× 100 = lambing percentage) is derived as follows (*average figures* only):
   Lambs born per 100 ewes lambing = 160
   Lambs born per 100 ewes put to ram = 150
   (93·5% of ewes put to ram bear lambs: 1·25% deaths, 5.25% barren)
   Lamb mortality: 9·5% (inc. 3·5% dead at birth or before seen)
   Lambs reared per 100 ewes lambing = 145
   Lambs reared per 100 ewes put to ram = 135
2. *Lamb Prices.* At any given level of management one would expect a lower lambing percentage to be associated with a faster growing lamb and in many cases a higher price per lamb. In the above table, however, it is assumed that this effect is largely offset by subsequent management, which is assumed to be better at the higher performance levels. Thus only a small decrease in price has been assumed as lambing percentage increases.
   Market prices were considerably (i.e. 70 to 80p) below the guide (guaranteed) prices in the second half of 1983, slowly closing during the first half of 1984. In 1984/5 the whole of the difference will continue to be made up to producers by the variable premium. The maximum payable weight for all certified sheep is 24·5 kg dw.
   Approximate monthly average guide prices for certified sheep for the 1984/85 marketing year are given below (pence per kg estimated dressed carcass weight). Compared with the 1983/4 scale these prices are higher from mid-December to mid-June, but lower from mid-June to mid-December, and particularly lower from mid-June to the end of August. They are level from early July to early October, instead of gradually falling, as before.

April 1984	256	October 1984	199
May	250	November	207
June	230	December	220
July	199	January 1985	237
August	198	February	251
September	198	March	258

The price for fat lamb *for the 1985 mid-season lamb crop* is assumed to be 200p, which assumes no increase over the above 1984 guide prices, with nearly all the lambs sold between the end of June and the end of October. This means a return of £36 for an 18 kg fat lamb. However, the average price given in the above table allows for a proportion sold (or retained) in the autumn as *store* lambs, increasing as lambing percentage and stocking rate increase.

A difference in price of £2 per lamb (i.e. a difference of approx. 11p per kg for an 18 kg lamb) causes a difference of approximately £18, £24 and £38 (7, 10, 16) to the low, average and high gross margins per hectare (acre) respectively.

3. Ewe annual compensatory premium; this E.E.C. payment per ewe is difficult to predict. £6.81 per ewe was paid for the 1983/4 marketing year in Great Britain, but the high level of E.E.C. sheep subsidy could lead to future cuts.

4. *Wool.* The guaranteed price for 1984 is 120p per kg. After deducting marketing costs producers are likely to receive an average net price of approx. 98p per kg. 100p per kg has been assumed for 1985 (weight 3·2 kg).

5. *Breed* will obviously have a large effect on lambing percentage, rate of liveweight gain (reflected in price per lamb), and amount of wool per ewe.

6. *Stocking Density.* The stocking rates assumed are based on land requirements *throughout the year.* With a given level of management one would expect higher stocking rates to be associated with a lower gross margin per ewe. The assumption made in the initial table, however, is that management performance is affecting both factors together.

The following figures are the *Gross Margins (£) per hectare (acre)* at six different stocking rates at the three production levels quoted, *assuming* seed and fertilizer costs vary with the stocking rate, and that for this reason and because of better all-round management *all lambs are sold fat*—an optimistic assumption, particularly with high lambing percentages and stocking rates.

Stocking Density	Performance level			Forage V.Cs. assumed per hectare (acre) (£)
	Low	Average	High	
7 ewes per ha (2·85 per acre)	173(70)	211(85)	274(111)	35(14)
9 ewes per ha (3·65 per acre)	202(80)	251(102)	332(134)	65(26)
11 ewes per ha (4·45 per acre)	247(100)	306(124)	405(164)	80(32)
13 ewes per ha (5·25 per acre)	286(116)	356(144)	473(191)	100(40)
15 ewes per ha (6·05 per acre)	320(130)	401(162)	536(217)	125(51)
17 ewes per ha (6·85 per acre)	355(144)	447(181)	600(243)	150(61)

Farmers able to achieve average lambing percentages of 160 or more, with a stocking rate exceeding 14 per hectare (5·65/acre) (all the year), who are still able to sell most lambs fat, are thus able to achieve gross margins exceeding £500 per hectare (£200/acre) (especially if they have lower ewe depreciation charges than assumed in the main tables, as often appears to be the case), but these are exceptional. Others are able to achieve high per hectare figures by substantial use of arable by-products (e.g. autumn or spring grazing of grass grown primarily for seed) and catch crops (e.g. rape).

A stocking rate of 14 per hectare (5·65/acre) would require a stocking rate of around 22 ewes (with lambs) per hectare (9/acre) in the spring and early summer. If there are no grazing livestock other than sheep on the farm, some ewes, at the higher stocking rates, will have either to be agisted (away-wintered) or housed indoors, thus reducing the margin. Agistment costs around 26p per week plus transport, i.e. about £7 per year. Depreciation and Interest on new Housing (1·2 sq. m per ewe) is approximately £2·75 per ewe per year (10-year life); extra hay and perhaps concentrates will also be required. These extra costs have not been allowed for in the above table.

On the other hand, with only 7 or 8 ewes per hectare (2·75 to 3·25/acre) on a lowland farm of reasonable quality with no other grazing livestock, there should be surplus grass available in the late spring or early summer; this could be cut for hay or used for seed production. No allowance has been made for this in the above table.

51

7. *Replacement Costs.* It is assumed above that 22 per cent of the ewe flock is culled each year @ £27·50 each and that, allowing for 3 per cent mortality, 25 per cent are purchased at £60 each. Rams: 1 per 40 to 50 ewes, 3-year life, purchased @ £175, sold @ £35.

8. *Miscellaneous Costs* include lambing and shearing bonus. Contract shearing is approximately 60p per head, including rolling (but up to 75p for small flocks).

9. *Prices of Specialized Equipment:*

Troughs (2·75 m)	£35 to £40
Racks (2½ to 3 m)	£110 to £145
Foot Baths (3 m)	£55 to £70
Shearer (electric)	£380 to £760 (two heads)
Netting	45p to 75p per metre

10. *Fencing:* approximately 90p per metre + 40p labour.

11. *Home-reared tegs* (shearlings). Output: value £57·50 (allowing for mortality) less £34 for the lamb, plus £3 for wool = £26·50. Variable costs (including forage) = £12·50. Gross margin per head = £14, per forage hectare £175 (£71 per acre).

   If the figures for home-reared replacement tegs are included in the figures per ewe, the latter are increased approximately as follows: output by £6·50, gross margin (per ewe) by £3·50. The stocking rate in terms of ewes per hectare devoted to sheep will be about 15 per cent less.

12. *Labour:* see page 87

B. Other Sheep Systems (average performance level only)

System	Early Fat Lamb per ewe	Winter Fattening of Store Lambs per head	Upland Sheep per ewe	Hill Sheep per ewe
Lambs reared per ewe	1·27	—	1·22	0·97
	£	£	£	£
Average price per lamb sold ...	44·0	38·0	33·0	27·8
Lamb sales	55·9	38·0	41·2	19·5
Ewe premium	5·0	—	5·0	5·0
Wool	3·2	—	2·4	1·7
Cull ewes and rams	6·9	—	3·7	4·5
Subsidy	—	—	4·2	6·2
Sub-total	71·0	38·0	56·5	36·9
Less Livestock Purchases	18·1	31·0	9·8	1·3
Output	52·9	7·0	46·7	35·6
Variable Costs:				
Concentrates	14·0	2·2	5·5	3·3
	(90 kg)	(15 kg)	(37 kg)	(22 kg)
Vet. and Med.	2·5	0·2	1·9	1·5
Miscellaneous and Transport ...	1·7	0·3	1·2	2·3
Total Variable Costs (excl. Forage) ...	18·2	2·7	8·6	7·1
Gross Margin per ewe (or head) before deducting Forage Variable Costs ...	34·7	4·3	38·1	28·5
Forage Variable Costs (fert. and seed) ...	7·8	1·1	5·2	2·3
Gross Margin per ewe (or head) ...	26·9	3·2	32·9	26·2
Stocking Rate (No. per Forage Ha (Acre))	10·25	50	7·5	—
	(4·15)	(20)	(3·05)	
Gross Margin per Forage Hectare ...	276	160	247	—
Gross Margin per Forage Acre	(112)	(65)	(100)	—

Notes

Early Fat Lambs. 24 per cent culling of the ewe flock and 4 per cent ewe mortality are assumed; other replacement assumptions are as for Fat Lamb Production. In this system, 60 per cent of the lambs are sold before the end of May, and the remainder before the end of August. This may be compared with *Mid-Season* lamb production (see table on page 50), in which 75 - 80 per cent of the lambs are sold in June, July and August, and *Late* lamb production, in which only two-thirds or so of the lambs are sold fat, 60 per cent of total lambs being sold fat or as stores in October/November, or the stores retained for winter fattening. The gross margin per ewe tends to be slightly higher with the latter system compared with Mid-Season production, provided the proportion of stores is not too high but more grass is utilized per ewe, making per hectare results similar.

Winter Fattening of Store Lambs. The gross margin per head is highly variable, depending very much on the difference between the purchase and sale price of the lambs.

Hill Sheep. The flock is assumed to be mainly self-maintained; thus only about 0·7 lambs are sold per ewe per annum and the fleece of the yearling ewes are included in wool sales. Results obviously vary according to the height of the hill and severity of the winter.

Note. The figures for early fat lamb production, upland and hill sheep are largely based on the relative figures for these systems as compared with lowland mid-season fat lamb production obtained from the M.L.C. commercial flock recording results.

GRANTS FOR BEEF AND SHEEP (1984/5)

Beef Cows. There is a suckler cow subsidy of £24·74 per cow. To be eligible the farmer must earn at least 50 per cent of his income from agriculture and spend at least 50 per cent of his time farming and not sell milk or milk products from his holding or holdings (except for small quantities of dairy products sold direct from the farm to the consumer).

Hill Livestock Compensatory Allowances: (a) Cows. £44·50 a head on eligible cows and in-calf heifers maintained in regular breeding herds on hill land for the purposes of breeding store cattle. Cows kept for selling milk are not eligible.

(b) Sheep. £6·25 per head on ewes of an approved breed which form part of a specially qualified flock. £4·25 per head is payable on other ewes in respect of which an allowance may be paid.

The maximum rates of subsidy per hectare are £60 for cattle and £54 for sheep.

Note: For guidance premiums under the Agriculture and Horticulture Development Scheme, see page 147.

GRAZING LIVESTOCK UNITS

Dairy Cows	...	...	1·00	Ewes and Ewe Replacements	
Beef Cows (excl. calf)	...		0·75	(excl. suckling lambs):	
Bulls ...	...	...	0·65	light *weight	0·06
Other Cattle (excl. intensive beef):				medium * weight ...	0·08
0-1 year old	...	...	0·34	heavy * weight	0·11
1-2 years old	...	...	0·65	Rams	0·08
over 2 years old		...	0·80	Lambs:	
Barley Beef	...	...	0·47	0 to Fat or Store,	
				and Purchased Stores ...	0·04
				0 to Hoggets	0·08

* most lowland breeds are medium; few are light.

Notes

1. Total livestock units on a farm should be calculated by multiplying the above ratios by the *monthly livestock numbers averaged over the whole year, except* in the case of *lambs,* when *throughput* should be used.

2. The ratios are based on relative requirements of metabolisable energy. Strictly speaking, when calculating stocking density, allowances should also be made for differences in output (e.g. milk yield per cow or liveweight gain per head), breed (e.g. Friesians *v.* Jerseys), and quantities of non-forage feed consumed.

Source: Definitions of Terms used in Agricultural Business Management; (M.A.F.F., Dec. 1977).

Approximations

The following approximations will often suffice in calculating stocking rates, especially in view of the points made in note 2 above:

Dairy Cows	...	...	1·00	Lowland Ewes	
Beef Cows (excl. calf)	...		0·80	(inc. lambs under 6 months)	0·15
Other Cattle				Rams and Tegs (over 6 months)	0·15
over 2 years old...		...	0·80	Hill Ewes	0·1
Semi-Intensive Beef					
(6 to 15-18 months old)...			0·70		
Other Cattle 1 to 2 years old...			0·60		
Other Cattle					
under 1 year old		...	0·40		

These livestock units all relate to requirements over a twelve month period: thus in calculating total livestock units the ratios should be multiplied by *monthly livestock numbers averaged over the whole year.*

FORAGE VARIABLE COSTS
(£ per hectare (acre) per annum)

	Grass-Dairying(1)	Grass-Other(1)	Forage Maize(2)	Kale
Yield (tonnes/ha)	—	—	30 (silage)	50
Seed	10 (4)	10 (4)	60 (24)	17 (7)
Fertilizer	95 (38)	50 (20)	85 (35)	95 (38)
Sprays	10 (4)	5 (2)	35 (14)	18 (7)
Total	115 (46)	65 (26)	180 (73)	130 (52)

	Rape and Turnips	Mangolds	Turnips and Swedes	Cabbage
Yield: tonnes/ha (tons/acre) ...	—	100 (40)	65 (26)	90 (36)
Seed/Plants	20 (8)	35 (14)	15 (6)	145 (59)
Fertilizer	90 (37)	115 (47)	95 (39)	190 (77)
Sprays	—	45 (18)	25 (10)	35 (14)
Total	110 (45)	195 (79)	135 (55)	370 (150)

(1) These are *average* figures only. Intensively grazed grass will have much higher fertilizer costs in particular—approaching or possibly even exceeding £185 (75) for dairying. The seed costs will vary according to the proportion, if any, of permanent pasture and the length of the leys. Fertilizer inputs are often less on permanent pasture too, but this depends largely on the attitude of the farmer/manager, which will also be reflected in the stocking rates and productivity levels per animal achieved. Note that the dairying figure is the average for the grass devoted to the *whole herd*, i.e., followers as well as cows; the figure for cows alone will be higher (approx. £128 (52) total forage variable costs).

(2) Contract work on maize: drilling £26 (11); harvesting (inc. carting and clamping) 100-145 (40-58).

Source (excl. leys): based substantially on Fodder Crops, by J. A. L. Dench and W. I. Buchanan, Agricultural Enterprise Studies, Economic Report No. 50, University of Reading, 1977 (updated by author).

Labour: grass, pages 80-1; kale, page 82; conservation labour, page 80. Conservation machinery, page 90.

Silage and Hay Costs

The average costs of producing and harvesting, on a full costs basis (i.e. including rental value of the land, all labour, share of general overheads, etc.) are approximately as follows:

Hay: £47·50 per tonne; Silage: £14·50 per tonne.

Approximately half the costs are for production and half for harvesting. For further details see the report quoted on page 81.

FODDER CROPS, GRASSES AND CLOVERS: SEED PRICES (1984) AND SEED RATES

Crop	Price	Seed Rate per hectare
Fodder Kale	£3·50 to £5·25 per kg (£7·00 to £10·50 graded)	3·4 to 4·5 kg (1·1 to 1·7 graded)
Swede	£6·00 per kg (£12·00 graded)	3·0 to 4·0 kg (less if graded)
Turnip	£3·00 per kg (£6·00 graded)	3·0 to 4·0 kg (less if graded)
Mangold	£3·25 per kg (£6·50 graded)	8 to 11 kg (less if graded)
Rape	£1·50 to £1·60 per kg	3·8 kg drilled 7·5 kg broadcast
Mustard	£0·70 per kg	22 to 28 kg
Rape and Turnips	£18· to £22 per hectare	10 to 11 kg rape 1 to 2 kg turnips
Rape, Kale and Turnips	£23 to £27 per hectare	—
Fodder Turnip	£1·50 to £2·50 per kg	9 kg broadcast
Forage Maize—Silage	£60 to £65 per hectare	110,000 to 120,000 seeds
Forage Maize—zero grazed	£70 to £85 per hectare	130,000 to 160,000 seeds
Arable Silage	£62 per hectare	125 kg oats, 60 kg tares
Tares	£27 per 50 kg	—
Italian Ryegrass	£1·20 to £1·50 per kg	—
Perennial Ryegrass	£1·20 to £1·50 per kg	—
Cocksfoot	£1·25 per kg	—
Timothy	£1·60 to £3·40 per kg	—
Meadow Fescue	£1·25 per kg	—
Broad Red Clover	£2·50 per kg	18 to 22 kg
Late-Flowering Red Clover	£1·75 per kg	18 to 22 kg
White Clover	£3·20 to £7·50 per kg	—
Kent Wild White Clover	£5·15 per kg	—
Alsike Clover	£1·00 per kg	11 kg
Lucerne	£4·30 per kg	18 to 22 kg
Rye	£12 per 50 kg	220 kg
Rye and Ryegrass	£57 per hectare	125 kg rye, 22 kg Italian ryegrass
1 year leys	£40 to £45 per hectare	—
2-3 year leys	£40 to £45 per hectare	—
3-5 year leys	£40 to £50 per hectare	—
Game cover	£25 per hectare	—
Horse grazing	£38 per hectare	—

4. PIGS AND POULTRY

PIGS

1. Breeding (to 25 kg liveweight)

Performance Level	Average			High	
	per sow	per weaner		per sow	per weaner
	£	£		£	£
Weaners: 19·5 (1) @ £26·50	517	26·50	22·5 (2) @ £26·50	596	26·50
LESS Livestock Depreciation (3)	12	0·60		17	0·75
OUTPUT	505	25·90		579	25·75
Variable Costs:					
Food (4)	370	18·95		370	16·45
Miscellaneous (5)	35	1·80		40	1·80
TOTAL VARIABLE COSTS	405	20·75		410	18·25
GROSS MARGIN (per year)	100	5·15		169	7·50

Notes

1. Weaners per sow—average: 9·05 reared per litter, 2·15 litters per year = 19·5 weaners per sow per year.

2. Weaners per sow—high: 9·55 reared per litter, 2·35 litters per year = 22·5 weaners per sow per year.

3. Livestock depreciation assumes approx. £15 per head difference between in-pig gilt price (approx. £115) and cull value per sow (approx. £100) and average of 6 litters per sow life. Sow mortality 4%. "High" compared with "Average"; higher gilt and boar purchase prices and fewer sows per boar assumed (22 v. 24).

4. Food—1·95 tonne per sow, including boar (approx. 0·05 tonne per sow) and creep feed (approx. 40% of total). Price of feed consumed: £190 per tonne; (average of home-mixed and purchased compounds).

5. Includes vet. and med., £12.

6. *Direct Labour Cost* per sow: average £100, good £70. See further page 87.

7. *Building Costs:* see pages 118, 120.

PIGS

2. *Fattening* (from 25 kg liveweight)

A. *Average Performance*

	Pork £	Cutter £	Bacon £
Sale Value	52·70	64·05	71·95
LESS Weaner Cost	26·50	26·50	26·50
Mortality charge	0·40	0·45	0·50
OUTPUT	25·80	37·10	44·95
Variable Costs:			
Food	22·55	31·80	36·20
Miscellaneous	1·00	1·25	1·35
TOTAL VARIABLE COSTS	23·55	33·05	37·55
GROSS MARGIN	2·25	4·05	7·40
Liveweight (kg)	69	85	93
Deadweight (kg)	49	62·5	69·5
Killing out (%)	71	73·5	74·5
Price per kg deadweight (p) ...	107·5	102·5	103·5
Food Conversion Rate (n.b. from 25 kg)	3·0	3·2	3·3
Food per pig (kg)	132	192	224
Average Cost of Food per tonne	£171	£165·5	£161·5
Food Cost per kg Liveweight Gain ...	51·2p	53·0p	53·2p
Fattening period (weeks)	12	16	17·5
Mortality (per cent)	2·0	2·3	2·3
Direct Labour Cost per pig	£1·95	£2·85	£3·20
B. *High Performance* (Food Conversion)			
Food Conversion Rate (n.b. from 25 kg)	2·4	2·7	2·8
Food per pig (kg)	106	152	190
Food Cost per pig	£18·15	£26·80	£30·70
Food Cost per kg Liveweight Gain ...	41·2p	53·0p	45·1p
Gross margin per pig	£6·65	£9·05	£12·90

Notes

Labour: see page 87.

Building Costs: see pages 118, 120.

Acknowledgement: These data are largely based on the latest published results from the Cambridge Pig Management Scheme, produced by R. F. Ridgeon, Agricultural Economics Unit, Dept. of Land Economy, Cambridge University and to a lesser extent on Meat and Livestock Commission figures, but the pig price and feed price assumptions are entirely the author's responsibility. Small differences in the relationship between these can of course cause large differences in margins. The weaner price is crucial as regards the relative margins between breeding and fattening.

*N.B. No attempt has been made in this section to forecast the **actual** position of the pig cycle during 1985. The figures represent only what the **average** trend figures are likely to be in that year, given neither an "up" nor a "down" stage prevailing for much of the year.*

EGG PRODUCTION
(brown egg layers, 52 week laying period, battery producers)

Performance Level				Average		High	
				per bird	per doz eggs	per bird	per doz eggs
				£	p	£	p
Egg Returns				10·75	50·0	11·75	50·0
Less Livestock Depreciation				1·70	7·9	1·70	7·2
Output (per year)				9·05	42·1	10·05	42·8
Variable Costs:							
Food				7·05	32·8	7·05	30·0
Miscellaneous				0·65	3·0	0·65	2·8
Total Variable Costs				7·70	35·8	7·70	32·8
Gross Margin				1·35	6·3	2·35	10·0

Notes

1. Hen-housed data are used throughout, i.e. the total costs and returns are divided by the number of birds housed at the commencement of the laying period.

2. The average price assumed (for 1985), 50p per dozen, is similar to 1984 levels. Various differentials and bonuses are available, and farmer-to-retailer prices are well above packer-to-producer levels.

   The *yields* assumed are.
Average	...	...	258 (21·5 dozen)
High	...		282 (23·5 dozen)

3. Livestock depreciation—the average point of lay pullet is priced at £2·25 (18 weeks old) less £0·55 for culls; (allowance has been made for mortality).

4. The food price assumed (for 1985) is £160 per tonne (average of home-mixed rations and purchased compounds). The feed cost is dependent on breed, type of house, environmental conditions and type of ration.
   Quantity of feed used = 44 kg.

5. Miscellaneous costs in this case include overhead costs specific to this enterprise.

6. *Direct Labour Costs:* average 75p per bird, premium 60p. See page 87.

   Housing Costs: see page 118. Deadstock depreciation averages about 75p per bird.

   Acknowledgement: see page 62.

REARING PULLETS
(Average per bird reared)

	£
Value of 18 week old bird	2·25
LESS Chicks 1·02 (1) @ 49p (including levy)	0·50
OUTPUT	1·75
Variable Costs:	
Food: 6·6 kg @ £164 per tonne	1·08
Miscellaneous (2)	0·27
TOTAL VARIABLE COSTS	1·35
GROSS MARGIN	0·40

1. Assumes 4 per cent mortality, but 2 per cent allowed in price.
2. Excluding transport (11p).

Labour 13p; *deadstock depreciation* 22p.

TABLE POULTRY

A. *Broilers* (per bird sold at 50 days)

	p
Returns 2·1 kg per bird @ 61·5p per kg L.W.	129·2
LESS Cost of Chick	20·0
OUTPUT	109·2
Variable Costs:	
Food: 4·4 kg per bird @ £210 per tonne	92·4
Heat, Light, Miscellaneous	14·0
TOTAL VARIABLE COSTS	106·4
GROSS MARGIN	2·8

Capital cost of housing and equipment: £3·00 per broiler space (depreciation cost approximately 3·8p per bird sold).

Labour: 4·5p, excluding catching and cleaning out (2·7p); see page 87.

Housing Costs: see page 118.

B. *Turkeys* (per bird sold) (1)

Size (2)	Light £	Medium £	Heavy £
Returns (Christmas) (3)	9·15	10·95	20·15
Returns (All Year Average) (3)	7·30	8·75	17·05
Less Cost of Poult	1·45	1·45	1·40
OUTPUT (Christmas)	7·70	9·50	18·75
OUTPUT (All Year Average)	5·85	7·30	15·65
Variable Costs:			
Food (£210 per tonne)	3·75	5·40	13·40
Miscellaneous	0·95	1·15	2·15
TOTAL VARIABLE COSTS	4·70	6·55	15·55
GROSS MARGIN (Christmas)	3·00	2·95	3·20
GROSS MARGIN (All Year Average)	1·15	0·75	0·10
Killing Age (weeks)	16	20	24
Deadweight (kg)	6·1	7·3	15·5
Food Conversion Factor	3·0	3·6	3·4
Food per bird (kg)	16·4	23·4	58·0

(1) 10% mortality allowed for in cost of poult and feed figures.
(2) Light and medium: hen birds; heavy: stags.
(3) Price per kg D.W.: Christmas: hens 150p, stags 130p; All Year Average: hens 120p, stags 110p.

C. *Capons* (per bird sold at 14 weeks; Christmas—males only)

	£
Returns 5·10 kg @ 88p per kg.	4·49
Less Cost of Chick	0·34
OUTPUT	4·15
Variable costs:	
Food: 14·8 kg per bird @ £190 per tonne	2·81
Miscellaneous	0·26
TOTAL VARIABLE COSTS	3·07
GROSS MARGIN	1·08

D. Ducks (Aylesbury: per bird sold at 8 weeks)

	£
Returns 3 kg @ 120p per kg D.W.	3·60
LESS Cost of Duckling	0·60
OUTPUT	3·00
Variable Costs:	
Food: 10·35 kg per bird @ £195 per tonne	2·02
Miscellaneous	0·46
TOTAL VARIABLE COSTS	2·48
GROSS MARGIN	0·52

N.B. No allowance made above for mortality (average 8%).

Acknowledgement: The figures in the whole of the poultry section are as estimated by the Poultry Department of ADAS.

II. LABOUR

1. LABOUR COST

1. Statutory Minimum Wage Rates
(from June 3, 1984)

The minimum weekly rates relate to a 40-hour five-day standard week worked on any days between Monday and Saturday.(1) The rates apply to both men and women.

Grades I & II Age	Appointment Grade I Rate	Appointment Grade II Rate	Craftsman (2) Rates	Appointment Grades and Craftsman
		Weekly Rates		Overtime Rate per hour
	£	£	£	£
20 and over	111·78	103·50	95·22	3·57
19 ... (3)			85·70	3·21
18 ... (3)			76·18	2·86

Age	Whole-time Weekly Rate	Whole-time Overtime Rate per hour	Regular part-time over 30 hours per week (excl. overtime) Rate per hour (excl. overtime)	Regular part-time 30 hours or less per week (excl. overtime) Rate per hour (excl. overtime)	Overtime Rate per hour (excl. overtime)	Seasonal workers Rate per hour (excl. overtime)	Seasonal workers Overtime Rate per hour
	£	£	£	£	£	£	£
20 and over	82·80	3·11	2·07	1·97	2·95	1·76	2·64
19 ...	74·52	2·79	1·86	1·77	2·65	1·58	2·38
18 ...	66·24	2·48	1·66	1·57	2·36	1·41	2·11
17 ...	53·82	2·02	1·35	1·28	1·92	1·14	1·72
16 ...	45·54	1·71	1·14	1·08	1·62	97	1·45
15 ...	41·40	1·55	1·04	98	1·47	88	1·32
14 ...	—	—	—	93	—	84	—
13 ...	—	—	—	88	—	79	—

Other payments:	Age:	20+	19	18	17	16	15
Night Work Supplements per hour (p)		41	37	33	27	23	21
Stand-by Payments per day (£)		8·28	7·45	6·62	5·38	4·55	4·14

1. Holidays with pay (Regular Workers): 20 days for workers with 52 weeks' continuous service. The minimum holiday pay entitlement is at least 125% of the appropriate minimum rate for whole-time workers.

2. In early 1984 approximately 28 per cent of the regular whole-time male labour force in England and Wales were classified as craftsmen (plus 3·5 per cent as Grade I and 6 per cent as Grade II). However, many other workers receive basic wages above the "ordinary" rates.

3. These rates apply only to craftsmen who are qualified former Board apprentices.

4. Certain conditionally accepted pre-college students may be paid 75% of the appropriate minimum rate for age (for a maximum of one year).

2. Average Earnings(1)
(1985: estimated)(2)

Type of Worker	Average Total Earnings		Total Hours(3)
	Annual £	Per Week £	Per Week
All Hired Men	6805	130·90	47·1
Foremen	8225	158·20	46·1
Dairy Cowmen	8395	161·40	53·6
Tractor Drivers	7030	135·15	48·4
General Farm Workers	6250	120·15	46·1
Horticultural Workers ...	5885	113·20	43·0

1. Hired regular whole-time workers, England and Wales.
2. 1983 calendar year figures, plus 11 per cent.
3. Hours worked plus statutory holidays (in 1983).

Source: Wages and Employment Enquiry, M.A.F.F., with author's adjustments.

3. Typical Annual Labour Cost
(regular worker of 20 or more: from June 3, 1984*)

		Average Annual Cost £	Average Weekly Cost £	Average Hourly Cost(1) £
Minimum Wage (non-craftsman rate)		4389	84·40(2)	2·39
National Insurance Contribution (10·45 per cent of earnings) ...	459			
Employer's Liability Insurance (0·62%)	27	486	9·35	
		4875	93·75	2·65
Overtime, average 7·1 hours per week @ £3·11 (+ NIC, ELI)		1275	24·55	
		6150	118·30	2·78
"Premium" over basic rate, average £12·00 per week (3) (+ NIC, ELI)		695	13·35	
Total		6845	131·65	3·10

(NIC = National Insurance Contributions; ELI = Employer's Liability Insurance)
1. Hours, excluding overtime, based on 46 weeks (40 hours) per year, i.e. statutory holidays and a few days' illness have been deducted.
2. Including additional holiday pay.
3. Including craftsman addition if paid.
4. Annual cost of cottages, value of perquisites, etc., would have to be added where appropriate.

* For 1985 add 5 per cent (est.).

4. Assessing Annual Labour Requirements

The regular labour staff required for a farm is sometimes assessed by calculating the total number of Standard Man-Days (Man-Work Units), as given on page 154. The number of days supplied by casual labour are first deducted, then 15 per cent is added for general maintenance work; it is assumed that 300 Standard Man-Days are provided annually per man; allowance is made for any manual labour supplied by the farmer himself. Alternatively, no addition is made for maintenance work and 300 SMD are assumed to be provided by stockmen and 250 by other workers. (1 SMD = 8 labour hours a year.)

This is a very rough and inaccurate calculation since it makes no allowance for seasonality and the special circumstances of an individual farm, such as soil type, level of mechanization, and condition and layout of the buildings.

The following sections supply the type of data that should be used in assessing labour requirements.

2. LABOUR HOURS AVAILABLE FOR FIELD WORK
(per man per month)

	Total Ordinary Hours (1)	Adjusted Ordinary Hours (2)	% Workable	Available Ordinary Hours (3)	Available Overtime Hours (4)	Total Available Hours	Total Available "8-hour Days" (5)
January	177	148	50	74	28(61)	102(135)	13(17)
February	160	134	50	67	33(55)	100(122)	12½(15)
March	172	149	60	89	69(82)	158(171)	20(21½)
April	161	139	65	90	86	176	22
May	171	151	70	106	110	216	27
June	170	150	75	112	112	224	28
July	177	157	75	118	113	231	29
August	169	150	75	112	104	216	27
September	172	152	70	106	82(69)	188(195)	23½(24½)
October	177	153	65	99	63(83)	162(182)	20(23)
November	172	144	50	72	26(59)	98(131)	12(16½)
December	161	135	50	67	25(65)	92(132)	11½(16½)

(1) 40 hour week, less public holidays. No deductions have been made for other holidays because they may be taken at various times of the year.

(2) After deducting (a) for illness (10 per cent Nov. to Feb., 7½ per cent March, April and Oct., 5 per cent May to Sept.), and (b) for contingencies and non-delayable maintenance (½ hour per day).

(3) Adjusted Ordinary Hours × percentage Workable.

(4) Maximum 4 overtime hours per day summer, 3 hours winter, and 12 to 14 hours' work at weekends, according to season. Same adjustments for illness and percentage workable as for ordinary hours. Figures in brackets indicate hours available if headlights used up to limit of overtime stated. The percentage overtime (without headlights) available from weekend work as opposed to evenings = (January to December respectively): 100, 78, 58, 50, 40, 40, 41, 42, 53, 67, 100, 100.

(5) Total available hours ÷ 8.

Notes

1. *These figures relate to medium land. The percentage workability will be higher with light soils and less with particularly heavy soils.* On heavy soils, of course, the land may be virtually 100 per cent unworkable between late November and early March (or still later, according to the season), particularly if undrained. A rough estimate of variations in workability according to soil type (compared with the figures in the above table) are as follows. Heavy land—March, October, November: one-third less; April: one-fifth less; September: 10 per cent less; May to August: no difference. Light land—October to April: one-sixth more; May and September: 10 per cent more; June to August: no difference.

2. When these figures are used for farm planning, it must be remembered that indoor work, e.g. livestock tending or potato riddling, can be continued over the full working-week, i.e. the hours available are the Adjusted Ordinary Hours, plus overtime. Also, some handwork in the field has to continue even in rain, e.g. sprout picking.

3. To be precise, percentage workability varies according to the particular operation, e.g. compare ploughing and drilling.

4. Furthermore, some operations are limited by factors other than soil workability, e.g. combine-harvesting by grain moisture content.

5. Factors touched upon briefly above are discussed fully in Duckham's "The Farming Year".

3. SEASONAL LABOUR REQUIREMENTS FOR CROPS AND GRASS

On the following pages, data on labour requirements for various farm crops and types of livestock are given. Two levels are shown: average and premium. *The average figures relate to the whole range of conditions and farm size. The premium rates do not denote the maximum rates possible,* for instance by the use of especially high-powered tractors under ideal conditions, but relate to rates of work estimated to be obtainable of the whole season, averaging good and bad conditions, with the use of wide implements, largish tractors (40 to 55 kW) and high capacity equipment in 8 hectare fields and over, where no time is wasted. **Most farmers with more than 125 hectares of arable land are likely to achieve the premium levels shown. Those with over 250 hectares will have still bigger machines and therefore faster work rates, and thus require about 20 per cent less labour than even the premium levels given.**

The rates of work include morning preparation, travelling to and from the fields, and allow for minor breakdowns and other stoppages. They relate broadly to medium and medium-heavy land; some jobs, such as ploughing, may be done more quickly on light soils. Operations such as combine harvesting can obviously vary according to many factors to do with the topography and other natural features of the farm.

The usual times of year when each operation takes place are shown; these relate to lowland conditions in the south-eastern half of Britain. They will obviously vary between seasons, soil types, latitude and altitude. In particular, on light land, land can be ploughed over a longer winter period and a high proportion of cultivations for spring crops may be completed in February in many seasons. All such factors must be allowed for in individual farm planning. Conditions in different seasons will also affect, for instance, the number and type of cultivations required in seedbed preparation. Typical monthly breakdowns of requirements are given for various crops.

To illustrate the type of questions that need to be asked for full details of seasonal labour requirements on the individual farm, "Critical Questions affecting Timing" are listed for cereals and main crop potatoes. Similar questions would, of course, need to be asked for other crops.

WINTER WHEAT

Operations	Labour-Hours per hectare		Time of Year
	Average	Premium	
Plough (1)	2·9	2·0	July to October (according to previous crop)
Seedbed Cults. (2 cults.) ...	2·2	1·5	September to October (according to previous crop) (half August if ploughed in July)
Combine Drill, Cart Seed and Fertilizer, Harrow in ...	2·0	1·5	Mid-September to 1st week November (according to previous crop and soil)
Top Dress and Roll	1·1	0·7	Top Dress March or April, Roll mid-March to mid-April
Spraying	1·1	0·7	Spring/early summer
Combine, Cart Grain, Barn Work	3·5	2·3	Mid-August to 1st week September
Later Barn Work (2)	0·7	0·4	September to June
Total	13·5	9·1	
Straw: Bale	1·3	0·9 ⎫	Mid-August to end
Cart	4·5	3·0 ⎭	September

Typical Monthly Breakdown

Month	Average	Premium	Notes
October ...	4·8	3·3	Approx. ⅔ of Ploughing, Cults., Drill, Harrow
November ...	0·8	0·6	10-15% of Ploughing, Cults., Drill, Harrow
December ...	—	—	
January ...	—	—	
February ...	—	—	
March ...	0·6	0·4	Part Top Dress and Roll
April	1·1	0·7	Part Top Dress and Roll; Spraying
May	0·5	0·3	Spraying
June	—	—	
July	—	—	
August ...	2·6 (+3·1 Straw)	1·7 (+2·1 Straw)	¾ of harvesting
September (harvest) ...	0·9 (+2·7 Straw)	0·6 (+1·8 Straw)	¼ of harvesting
September (prepn. drill)	1·5	1·1	20-25% of Ploughing, Cults., Drill, Harrow

Notes
1. A high proportion of cereal crops are now being direct drilled or drilled after reduced, or minimal, cultivations, i.e. without traditional ploughing. Direct drilling reduces man-hours per hectare by about 4 (average) or 3 (premium), and minimal cultivations by about 2 (average) and 1·5 (premium).
2. Later barn work excluded from monthly breakdown.

Seasonal Labour Requirements

SPRING BARLEY

Operations	Labour-Hours per hectare		Time of Year
	Average	Premium	
Plough (1)	2·9	2·0	September-March (according to previous crop and soil type)
Seedbed Cults. (3 cults.) ...	2·4	1·7	March (½ in second half February on light land)
Combine Drill, Cart Seed and Fertilizer, Harrow ...	1·8	1·3	March (¼ at end February on light land)
Roll	0·6	0·5	April (or straight after Drilling)
Spray	0·5	0·3	May
Combine, Cart Grain, Barn Work	3·5	2·3	Last three-quarters of August (affected by variety as well as season)
Later Barn Work (2)	0·7	0·4	September to June
Total	12·4	8·5	
Straw: Bale (unmanned sledge)	1·3	0·9 ⎫	Mid-August to end
Cart	4·5	3·0 ⎬	September

Typical Monthly Breakdown

Month	Average	Premium	Notes
October ...	0·8	0·5 ⎫	Ploughing. How much in
November ...	1·3	1·0 ⎬	October depends on
December ...	0·8	0·5 ⎭	area of Winter Wheat, Potatoes, etc.
January ...	—	—	
February ...	—	—	
March ...	4·2	3·0	All Cults. and Drilling (nearly half in February on light land)
April	0·6	0·5	Roll
May	0·5	0·3	Spray
June ...	—	—	
July ...	—	—	
August ...	3·5 (+3·2 Straw)	2·3 (+2·1 Straw)	
September ...	— (+2·6 Straw)	— (+1·8 Straw)	

Notes
1. See note 1 on page 68.
2. Later barn work excluded.

WINTER BARLEY

As for winter wheat, except that:

Ploughing unlikely to start before cereal harvest, as usually follows a cereal crop.

Harvesting usually some weeks earlier: end July/beginning August.

WINTER OATS

As for winter wheat, except that:

Drilling completed at least two weeks earlier (mid-September to mid-October).

Harvesting earlier (first half of August).

SPRING WHEAT

As for spring barley, except that:

Drilling on average is two weeks earlier (should be finished in March)—lose more if late than barley.

Harvesting, on average, is two weeks later (two-thirds in September, on average).

SPRING OATS

As for spring barley, except that:

Drilling is, on average, two weeks earlier.

Harvesting is later than spring barley, earlier than spring wheat: end August/beginning September.

Seasonal Labour Requirements

Critical Questions affecting Timing (Autumn-sown Cereals)

1. Previous crops (affects time available for ploughing and cultivations).
2. Will the crop be ploughed traditionally, chisel ploughed, minimally cultivated, or direct drilled?
3. Earliest and latest drilling date, by choice.
4. Effect on yield if drilling is delayed.
5. In the spring: (a) whether crop is rolled, and when.
   (b) whether crop is harrowed, and when.
   (c) time of top dressing.
5. (a) Average period for harvesting.
   (b) Earliest dates for starting and finishing harvest, and latest dates for starting and finishing harvest, ignoring extreme seasons (one year in ten).

Critical Questions affecting Timing (Spring-sown Cereals)

1. Previous crops.
2. Will the crop be ploughed traditionally, chisel ploughed, minimally cultivated, or direct drilled?
3. Months when winter ploughing is possible, on average. (Where relevant).
4. Is spring ploughing satisfactory? (Where relevant).
5. Average period of cultivations and drilling.
6. Earliest dates for starting and finishing spring cultivations/ drilling and latest dates for starting and finishing cultivations/ drilling, ignoring extreme seasons (one year in ten).
7. Effect on yield if drilling is delayed.
8. Is the crop rolled (a) within a few days of drilling or (b) later?
9. (a) Average period of harvesting.
   (b) Earliest dates for starting and finishing harvest, and latest dates for starting and finishing harvest, ignoring extreme seasons (one year in ten).

MAINCROP POTATOES

Operations	Labour-Hours per hectare (30 tonne crop)		Time of Year
	Average	Premium	
Plough	2·9	2·0	September to December
Seedbed Cults. (3)	2·4	1·7	March, early April
Load, Cart, Apply Fertilizer	1·3	0·9	March
Load and Cart Seed and Plant (machine)	15·0(1)	4·0(2)	Last quarter of March, first three-quarters of April
Tractor hoe (3)/harrow (2), mould up	6·5	0·8(3)	May, June, first half July
Spray (blight, 3 times) ...	2·6	1·5	July, first half August
Burn off Haulm	0·8	0·6	End September, early October
Harvest, Cart, Clamp ...	35·0(4)	35·0(5)	End September, October
Work on Indoor Clamp ...	6·0	4·0	November
Riddle, Bag, Load	50·0	40·0	October to May

(1) Hand-fed 2- or 3-row planter, including approx. 10 hours that could be casual labour.
(2) Automatic 2-row planter.
(3) Weedkiller spraying; minimal after-cultivations.
(4) Spinner or elevator digger, excluding 80 hours for picking—usually casual labour.
(5) Mechanical harvester, excluding 30 hours for picking off on harvester—usually casual labour. Less than this, or even none, may be needed on clod- and stone-free soils.

Typical Monthly Breakdown (30 tonne crop)

Month	Average	Premium	Notes
October ...	28·4	28·3	80% of harvest, ½ burn off
November ...	8·2	5·5	Clamp work and ¾ plough
December ...	0·7	0·5	¼ plough
January ...	—	—	
February ...	—	—	
March	6·2	2·8	All fertilizer, ½ cults., ¼ plant
April	12·5	3·8	½ cults., ¾ plant
May	1·6	0·8	¼ after-cults., spray
June	3·3	—	½ after cults.
July	3·4	1·0	¼ after-cults., 2 blight sprays
August ...	0·8	0·5	1 blight spray
September ...	7·4	7·3	20% harvest, ½ burn off

Note: These figures exclude labour for picking and riddling.

SECOND EARLY POTATOES

Operations	Labour-Hours per hectare Average	Premium	Time of Year
Plough	2·9	2·0	September to December
Seedbed Cults.	2·4	1·7	March
Load, Cart and Apply Fertilizer	1·3	0·9	March
Load and Cart Seed and Plant	15·0	4·0	Half 2nd half March, half 1st half April
After-Cultivations/Spray ...	4·5	0·8	End April, May, early June
Harvest	30·0(1)	30·0(2)	Mid-July to end August

(1) Spinner or elevator-digger, excluding 18 picking and 7 riddling—usually casual labour.
(2) Mechanical harvester, excluding 7 picking and 6 riddling—usually casual labour.

Typical Monthly Breakdown

Month	Average	Premium	Notes
October ...	—	—	
November ...	2·2	1·5	¾ plough
December ...	0·7	0·5	¼ plough
January ...	—	—	
February ...	—	—	
March ...	11·2	4·6	All cults. and fert., ⅓ planting
April	8·2	2·0	½ planting + c. 15% after-cults.
May	2·9	0·8	} Remaining after cults., spray
June	0·9	—	
July	10·0	10·0	⅓ harvest, etc.
August ...	20·0	20·0	⅔ harvest, etc.
September ...	—	—	

Note: These figures exclude labour for picking and riddling.

EARLY POTATOES

Operations	Labour-Hours per hectare		Time of Year
	Average	Premium	
Plough	2·9	2·0	September to December
Seedbed Cults.	2·4	1·7	Late February, early March
Load, Cart, Apply Fertilizer ...	1·3	0·9	Late February, early March
Load and Cart Seed and Plant	17·0	5·0	1st half March (some in February on light land or in early season)
After-Cultivation/Spray ...	43·5	0·8	April, early May
Harvest, bag, load	35·0(1)	30·0(2)	2nd week June onwards. All June or till mid-July

(1) Excluding 85 picking—usually casuals.
(2) Excluding 65 picking—usually casuals.

Typical Monthly Breakdown

Month	Average	Premium	Notes
October ...	—	—	
November ...	2·2	1·5	¾ plough
December ...	0·7	0·5	¼ plough
January ...	—	—	
February ...	1·9	1·3	½ cults. and fertilizer
March ...	18·8	6·3	½ cults. and fertilizer; all planting
April	2·3	0·8	} After-cults.
May	1·2	—	
June	35·0	30·0	Harvest, etc.
July ...	—	—	
August ...	—	—	
September ...	—	—	

Note: These figures exclude labour for picking.

Seasonal Labour Requirements

SUGAR BEET

Operations	Labour-Hours per hectare Average	Premium	Time of Year
Plough	2·9	2·0	September to December
Seedbed Cults. (1)	3·9	2·8 ⎤	Mainly March (some early April. Some late February
Load, Cart, Apply Fertilizer	1·3	0·9 ⎦	in good seasons)
Drill (and Flat Roll)	2·6	1·7	Late March and April, especially early April
Spray (weedicide) (2) ...	2·0	3·0	Late March/April
Hand hoeing (3,7)	15·0	—	Mainly 2nd half May, 1st half June (mainly May on light land)
Tractor Hoe (4)	6·0	—	May, June, early July (may start late April with March drilling)
Spray (aphis)	0·6	0·3	July
Harvest (machine) (5,7) ...	26·0	16·0	End September, October, November
Load (6)	7·0	3·0	End September to early January

Notes

1. Seedbed Cults. = 2 heavy cults., once medium and once light harrows, once rolled.
2. Spraying (weedicide). Average: pre-emergence band spraying. Premium: sprayed twice.
3. Hand Hoeing. Average — once through the crop (casual labour may be used). Premium = no hand hoeing. A precision drill is assumed in both cases.
4. Tractor Hoeing. 3 times, with mid-mounted hoe (1 man).
5. Harvesting. Average = 1 man harvester, 2 carting and clamping. Premium = 1 man tanker-harvester, beet dumped; or 2-row harvester.
6. Loading. Average = hand loading. Premium = loading with tractor and foreloader.
7. Reduce hand hoeing and harvesting times by 20 per cent on light land.

Typical Monthly Breakdown

Month		Average	Premium	Notes
October	...	13·5	7·9	45% harvest; + loading
November	...	15·7	9·4	45% harvest; ¾ ploughing; + loading
December	...	2·5	1·2	¼ ploughing; + loading
January	...	0·8	0·4	Loading
February	...	—	—	
March	...	5·4	4·2	Fertilizer, most of cults., some drilling
April	...	4·4	4·2	Some cults., most of drilling
May	...	10·0	—	½ thinning, 40-45% tractor hoeing
June	...	10·0	—	½ thinning, 40-45% tractor hoeing
July	...	1·6	0·3	Rest of tractor hoeing; spraying (aphis)
August	...	—	—	
September	...	3·4	2·1	10% harvesting; + loading

VINING PEAS

Operations	Labour-Hours per hectare Average	Premium	Time of Year
Plough	2·9	2·0	September to December
Cults., Fert. and Drill ...	2·5	1·8	Mid-Feb. to April
Post Drilling and Spraying	1·5	1·0	
Harvesting	20·0	15·0	July and early August

Note

Drilling is staggered in small areas through the season, ranging from early varieties to late varieties.

DRIED PEAS

Month	Labour-Hours per hectare	Operation
October ...	1·2	⎫
November ...	0·7	⎬ Stubble cult.; Plough
December ...	0·2	⎭
January ...	—	
February ...	0·2	Cult. twice, harrow; drill and fert. (80 per
March ...	3·2	cent March); light harrow and roll;
April	1·2	spray
May	2·5	⎫
June	0·2	⎬ Scare pigeons; spray
July	2·2	⎫ Possibly spray desiccant; combine and
August ...	2·5	⎬ cart; dry
September ...	0·7	Stubble cult.

Assumes direct combining. Windrowing up to 2·5 more hours. Drying on 4-poles extra 25 to 30 hours.

Source: J. A. L. Dench with co-authors, "Break Crops", Agricultural Enterprise Studies in England and Wales, Economic Report No. 13, University of Reading, 1972.

OILSEED RAPE

A. Winter

Month	Labour-Hours per hectare	Operations
October ...	⎫	
November ...	0·3	Spray herbicide
December ...	⎭	
January ...	—	
February ...	—	
March ...	⎫ 0·7	Top dress twice
April ...	⎭	
May ...	—	
June ...	—	
July ...	1·3	Windrow (1st half July); combine (½ 2nd
August ...	2·3	half July; ½ 1st half Aug.); straw, dry
August ...	1·3	Cults.; drill and fert.; harrow, roll; barn
September ...	2·1	work (0·5)

B. Spring-sown

Month	Labour-Hours per hectare	Operations
October ...	2·3	End harvest (2·0), stubble cult. and start ploughing (0·3)
November ...	⎫	
December ...		
January ...	1·3	Plough
February ...	⎭	
March ...	1·0	Finish plough; cult. twice, heavy harrow
April ...	2·1	or sp. tine cult.; drill and fert. (85 per cent March); light harrow, roll
May ...	0·5	
June ...	0·3	
July ...	—	
August ...	—	
September ...	1·7	Combine, straw, dry (1·2); stubble cult. (0·2); barn work (0·5)

FIELD BEANS

A. Spring Beans

Operations	Labour-Hours per hectare		Time of Year
	Average	Premium	
Plough	2·9	2·0	September to December
Seedbed Cults.	2·5	1·6	End Feb., early March
Load, Cart, Apply Fertilizer	0·7	0·4	End Feb., early March
Drill	1·4	1·0	Late February, March (early if possible)
Spray (weed control) ...	0·5	0·3	Few days after drilling
Spray (blackfly)	0·5	0·3	June
Combine (tanker) and cart and barnwork	4·0	2·7	September

B. Winter Beans

Operations	Labour-Hours per hectare		Time of Year
	Average	Premium	
Plough	2·9	2·0	September to October
Seedbed Cults. ...	2·2	1·4	End Sept., October
Load, Cart, Apply Fertilizer	0·7	0·4	End Sept., October
Drill	1·5	1·1	October
Spray (weed control) ...	0·5	0·3	Few days after drilling
Combine (tanker) and cart and barnwork	4·0	2·7	August

HERBAGE SEEDS (first production year)

A. Undersown

Operations	Labour-Hours per hectare		Time of Year
	Average	Premium	
Undersow	0·8	0·6	March, April
(Roll)	(0·6	0·4)	(Straight after drilling—the cereal crop would probably be rolled anyway)
Load, Cart, Apply Fertilizer	0·7	0·5	September
	0·6	0·5	Late February, March
Harvest (by Combine): Mow	1·6	1·1	3 to 4 days before combining
Combine and Cart ...	4·5	3·5	Ryegrass { S22 and S24: mid-July; S101: second half July; S23 and White Clover: late July, early August
	6·0	4·5	Meadow Fescue: early July
	7·0	5·0	Cocksfoot: early July
	10·0	7·0	Timothy: mid-August
			Red Clover: late September

B. Direct Drilled in Autumn

Operation	Labour-Hours per hectare		Time of Year
	Average	Premium	
Plough	2·9	2·0	Depends on previous crop— Usually July or August
Seedbed Cults. ...	2·8	2·0	
Load, Cart, Apply Fertilizer	0·7	0·5	
Drill (with harrows behind)	0·8	0·6	As early as previous crop allows. This may be up to mid-September for rye-grasses without detriment to the subsequent yield.
Roll (soon after drilling) ...	0·6	0·5	Meadow fescue and cocksfoot are best sown
Harvest	See above (Undersown)		no later than July and it is risky to sow timothy much later than this.

GRASS

A. Production

Operations	Labour-Hours per hectare Average	Premium	Time of Year
Plough	2·9	2·0	Autumn drilling: may not plough
Seedbed Cults.	3·5	2·5	
Load, Cart, Apply Fertilizer	0·6	0·4	
Drill*	0·8	0·6	Mid-March to mid-April (1) or end July to mid-Sept.
Roll	0·6	0·5	Soon after drilling
Load, Cart, Apply Fertilizer*:			
(three lots) ...	1·8	1·2	March to mid-August (2)
Top*	1·4	0·9	Mid-June to mid-July; if grazed only

Notes
1. Direct drilling in spring may continue to mid-May to enable extra cleaning cultivations or the application of farmyard manure.
2. P. and K. may be applied in September—especially on undersown ley in year sown.
* Only these operations apply where the seeds are undersown in a spring cereal crop soon after drilling. One extra harrowing and rolling are needed if undersown in an autumn-sown cereal crop.

B. Conservation

Operations	Labour-Hours per hectare Average	Premium	Time of Year
Hay (5·5 tonnes per hectare)			
Mow	1·4	1·1	
Turn, etc.	3·1	2·3	Two-thirds June, one-third
Bale	1·4	1·0	July
Cart	7·3	5·5	
Total per hectare	13·2	9·9	
Total per tonne ...	2·4	1·8	
Silage (17 tonnes per hectare)			
Mow	1·3	1·0	
Turn, etc.	0·7	0·5	Two-thirds May, one-third
Load	2·4	1·8	June
Cart	3·3	2·5	
Clump	2·5	1·8	
Total per hectare	10·2	7·6	
Total per tonne	0·6	0·45	

Specialized Equipment Prices for Grass Conservation: see page 90.

Seasonal Labour Requirements

Typical Monthly Breakdown

A. Production (figures averaged over the life of the ley)

	1-year ley undersown		3-year ley undersown		1-year ley direct drilled in spring		3-year ley direct drilled in autumn (1)	
	Av.	Prem.	Av.	Prem.	Av.	Prem.	Av.	Prem.
March	0·9	0·5	0·7	0·5	0·6	0·3	0·6	0·3
April	0·9	0·5	0·7	0·5	0·6	0·3	0·6	0·3
May	0·6	0·3	0·6	0·3	0·6	0·3	0·6	0·3
June	0·6	0·3	0·6	0·3	0·6	0·3	0·6	0·3
July	0·6	0·3	0·6	0·3	0·6	0·3	0·6	0·3
August	0·3	0·2	0·3	0·2	5·0	3·4	1·9	1·4
September ...	0·6	0·3	0·3	0·2	3·2	2·2	1·4	1·0

Note
1. On land ploughed after a cereal crop, drilled early August to mid-September.

	1-year ley direct drilled in autumn (1)		3-year ley direct drilled in spring		Permanent Pasture	
	Av.	Prem.	Av.	Prem.	Av.	Prem.
March	3·0	2·1	1·4	1·0	0·6	0·3
April	1·8	1·2	0·9	0·7	0·6	0·3
May	0·3	0·3	0·6	0·3	0·6	0·3
June	0·6	0·3	0·6	0·3	0·6	0·3
July	0·6	0·3	0·6	0·3	0·6	0·3
August	0·3	0·2	0·2	0·2	0·3	0·2
September ...	—	—	—	0·2	0·2	0·2
October ...	0·9	0·5	0·6	0·3	—	—
November ...	1·4	1·0	1·0	0·3	—	—
December ...	0·7	0·5	0·6	0·2	—	—

B. Conservation *

	Hay				Silage			
	per hectare		per tonne		per hectare		per tonne	
	Av.	Prem.	Av.	Prem.	Av.	Prem.	Av.	Prem.
May ...	—	—	—	—	6·8	5·1	0·4	0·3
June ...	8·8	6·6	1·6	1·2	3·4	2·5	0·2	0·15
July ...	4·4	3·3	0·8	0·6	—	—	—	—

* For further details of labour and machinery inputs and costs see Burns, S.M., Lewis, M. R. and Rendell, J., Grass Conservation, 1980. University of Reading, Dept. of Agricultural Economics and Management, Economic Report No. 82

KALE (growing only)

A. Maincrop

Operation	Labour-hours per hectare Average	Premium	Time of Year
Plough	2·9	2·0	September onwards
Seedbed Cults.	3·7	2·5	March, April, early May
Fertilizer	1·0	0·6	April, early May
Drill	1·3	1·0	May
Roll	0·6	0·5	Straight after drilling
Spray (weedkiller)	0·5	0·3	6 weeks after drilling

B. Catch Crop

Kale may be drilled up to the first week of July; the crop will be smaller but either an early bite or silage crop may have been taken from a ley earlier in the year, or the ground may have been fallowed and thoroughly cleaned during the spring and early summer. The smaller crop is also easier to graze using an electric fence.

The above operations will still apply although the times of the year will obviously be different, but there may be an additional three or so rotavations and two or three heavy cultivations if fallowed for the first half of the year or ploughed after an early bite. This means approximately an extra 12 (average) or 9 (premium) man-hours per hectare in April, May, June.

FIELD-SCALE VEGETABLES

(Labour hours per hectare unless otherwise stated)

Cabbage Transplanting. Hand 150-160. Spring cabbage, Sept.-Oct.; summer, April; autumn, May-June.

Machine (3·5 gang). Spring cabbage 75, summer 85, autumn 100.

Pulling and dipping plants. 20 per hectare transplanted.

Cabbage Harvesting. Early spring cabbage, 210, Feb.-April; hearted spring, 250, April-June; summer, 220, June-July; autumn, 220, Oct.-Dec.

Brussels Sprouts Transplanting. 45 (machine) to 55 (hand), May-June.

Brussels Sprouts Picking. 320-400: picked over 3-5 times, maximum approx. 3 hectares per picker per season. Early sprouts, Aug.-Dec.; late, Nov.-Mar.

Peas Hand Pulling. 475-525 (150 per tonne). Early, June; maincrop, July-Aug.

Runner Beans (Picked) Harvesting. 625 (175 per tonne), July-Sept.
Runner Beans (Stick) Harvesting. 675, July-Sept.
Runner Beans (Stick) Erecting Canes and String. 100-150, May-June.

Carrot Harvesting. Elevator-digger: 260 (1 man + 12 casuals, 20 hours per hectare). Earlies, July-Aug.; maincrop, Sept.-Feb. Harvester: 30 (3 men, 10 hours per hectare). Riddle and Grade: 1½ per tonne), Dec.-Feb.

Beetroot Harvest and Clamp. 25, Oct.-Dec. 12-15 man-hours per tonne to wash and pack.

Source: The Farm as a Business, Aids to Management, Section 6: Labour and Machinery (M.A.F.F.). (N.B. This data is now nearly 15 years old, but it is still the latest known to the author.)

4. LABOUR FOR FIELD WORK: Gang Sizes and Rates of Work

Basic information on *Rates of Work* is given on pages 93 to 95, where both "average" and "premium" rates for many operations are listed.

The following data relate to rates of work with gangs of different sizes. The rates of work are *averages* for good and bad conditions throughout the season, including preparation time and travelling to the field, and *assume an 8-hour day, unless otherwise stated.* Obviously these rates can be exceeded by overtime work in the evenings.

Combine Drilling

2 men, autumn	10 hectares per day
2 men, spring	12 hectares per day
1 man, autumn	8 hectares per day
1 man, spring	9 hectares per day

Combine Harvesting

Gang size can vary from 1 to 4 men per combine (excluding straw baling) according to the number of men available, size and type of combine, distance from grain store, crop yield, type of grain drier, and degree of automation in the grain store. The main possibilities, assuming a tanker combine are:

1 man: all jobs (trailer in field)
2 men: 1 combining, 1 carting and attending to grain store
3 men: 1 combining, 2 carting and attending to grain store
3 men: 1 combining, 1 carting, 1 attending to grain store
4 men: 1 combining, 2 carting, 1 attending to grain store

Three men is most typical, although two is quite feasible with a fully automated grain store with in-bin or floor drying, unless transport times are excessive owing to distance or lack of good connecting roads. Four men is most usual with two tanker combines, but an extra man is normally needed with a continuous drier.

Except in the case of the small area cereal producer operating on his own, the rate of work will normally depend on the speed of the combine, sufficient tractors and trailers being provided to ensure that combining does not have to stop because of their absence.

Assuming an 8-hour combining day, typical rates of work are:

Small combine (1·5 to 1·8 m. cut) 1 man "gang"	2 ha a day
Small combine (1·5 to 1·8 m. cut) 2 or 3 man "gang"	3 ha a day
Medium combine (2 to 2·6 m. cut) 1 man "gang"	3·25 to 4·25 ha a day
Medium combine (2 to 2·6 m. cut) 2 or 3 man "gang"	4·25 to 5·5 ha a day
Large combine (3 to 3·7 m. cut, above average throughput)	
2 or 3 man "gang"	7 to 9 ha a day
Very large combine (3·7 to 4·3 m. cut, high throughput)	
2 to 4 man "gang"	8 to 10·5 ha a day

Straw Carting

2 men, 1 or 2 tractors and trailers	2·5 to 3·25 ha a day
3 men, 1 to 3 tractors and trailers	3·25 to 5 ha a day
1 man, 1 tractor with front and rear carriers	2·5 ha a day

Potato Planting

Hand planting (chitted seed) 3 men, 16 women	2 ha a day
Hand planting (unchitted seed) 2 men, 12 women	2 ha a day
(women working a 6-hour day only)	
2-row planter (chitted seed) 3 workers	1 ha a day
3-row planter (chitted seed) 4 or 5 workers	1·75 ha a day
2-row planter (unchitted seed) 3 workers	1·5 ha a day
3-row planter (unchitted seed) 4 workers	2·25 ha a day
2-row automatic planter (unchitted seed) 1 worker	2·5 ha a day
(part-time help loading and carting seed additional; this may be full time if fertilizer is applied with an attachment to the planter)	

Potato Harvesting

Hand harvesting (piecework) 3 to 5 men, 10 to 15 women	0·65 to 0·85 ha a day
(women working a 6-hour day only)	
Machine harvesting (1-row) 4 men, 3 women	0·65 to 0·75 ha a day
Machine harvesting (2-row) 5 men, 3 women	1 to 1·25 ha a day
(lower end of range for heavy land, upper end for light land and good work organization)	

Potato Riddling

3 to 5 workers	10 to 15 tonnes a day

Sugar Beet Harvesting (1-row)

Gang can vary from 1 to 5 (1 or 2 on harvester, 2 or 3 carting, 1 at clamp) but is usually 3 or 4.

3 or 4 men	0·9 ha a day
2 men	0·8 ha a day
1 man	0·7 ha a day
(add 20 per cent for light loams and silts)	

Vining Peas

Drilling (2 men)	6 to 9 ha a day
1·85 m. cutter (1 man)	1·25 to 2·25 ha a day
Carting and vining (static viner) 6 to 9 men	0·8 to 1·1 ha a day
Mobile viner, 4 men	1·7 to 2·5 ha a day

Carting Hay Bales

2 men, 1 or 2 tractors and trailers	7 to 9 tonnes a day
3 men, 1 to 3 tractors and trailers	9 to 14 tonnes a day

Silage-Making with Forage Harvester (excl. mowing, but inc. clamping; 6 tonne crop assumed)

1 man gang (1)	1·25 ha a day
2 man gang (1,3)	2·25 ha a day
3 man gang (1,3)	3·5 ha a day
4 man gang (2,3)	4·5 ha a day
(1) trailers towed behind, in line	
(2) trailers towed alongside	
(3) man with buckrake at clamp full-time	

Farmyard Manure Spreading

1 man: front loader and mechanical spreader	28 tonnes a day
4 men: front loader and 3 mechanical spreaders	90 tonnes a day

Sources include: The Farm as a Business, Aids to Management, Section 6: Labour and Machinery (M.A.F.F.). (N.B. The above data is now nearly 15 years old.)

5. LABOUR FOR LIVESTOCK

DAIRY COWS

Herd size (no. of cows)	60	80	100 or more
	hours per cow per month		
January	3·6	3·3	2·9
February	3·6	3·3	2·9
March	3·6	3·3	2·9
April	3·5	3·0	2·7
May	3·0	2·7	2·4
June	3·0	2·7	2·4
July	3·0	2·7	2·4
August	3·0	2·7	2·4
September	3·0	2·7	2·4
October	3·5	3·0	2·8
November	3·6	3·3	2·9
December	3·6	3·3	2·9
Total per cow per year	40	36	32
Total hours per year	2400	2880	3200
„ „ per week	46	55½	61½
Total cost per annum (1)	£7900	£9800	£11250
„ „ per week	£152	£188·50	£216·50
„ „ per cow	£132	£122·50	£112·50
Cost per litre: 4500 litres/cow ...	2·93p	2·72p	2·50p
„ „ „ : 5250 „ „ ...	2·51p	2·33p	2 14p
„ „ „ : 6000 „ „ ...	2·19p	2·04p	1·88p
„ „ „ : 6750 „ „ ...	1·95p	1·81p	1·67p

Note

1 These costs are *estimates for 1985* and are based on the average number of direct hours of work per cow for different herd sizes obtained from University costings; they do not include fieldwork, such as hay and silage making. The costs include craftsman addition and any other premiums paid, overtime, national insurance payments, and holidays with pay. They also include the cost of relief milking, including during annual holidays.

DAIRY FOLLOWERS AND BEEF

A. Calves (per head, early weaning)

Age Group	Labour hours per month Average	Premium
0-3 months	2·6	1·9
3-6 months	1·0	0·7
(av. 0-6 months	1·8	1·3)
6-12 months, yarded	1·3	0·6
6-12 months, summer grazed	0·3	0·2
(av. 0-12 months, during winter (1)	1·5	1·0)
(av. 0-12 months, during summer (1)	1·0	0·8)

Note
1. Assuming 6- to 12-month olds yarded in winter and grazed in summer, and calvings or calf purchases fairly evenly spaced throughout the year.

B. Stores (per head)

Yearling, yarded	1·2	0·7
2 year olds and over, yarded	1·9	1·0
Outwintered store	0·9	0·7
12 months and over, summer grazed	0·2	0·1

C. Dairy Followers

(Per "replacement unit", i.e. calf + yearling + heifer.) (1)

During winter	3·7	2·1
During summer	1·4	0·9

Note
1. Assuming calvings fairly evenly spaced throughout the year.

D. Beef Fattening (per bullock fattened)

Yarded	2·1	1·2
		(0·9 Self-feeding)
Summer Grazed	0·2	0·1
Barley Beef	0·8	0·6

E. Suckler Herds (per cow)

Single suckling (av. whole year)	0·9	0·6
Multiple suckling (av. whole year)	2·9	2·5

F. Veal Calves

130-150 per worker	1·5	1·2

SHEEP
(per ewe)

							Labour hours per month Average	Premium
January	...	...	...	...	...	...	0·3	0·25
February	...	...	...	...	...	...	0·3	0·25
March	...	...	...	...	...	...	1·0(1)	0·75
April	...	...	...	...	...	...	0·4	0·3
May	...	...	...	...	...	...	0·3	0·25
June	...	...	...	...	...	...	0·4(2)	0·3
July	...	...	...	...	...	...	0·2	0·15
August	...	...	...	...	...	...	0·2	0·15
September	...	...	...	...	...	...	0·25	0·15
October	...	...	...	...	...	...	0·25	0·15
November	...	...	...	...	...	...	0·2	0·15
December		...	...	...	...	...	0·2	0·15
Total	...	...	...	...	...	...	4·0(3)	3·0

Notes
1. Assuming mainly March lambing.
2. 0·3 if shearing is by contract.
3. A full-time shepherd can look after 400 ewes, with lambs (average), to 600 (premium), with help of extra man at lambing time (4 to 6 weeks) and extra men during dipping (one day) and at shearing time. The above labour-hour figures would thus be higher if only full-time shepherds were considered, since 400 ewes per man equals more than 5·5 hours per ewe per year. (With a full-time assistant a shepherd can look after 1,000 ewes or more.)

PIGS

	Labour hours per month Average	Premium
Breeding only, per sow	2·7	1·8
(Average 80 per man, Premium 120)		
Fattening only, in fattening house, per 10 (1)	3·6	2·4
(Average 600 per man, Premium 900)		
Fattening only, in yards, per 10 (1)	2·5	1·7
(Average 1,000 per man, Premium 1,500)		
Breeding and Fattening for pork, per sow	5·8	3·7
(Average 40 sows and progeny per man, Premium 65)		
Breeding and Fattening for bacon and heavy hogs, per sow	6·2	4·0
(Average 35-40, Premium 60)		

Note
1. Numbers (fattening only) refer to the numbers being fattened at a time, not to the total number produced during the year.

POULTRY

	Labour hours per month
3,000 laying hens per worker	7·5 per 100
5,000 laying hens per worker	5·0 per 100
8,000 laying hens per worker	3·25 per 100
12,000 laying hens per worker (automatic egg collection)	2·25 per 100
20,000 table birds per year per worker	0·75 per 100 produced
50,000 table birds per year per worker	0·5 per 100 produced

III. MACHINERY

1. AGRICULTURAL MACHINERY PRICES

(Estimated Spring 1985 prices for new machinery, excluding V.A.T.)

1. *Tractors*

(a) Two-Wheel Drive   £

27-34 kW (36-45 hp)	8,000-9,000
35-40 kW (47-54 hp)	9,000-10,000
43-49 kW (57-66 hp)	10,000-11,000
50-56 kW (67-75 hp)	11,000-13,000
57-66 kW (76-89 hp)	12,000-15,000
67-75 kW (90-100 hp)	15,000-17,000
76-90 kW (101-120 hp)	17,500-21,000
93-104 kW (125-140 hp)	19,500-23,000
112-130 kW (150-175 hp)	22,500-26,500

(b) Four-Wheel Drive

43-50 kW (57-67 hp)	12,000-14,000
56-65 kW (75-87 hp)	14,000-17,000
66-75 kW (88-100 hp)	17,500-21,000
76-90 kW (101-120 hp)	21,000-25,000
95-100 kW (127-134 hp)	25,000-29,000
115-134 kW (154-180 hp)	30,000-37,000

(c) Crawlers

30-37 kW (40-50 hp), inc. linkage	9,000-10,000
45-53 kW (60-70 hp), inc. linkage	13,000-15,000
82-100 kW (110-134 hp), inc. linkage	26,000-32,000

2. *Cultivating Equipment*

(a) Ploughs

Mounted 2-furrow	1,000-1,200
Mounted 3-furrow	1,350-1,700
Mounted 4-furrow	1,700-2,300
Mounted 5-furrow	2,300-2,700
Semi-mounted 5-furrow	3,800-4,600
Semi-mounted 6-furrow	4,600-5,700
Reversible 2-furrow	2,000-2,500
Reversible 3-furrow	2,600-3,800
Reversible 4-furrow	3,300-4,400

(b) Other Cultivating Equipment

Chisel Plough (2-3 m)	700-1,100
Heavy Cultivator (2·4-4·0 m)	1,000-1,500
Spring-tine Cultivator (2·4-3·7 m)	550-750
Spring-tine Cultivator (3·9-5·3 m): 3 section folding ...	1,300-1,700
Spring-tine Cultivator (5-6 m): 3 section hydraulic folding	1,900-2,300
Rotary Harrows (2·5-3 m)	1,050-1,300
Disc Harrows (2-2·8 m): light	1,100-1,300
Disc Harrows (3-3·7 m): heavy-trailed	2,300-2,700
Harrows (2·1-6·1 m): light-medium	300-700
Rotary Cultivator (up to 45 kW tractor)	1,600-2,000
Rotary Cultivator (up to 50-75 kW tractor)	2,000-2,700
Power Harrow (2·5-3 m)	2,300-2,700
Rolls: single, Cambridge or flat, 2·5 m	650-725
Rolls: triple gang, Cambridge or flat, 4·3-4·9 m	1,400-1,700

3. *Fertilizer Distributors, Seed Drills, Sprayers*

(a) Fertilizer Distributors

Mounted Spinner (up to 600 kg hopper)	400-800
Trailed Spinner (1-2 tonne hopper)	1,800-2,600
Pneumatic Spreader (10·0-12·0 m)	2,750-3,250

(b) Seed Drills

21-33 row mounted	1,800-2,700
Mounted grass seed broadcaster (2·4-4·6 m)	400-700
Spacing drill: 4 row-5 row (pneumatic)	2,100-2,500
Spacing drill: 4 row-6 row (land wheel drive)	1,600-2,000

(c) Combine Drills

14-15 row trailed	2,900-3,500
23-25 row trailed	4,000-5,000

(d) Direct Drill

23-32 row (4 m)	9,000-10,000

(e) Sprayers

Mounted, 200-300 litre tank	450-600
Mounted, 350-500 litre tank	800-950
Mounted, 550-800 litre tank	1,200-2,200
Trailed, 1,000-1,500 litre tank	2,600-3,200
Trailed, 1,500-2,000 litre tank	3,500-4,500
Band sprayer (4-7 rows)	650-800

4. *Grass Conservation and Handling Equipment*

(a) Forage Harvesters, Buckrakes and Silage Cutters

Flail type (1·1-1·2 m)	1,600-2,000
Double chop	3,600-4,100
Fine and Precision chop (trailed)	4,400-6,500
Self-propelled (1·5-2·2 m pick-up 120-150 kW)	30,000-35,000
Buckrake (push off)	550-650
Silage Cutters: rear/front end loader mounted	2,400-2,700/1,700-2,000

(b) Haymaking Equipment

Mower (1·5 m, cutterbar type)	600-750
Mower (1·5-1·8 m, rotary type)	1,250-1,800
Mower Conditioner (1·65-1·9 m)	2,000-2,700
Side Rake	600-1,100
Rotary Haymakers (3·0-3·2 m)	950-1,200

(c) Haylage Equipment

Dump Box	5,000-5,500
Blower	2,100-2,600
Tower Silos, vitreous enamel and steel (before grant)	£67 per tonne stored

(assumes 1·4 m³ per tonne and largest silos available (1 per 200 cows, 5 to 6 months). Silos for 70 to 80 cows, 5 to 6 months, about 20 per cent extra. Usual feeding rate: 0·65 per tonne per cow per month.)

Spreader	650-700
Unloader: top/bottom	4,000-5,000/13,500-15,500
Forage Box (2-4 tonne)	4,400-6,400
Mixer-feeder Wagon (2-3 tonne)	9,000-12,000
Mechanical Feeders (30 m with motor)	3,800-4,700

5. *Grain and Straw Harvesting and Handling Equipment*

(a) Combines

	Engine size kW (hp)	Cutterbar width metres (feet)	
Conventional:	45-59 (60-79)	2·6-3.0 (8-10)	19,000-22,000
	60-74 (80-99)	2·6-3·0 (8-10)	23,000-27,000
		3·6-4·0 (12-13)	24,000-28,000
	75-89 (100-119)	3·0-3·4 (10-11)	28,000-33,000
		3·6-4·6 (12-15)	29,000-35,000
	90-111 (120-149)	3·0-3·4 (10-11)	34,000-40,000
		3·6-4·6 (12-15)	36,000-42,000
		4·9-6·0 (16-19)	38,000-46,000
	112-148 (150-199)	3·6-4·6 (12-15)	43,000-53,000
		4·9-6·0 (16-19)	44,000-54,000
	Over 150 (over 200)	4·3-6·1 (14-20)	56,000-63,000
Axial Flow:	90-120 (120-160)	4·0-4·6 (13-15)	36,000-44,000
	135-160 (180-213)	4·3-6·1 (14-20)	50,000-64,000

(b) Pick-up Balers (twine tying)
Small rectangular bales	3,000-4,300
Small rectangular bales, heavy duty models	4,500-5,800
Big round bales	7,000-8,500

(c) Bale Handling Equipment
Bale Sled	175-225
Bale Trailers	1,000-1,300
Accumulator, flat 8, mechanical	950-1,100
Loader, flat 8	550-650
Big Bale Spike	150-200
Big Bale Unroller	450-500
Bale Elevator	750-950

(d) Drying, Handling, Food Processing Equipment
Grain driers and Grain storage: see page 105	
Grain augers 100 mm, 3·3-7·3 m	250-350
Grain augers 150 mm, 3·3-7·3 m	500-700
Grain conveyors	600-750 + 60-70 per m
Elevators, sacks, 4·5-6·1 m	1,000-1,600
Hammer Mill, 3·75-7·5 kW automatic	900-1,200
Mill and Mixer, 1000kg, 3·7-5·5 kW	2,750-3,100
Mixer, 1,000 kg	1,400-1,800
Crushing Mill, 1·5-5·5 kW	750-1,000
Cuber, 5·5-7·5 kW	2,500-2,700

6. Potato and Sugar Beet Machinery

(a) Potato Machinery

Planter, 2-row automatic	1,600-2,000
Planter, 4-row automatic	3,600-4,000
Fertilizer attachment for 2 row	700-800
Haulm Pulveriser (2 m)	1,300-2,100
Elevator-Digger, 1 row	1,500-1,750
Elevator-Digger, 2 row	1,900-2,400
Harvesters: Tractor mounted, 1 row	7,500-8,700
Trailed, 1 row, manned	7,500-11,000
Trailed, 2 row, manned	18,000-24,000
Trailed, 1 row, unmanned	11,000-15,000
Trailed, 2 row, unmanned	16,500-24,000
Elevator (rubber belt)	3,000-3,400
Swing-Head Elevator	5,500-6,500
Sorters	1,400-2,200

(b) Sugar Beet Machinery

Precision Drill: 4 row-5 row (pneumatic)	2,100-2,500
Precision Drill: 4 row-6 row (land wheel drive)	1,600-2,000
Hoe: 4 row-6 row	1,200-1,500
Harvesters: Trailed, 1 row tanker	6,800-8,800
Trailed, 3 row	13,000-16,500
Trailed, 6 row	19,000-26,000
Self-propelled, 2-3 row, with power unit	38,000-42,000
Cleaner-loader, with engine	6,000-6,500

7. General

Trailer, 4 tonne tipping; grain/silage	1,300-1,400/1,500-1,600
Trailer, 6 tonne tipping; grain/silage	2,000-2,200/2,300-2,500
Trailer, 10 tonne tipping, tandem axle; grain/silage	3,500-3,900/4,000-4,500
F.Y.M. Spreaders, rear beaters (2·0-3·0m)	2,200-2,700
F.Y.M. Spreaders, side delivery (3·0-4·2m)	1,500-1,900
Loaders: rear/front mounted	550-650/1,200-1,700
Forklift (1·5-2·0 tonne)	1,400-1,900
Slurry Stores (metal), including base but before grant (assumes large store for 200 cows with a 15-week storage period; stores for 70-80 cows are £100-150 per cow)	£78 per cow
Slurry Tanker-Spreaders (3,000-4,000 litre)	3,000-3,500
Slurry-Tanker-Spreaders (4,000-4,800 litre)	4,000-4,800
Slurry pump	1,800-2,200
Yard scrapers	225-275
Hedger: hydraulic angling; flail head	2,500-2,700
Ditcher: fully slewing	3,200-3,700
Transplanter: 2 row-3 row	700-1,000
Carrier box	200-275
Post hole digger	750-850
Grassland Roll, solid filled (3-4 tonne)	800-1,000
Pasture topper (2·0-3·0m)	1,100-1,300

2. TYPICAL CONTRACTORS' CHARGES, AVERAGE FARMERS' COSTS AND RATES OF WORK FOR VARIOUS FARM OPERATIONS

Contractors' charges vary widely according to many factors: those given below are estimates for 1985 based on the guideline prices for 1984 plus 5 per cent. Farmer-contractors often charge less, since their overheads and machinery fixed costs are largely covered by their own farming operations, but the service may not always be so complete, including specialist advice.

Farmers' own costs vary even more widely; those given below (estimated for Spring 1985) are averages in every respect—covering different types of soil, size of farm, and so on; they are based on accounting cost procedures in that labour, tractor and machinery fuel, repairs and depreciation are included—but no allowance has been added for general farm overheads, interest on capital, supervision or under-occupied labour during slack times. They assume medium-sized tractors. The figures are given for interest only and should on no account be used for partial budgeting.

The contract charges and average farmers' costs are put side-by-side for tabular convenience, not to facilitate comparisons. Apart from the fact that contractors' charges must cover expenses omitted from the farmers' cost, the advisability or otherwise of hiring a contractor for a particular job depends on many factors, varying widely according to farm circumstances; furthermore, there are advantages and disadvantages not reflected in a cost comparison alone.

Wheeled tractors of 50-60 kW are assumed for the "Premium" rates of work (which will be achieved on most farms with more than 120 hectares of arable land); obviously, 75 kW or more wheeled tractors and crawlers could achieve still faster rates of work, particularly on light land. See further page 67, first paragraph.

All charges and costs below are *per hectare* unless otherwise stated.

Operation		Contract Charge	Average Farmers' Cost	Rate of Work (hectares per 8 hr. day)	
				Average	Premium
		£	£		
Ploughing (heavy/light soils)	...	36·00	24·00-35·00	2¼-3¼	3½-4½*
Deep Ploughing (over 225 mm)	...	52·00	40·00-54·00	1½-2	2½-3
Rotary Cultivating	...	23·00 per hour	53·00 (grass or stubble)	2	3
			30·00 (ploughed land)	3	5

Operation	Contract Charge	Average Farmers' Cost	Rate of Work (hectares per 8 hr. day) Average	Premium
	£	£		
Chisel Ploughing and Heavy				
Cultivating (first)	27·00 (once)	12·00	6	8*
(other)	39·00 (twice)	9·00	8	12*
Heavy Disc Harrowing (first) ...	19·00	13·50	7	9
(other) ...		12·00	8	10
Light Disc Harrowing (first) ...	15·00	8·75	8	10
(other) ...		7·75	9	11
Power Harrowing	22·00	15·80	5½	7
Spring tine Harrowing	14·00	6·35	10	16
Heavy Harrowing (Light Cult.) ...	16·00	9·00	8	12
Light Harrowing	11·00	3·50	15	22
Rolling (flat or ring 2·5 m) ...	16·00	7·50	8	11
(ring, set of 3, 5·0 m) ...	11·50	6·00	14	17
Fertilizer Distributing (including loading and carting):				
Spinner (125-375 kg/ha) ...	7·25 (fert. in field)	4·50	15	20
Spinner (500-1,250 kg/ha) ...	—	6·30 (2 men)	15	20
Full-width Distribution (125-375 kg/ha) ...	—	7·20	12	17
Full-width Distribution (500-1,250 kg/ha)	—	9·35 (2 men)	12	17
Drilling/Planting:				
Cereals (1 man only)	18·00 seed & fert. in field	9·00	11	15
Cereals (Combine, 1 man) ...	24·00 field	13·85	9	12
Grass	12·50	6·50	11	15
Roots (4-row)	—	26·50	3½	5
Sugar Beet—precision drill (5-row)	26·50	18·50	5	8
Sugar Beet + band spraying ...	—	32·00	3½	5½
Potato Planting	—	107·00 (inc. all labour & seed carting)	1½ (2 row) 2¼ (3 row)	1¾ 2¾
Potato Planting automatic ...	—	54·00	2½ (2 row)	3¼
Potato Ridging	—	13·00	5½	7
Spraying:				
Low Volume (excl. materials) ...	11·00	4·40	15	25
Medium Volume (excl. materials)	14·00	5·50	12	20
High Volume (excl. materials) ...	24·00	12·50	10	15
Tractor Hoeing Sugar Beet ...	26·00	19·00	4	6
Tractor Hoeing Potatoes	—	12·50	5½	7
Combine Harvesting (3·6 m) ...	63·00	58·00	¾-1¼	1-1¾
(+ carting to barn)	78·00	68·00	per hour	per hour

* For rates of work with extra large tractors, see page 95.

Operation	Contract Charge	Average Farmers' Cost	Rate of Work (hectares per 8 hr. day) Average	Premium
	£	£		
Pea Cutting	31·00	—	—	—
Oilseed Rape Harvesting:				
Windrow ...	28·00	—	—	—
Combine with pick-up attachment	81·00	—	—	—
Pick-up Baling (incl. string)	18 20p per bale	9·25 per tonne	0·8 per hour	1 per hour
Big Baling (round)	3·15 per bale	—	—	—
Grain Drying (by 6 per cent) ...	10·50 per tonne	8·50 per tonne	—	—
Grain Drying (by 10 per cent)	13·50 per tonne	10·00 per tonne	—	—
Cleaning without drying	6·70	—	—	—
Grain Storage	25-30p per tonne per week	(see page 105)	—	—
Potato Harvesting ... ... (incl. carting and loading into store)	—	500-600	0·7	1
Sugar Beet Complete Harvesting (with 1 row tanker)	—	108 (excl. carting)	1	1½
	—	170 (incl. carting)	—	—
Grass Mowing	16·00	14·20	5	8
Swath Turning/Tedding ...	12·00	6·60	10	15
Forage Harvesting:				
Full chop harvester (driver only)	42·00	—	—	—
Forage harvesting, carting and ensiling grass ...	90·00	—	—	—
Forage harvesting, carting and ensiling maize ...	100-120	—	—	—
F.Y.M.: Tractor and Spreader ...	16·00 per hour	—	—	—
F.Y.M.: Tractor and Loader ...	13·00 per hour	—	—	—
Lime Spreading	2·80 per tonne	—	—	—
Subsoiling	25-35	—	—	—
Hedge Cutting (flail head) ...	13·00 per hour	—	—	—
Tractor Hire (excl. driver):				
2 wheel drive, 56 kW (75 h.p.) ...	11·00	—	—	—
2 wheel drive, 75 kW (100 h.p.)	12·50	per hour —	—	—
4 wheel drive, 56 kW (75 h.p.) ...	12·00	—	—	—
4 wheel drive, 90 kW (120 h.p.)	15·50	—	—	—
Crawler, 90 kW (120 h.p.) ...	15·50	—	—	—
Trailer (with driver and tractor) ...	—	6·60 per hour	—	—

Rates of Work, Large Tractors (over 75 kW)   hectares per day

Ploughing   5

Chisel Ploughing and Heavy Cultivating (3·5 to 5·0 m)   12

3. TRACTOR HOURS
(per annum)

Crops

	per hectare	
	Average	Premium
Cereals	11	8
Straw Harvesting	4	2·5
Potatoes	50	40
Sugar Beet	45	30
Vining Peas	17	13
Dried Peas	13	10
Field Beans	13	10
Herbage Seeds:		
1 year undersown or 3 year direct drilled	7	5
1 year direct drilled	13	10
Hops (machine picked)	150	—
Kale (grazed)	9	7
Turnips/Swedes: folded/lifted	15/40	11/30
Mangolds	60	40
Fallow	14	7
Ley Establishment:		
Undersown	2	1
Direct Seed	8	5
Making Hay	12	8
Making Silage:		
1st·Cut	12	8
2nd Cut	9	6
Grazing:		
Temporary Grass	3	2·5
Permanent Grass	2	1·5

Livestock

	per head Average
Dairy Cows	6
Other Cattle over 2 years	5
Other Cattle 1-2 years	4
Other Cattle ½-1 year	2·25
Calves 0-½ year	2·25
Yarded bullocks	3
Sheep, per ewe	1·25
Store sheep	0·8
Sows	1·75
Other pigs over 2 months	1
Laying Birds	0·04

Notes

1. *Sources include* The Farm as a Business: Aids to Management, 6: Labour and Machinery. "Premium" figures apply where high performance machinery is used.
2. For Livestock, annual requirements are the per head requirements above multiplied by average numbers during the year (i.e. average numbers at end of each month).
3. A rough idea of the number of tractors required by a farm can be calculated as follows: up to 800 hours, 1; 800-2,000, 2; plus 1 for each additional 1,200 hours. As with labour, however, seasonal demands and numbers required at peak times are more important than the annual requirements as given above. These can be calculated from the seasonal labour data provided earlier in this booklet.

4. TRACTOR COSTS

(Estimates for Spring 1985)

	Wheeled Tractors			
	27-34 kW (36-45 h.p.)		43-49 kW (57-66 h.p.)	
Initial Cost	£8,500		£10,500	
	per year £	per hour £	per year £	per hour £
Depreciation	1,062	1·06	1,312	1·31
Tax and Insurance	90	0·09	102	0·10
Repairs and Maintenance	680	0·68	840	0·84
Fuel and Oil	1,000	1·00	1,682	1·68
Total	2,832	2·83	3,936	3·93

	Wheeled Tractors			
	57-66 kW (76-89 h.p.)		76-90 kW (101-120 h.p.)	
Initial Cost	£13,500		£20,000	
	per year £	per hour £	per year £	per hour £
Depreciation	1,687	1·69	2,500	2·50
Tax and Insurance	120	0·12	158	0·16
Repairs and Maintenance	1,080	1·08	1,600	1·60
Fuel and Oil	2,375	2·37	3,437	3·44
Total	5,262	5 26	7,695	7·70

	Crawler Tractors			
	45-53 kW (60-70 h.p.)		82-100 kW (110-134 h.p.)	
Initial Cost	£14,000		£26,000	
	per year £	per hour £	per year £	per hour £
Depreciation	1,750	1·75	3,250	3·25
Tax and Insurance	105	0·10	175	0·18
Repairs and Maintenance	1,120	1·12	2,080	2·08
Fuel and Oil	2,250	2·25	4,050	4·05
Total	5,225	5·22	9,555	9·56

Depreciation is based on the assumption that a tractor is sold or traded in for one-quarter of its original cost after six years. Annual Repair Costs have been calculated at 8 per cent of initial cost. No interest on capital has been included.

The hourly figures are based on a use of 1,000 hours a year. A greater annual use than this will mean higher annual costs but possibly lower hourly costs. Early replacement at a given annual use will increase depreciation costs per hour but should reduce repair costs. The hourly figures are averages for all types of work: heavy operations such as ploughing obviously have a higher cost than light work.

5. ESTIMATING ANNUAL MACHINERY COSTS

Annual machinery costs consist of depreciation, repairs, fuel and oil, contract charges, and vehicle tax and insurance. These can be budgeted in three ways, assuming there is no available information on past machinery costs on the farm:

(a) Per hectare, by looking up an average figure for the district, according to the size and type of farm. Approximate levels are shown in the tables of fixed costs (pages 106-7). This is obviously a very rough and ready measure.

(b) Per standard tractor hour. The crop area and livestock numbers can be multiplied by the appropriate standard (average) tractor hours per hectare and per head as given on page 96. The total can then be multiplied by the machinery cost per standard tractor hour as calculated from farm surveys. The following average figures (estimated for mid-1985) are based on 1982-83 levels in South-East England, plus 10% per cent.

Farm Type	Cost per Standard Tractor Hour
Mainly Sheep/Cattle, ... Intensive Arable—Vegetables	£7·75
Mainly Dairying, over 120 ha ... ... Sheep/Cattle and Arable ... ... Intensive Arable—Fruit	£9·25
Mainly Dairying, 60-120 ha ... ... Mainly Arable, over 200 ha ... ... Dairy and Arable, over 200 ha	£10·50
Mainly Dairying, over 120 ha ... ... Mainly Arable, 100-200 ha ... ... Dairy and Arable, under 200 ha ... ... Milk, Sheep/Cattle and Arable	£11·75
Mixed, with Pigs/Poultry	£15·50
Mainly Arable, under 100 ha	£16·50
Mainly Pigs/Poultry	£18·50

Premium levels are about 10 per cent lower.

Depreciation is based on the current (i.e. 'replacement') cost of machinery, not on the original (i.e. 'historic') cost.

The composition of the total cost varies with size and type of farm but averages approximately: depreciation $37\frac{1}{2}$ per cent; repairs, vehicle tax and insurance $27\frac{1}{2}$ per cent; fuel, including electricity, $22\frac{1}{2}$ per cent; contract work $12\frac{1}{2}$ per cent.

Again this calculation is a fairly rough and ready one, but is a useful check on the per hectare calculation.

(N.B. The standard tractor hour is used only as a convenient measure of machinery input. The costs incorporate not only tractor costs but all other power and machinery expenses, including field machinery and implements, fixed equipment, landrovers, vans, use of farm car, etc.)

(c) *Fully detailed calculation,* costing and depreciating each machine in turn, including tractors, estimating repairs and fuel costs for each, and adding the charges for any contract work.

The following tables, giving, for different types of machine, estimated life, annual depreciation, and estimated repairs according to annual use, are taken from "Profitable Farm Mechanisation", by C. Culpin.

ESTIMATED USEFUL LIFE (YEARS) OF POWER OPERATED MACHINERY IN RELATION TO ANNUAL USE

Equipment	Annual Use (hours)				
	25	50	100	200	300
Group 1:					
Ploughs, Cultivators, Toothed harrows, Hoes, Rolls, Ridgers, Simple potato planting attachments, Grain cleaners	12+	12+	12+	12	10
Group 2:					
Disc harrows, Corn drills, Binders, Grain drying machines, Food grinders and mixers	12+	12+	12	10	8
Group 3:					
Combine harvesters, Pick-up balers, Rotary cultivators, Hydraulic loaders	12+	12+	12	9	7
Group 4:					
Mowers, Forage harvesters, Swath turners, Side-delivery rakes, Tedders, Hedge cutting machines, Semi-automatic potato planters and transplanters, Unit root drills, Mechanical root thinners	12+	12	11	8	6
Group 5:					
Fertilizer distributors, Combine drills, Farm-yard manure spreaders, Elevator potato diggers, Spraying machines, Pea cutter-windrowers	10	10	9	8	7

99

Miscellaneous:									
Beet harvesters	...	...	...	...	11	10	9	6	5
Potato harvesters	...	...	...	...	—	8	7	5	—
Milking machinery	...	...	...	...	—	—	—	12	10

	Annual Use (hours)					
	500	750	1,000	1,500	2,000	2,500
Tractors	12+	12	10	7	6	5
Electric motors	12+	12+	12+	12+	12	12

DEPRECIATION: AVERAGE ANNUAL FALL IN VALUE

(per cent of new price)

(Source: V. Baker, Bristol University)

Frequency of renewal. Years	Complex. High Depreciation Rate e.g. potato harvesters, mobile pea viners, etc.	Established machines with many moving parts, e.g. tractors, combines, balers, forage harvesters	Simple equipment with few moving parts, e.g. ploughs, trailers
	%	%	%
1	34	26	19
2	24½	19½	14½
3	20*	16½*	12½
4	17½†	14½	11½
5	15‡	13†	10½*
6	13½	12	9½
7	12	11	9
8	11	10‡	8½†
9	(10)	9½	8
10	(9½)	8½	7½‡

* Typical frequency of renewal with heavy use.
† Typical frequency of renewal with average use.
‡ Typical frequency of renewal with light use.

Tax Allowances on Machinery. See page 139.

ESTIMATED ANNUAL COST OF SPARES AND REPAIRS AS A PERCENTAGE OF PURCHASE PRICE* AT VARIOUS LEVELS OF USE

	Approximate Annual Use (hours)				Additional use per 100 hours ADD
	500	750	1,000	1,500	
	%	%	%	%	%
Tractors	5·0	6·7	8·0	10·5	0·5

	Approximate Annual Use (hours)				Additional use per 100 hours ADD
	50	100	150	200	
	%	%	%	%	%
Harvesting Machinery:					
Combine Harvesters, self-propelled and engine-driven	1·5	2·5	3·5	4·5	2·0
Combine Harvesters, p.t.o. driven, metered-chop forage harvesters, pick-up balers, potato harvesters, sugar beet harvesters	3·0	5·0	6·0	7·0	2·0
Other Implements and Machines:					
Group 1:					
Ploughs, Cultivators, Toothed harrows, Hoes, Elevator potato diggers } Normal Soils	4·5	8·0	11·0	14·0	6·0
Group 2:					
Rotary cultivators, Mowers, Binders, Pea cutter-windrowers	4·0	7·0	9·5	12·0	5·0
Group 3:					
Disc harrows, Fertilizer distributors, Farmyard manure spreaders, Combine drills, Potato planters with fertilizer attachment, Sprayers, Hedge cutting machines	3·0	5·5	7·5	9·5	4·0
Group 4:					
Swath turners, Tedders, Side-delivery rakes, Unit drills, Flail forage harvesters, Semi-automatic potato planters and transplanters, Down-the-row thinners	2·5	4·5	6·5	8·5	4·0
Group 5:					
Corn drills, Milking machines, Hydraulic loaders, Simple potato planting attachments	2·0	4·0	5·5	7·0	3·0
Group 6:					
Grain driers, Grain cleaners, Rolls, Hammer mills, Feed mixers, Threshers	1·5	2·0	2·5	3·0	0·5

* When it is known that a high purchase price is due to high quality and durability or a low price corresponds to a high rate of wear and tear, adjustments to the figures should be made.

6. IRRIGATION COSTS
(Estimated for 1985)

A. Capital Costs
(before deducting grant)

1. *Pumps* (delivering from 27 to 110 cubic metres per hour from a surface water source)

Tractor driven, with accessories	£1,400-2,000
Diesel units	£4,800-12,000
Electrically driven units (excluding power supply)	£3,250-6,500

2. *Pipelines* (per m)

Portable: (excl. valves) 75 mm, £4·60; 100 mm, £6·20; 125 mm, £8·50; 150 mm, £12·30; (incl. valves) 75 mm, £7·00; 100 mm, £8·40; 125 mm, £10·70; 150 mm, £15·00.

Permanent (P.V.C. pipe and laying, before grant): 100 mm, £10·00; 150 mm, £12·00. Hydrants: 100 mm, £210; 150 mm, £285.

3. *Application Systems*

Sprinkler lines: a 1 hectare setting of a conventional sprinkler line costs approximately £3,900 to £4,400. For each hectare cover of sprinklers 30 to 40 hectares can normally be irrigated in a 10-day cycle; grid systems which are left *in situ* for the whole or part of the irrigation season cost approximately £1,780 per hectare.

Self travellers: hose reel equipment capable of irrigating 20-25 hectares in a 10-day cycle (two moves each day and operating for 22 hours per day) cost approximately £7,500. Larger machines capable of irrigating 32, 50 and 60 hectares in a 10-day cycle cost approximately £10,000, £14,000 and £16,000 respectively.

4. *Total*

If no source works are needed, as with water from a river, or pond, total capital costs can be as low as £500 for each hectare requiring irrigation at regular intervals, but are more typically £800 to £1,100. Irrigation schemes may be eligible for grant aid. Rates of grant depend upon the particular Capital Grant Scheme (see pages 145-6) and whether expenditure is on permanent or portable equipment.

5. Source Works

Boreholes typically cost £120 to £150 per m depth and require expensive submerged pumps. An overall cost, including electricity supply, pump and well head, to irrigate 4 hectares with 25 mm of water per day would be in the region of £20,000 to £27,000. £500 to £750 per hectare can easily be added to capital costs.

The least expensive large reservoirs typically cost 50p per cubic metre of storage capacity, with smaller reservoirs costing as much as £2.50 per cubic metre where lining is required. £1 per cubic metre equals £1,000 per hectare irrigated (£800 if grant aided at 20 per cent) if enough water is stored to apply 100 mm per hectare.

B. Operating Costs

A typical cost per 25 mm per hectare for a conventional sprinkler system where no source works are required would be: depreciation and interest £39; labour (5 man-hours per hectare), pumping, etc.,£35; total £74. That is approximately £220 per hectare if 3 applications of 25 mm were applied, on average, per year.

Charges by water authorities would add, for example, £2·50 per 25 mm per hectare if £10·00 p.m.l. were charged.

Mains water at £200 p.m.l. would add £50 per 25 mm per hectare to running costs.

Source works at £700 per hectare, after grant, together with mainly permanent pipelines, would increase the above depreciation and interest figure to £70 per 25 mm per hectare, but variable costs would be lower—about £20; total £90 per 25 mm per hectare. That is approximately £270 per hectare with 3 applications of 25 mm per year.

Note:

The (approximate) imperial equivalents for metric values commonly used in irrigation are as follows:

1 cubic metre=1,000 litres=220 gallons.

A pump capacity of 100 cubic metres per hour is equivalent to 22,000 gallons per hour (366 gallons per minute).

In terms of water storage 1,000 cubic metres (1 million litres) is equivalent to 220,000 gallons (1 million gallons=4,546 cubic metres).

1,000 cubic metres is sufficient to apply 25 millimetres of water over 4 hectares, which is approximately equivalent to applying 1 inch over 10 acres.

7. FIELD DRAINAGE

(Estimated for 1985)

(Costs before deducting grant*)

1. Installation (costs per metre of excavating a trench, supplying and laying the pipe and backfilling with soil).

		£ per metre
Plastic pipes:	60mm diameter	0·90—1·00
	80mm diameter	0·95—1·05
	100mm diameter	1·15—1·35
	125mm diameter	1·50—1·70
	150mm diameter	1·90—2·30
	250mm diameter	8·50—9·25
Clay pipes:	75mm diameter	1·10—1·25
	100mm diameter	1·25—1·50
	150mm diameter	1·70—1·95

Supplying and laying permeable backfill to within 360mm of ground level will add between 85p and £1·00 per metre to costs.

Digging new open ditches (1·8m top width, 0·9m depth) costs £1·50-£1·75 per metre compared with improving existing ditches at £1·00 to £1·10 per metre.

Subsoiling or mole draining will cost in the region of £40-£50 per hectare.

2. *Total*

Costs per hectare for complete schemes will vary depending on the distance between laterals, soil type, size of area to be drained, region of the country and the time of year when the work is to be undertaken. The cost of a scheme with 20m spacing between laterals and using permeable backfill will typically be in the range £1,000 to £1,300 per hectare (£400-£525 per acre). Backfilling with soil, rather than with permeable material such as washed gravel, may reduce the cost by almost half but is only possible on certain types of soil. Equally, certain soil types which are particularly suitable for mole drainage may permit spacing between laterals to be increased to 40m or even 80m in some instances. Where this is possible costs will be reduced proportionately.

* For rates of grant for field drainage see pages 145-6.

8. GRAIN DRYING AND STORAGE COSTS
(Estimated for 1985)

A. Drying

Capital Costs: vary widely according to type and capacity of drier; a typical range is £22 to £30 per tonne dried annually.

Annual fixed costs: depreciation and interest £3·25 to £4·40 per tonne.

Running costs: fuel and repairs, approx. £3·20 per tonne (6 per cent moisture extraction) for oil-fired driers or where little heat is used in ventilated plants; £5·40 to £7·20 for electrically-heated driers. Labour, 65p to £1·60 per tonne.

Total operating costs: average £8·00 to £9·50 per tonne (6 per cent).

B. Storage

Capital Costs: from less than £30 per tonne (inexpensive storage in an existing building) to £125 per tonne for an elaborate plant.

Typical costs are given on page 118.

Depreciation and Interest: £80 per tonne depreciated over 10 years, with 12 per cent interest, equals £14·15 per annum; over 15 years, £11·75. (In highly mechanized bulk plants, part of this may be charged against harvesting rather than entirely against storage).

Fuel and Repairs: £1·25 per tonne.

Extra Drying: Additional drying costs will be borne if storage necessitates further moisture reduction. Average £1·60 per tonne where own drier, £3·00 if dried on contract.

Loss of Weight: the value of the weight of grain lost should be charged if storage requires extra drying. 2 per cent = £2·40 to £2·70 per tonne.

Interest on Grain Stored: from 87·5p (£105 per tonne grain, at 10 per cent) to £1·55 (£125 per tonne grain, at 15 per cent) per month.

Contract Storage: typical charges per tonne per week are 25p for feed grains and 30p for malting barley, where the identity of consignments is retained.

IV. MISCELLANEOUS DATA

1. FIXED COSTS

The following are a *broad indication* of the levels of fixed costs per hectare (£) for various types and sizes of farm, estimated for 1985. *All can of course vary widely according to many factors, especially the intensity of farming.* More specific data relating to local types of farm can be derived from data published annually by agricultural economics departments of the Universities.(1)

The term "fixed costs" refers to those costs that are unallocated in determining enterprise gross margins.These costs can and will alter when substantial changes are made in a farm plan—and some of them (e.g. a full-time cowman, or the costs of a potato harvester), both can and should be allocated to specific enterprises when budgeting major changes—but they alter in a different way from the "variable costs" as defined in gross margin analysis. The fixed resources are often described as "lumpy" because when they change in quantity and therefore cost they do so only in large "chunks" at a time, e.g. the annual wage of an extra man, the annual depreciation on a new machine or building; they will often stay the same when small changes in cropping and livestock numbers occur. In contrast, the "variable costs" vary roughly in proportion to such changes, however small.

	Mainly Dairying			Dairying and Arable		
	Under 50 hectares	50-100 hectares	Over 100 hectares	Under 100 hectares	100-200 hectares	Over 200 hectares
Labour	310	255	220	245	220	180
Machinery	225	210	195	210	200	175
Rent and Rates ...	125	120	110	120	110	100
General Overheads	90	80	70	70	55	50
Total	750	665	595	645	585	505

	Mainly Cereals			Mixed Cropping		
	Under 100 hectares	100-200 hectares	Over 200 hectares	Under 100 hectares	100-200 hectares	Over 200 hectares
Labour	150	125	115	205	155	140
Machinery	170	160	150	210	195	180
Rent and Rates ...	100	95	95	115	110	110
General Overheads	45	40	35	55	50	45
Total	465	420	395	585	510	475

(1) For example, Farm Business Statistics for South-East England, Wye College.

	Mainly Sheep/Cattle			Sheep/Cattle and Arable		
	Under 100 hectares	100-200 hectares	Over 200 hectares	Under 100 hectares	100-200 hectares	Over 200 hectares
Labour	140	125	115	150	130	120
Machinery	115	100	92·5	140	120	125
Rent and Rates ...	90	85	80	95	90	90
General Overheads	40	35	27·5	45	40	35
Total	385	345	315	430	380	370

	Arable and Pigs/Poultry			Livestock Rearing	
	Under 50 hectares	50-150 hectares	Over 150 hectares	(per *adjusted* hectare)	
				Upland	Hill
Labour	410	280	185	90	65
Machinery	400	265	205	55	30
Rent and Rates ...	150	135	120	50	25
General Overheads	135	105	75	20	10
	1095	785	585	215	130

Notes

Labour: Paid regular labour *plus the value of unpaid family labour,* including the value of the farmer's manual labour and that of his wife. *Casual labour specific to an enterprise is also included,* although this is normally regarded as a variable cost in gross margin analysis; **(n.b., this is the first edition in which this has been done).**
Machinery: Note that depreciation is based on the current (i.e. 'replacement') cost of machinery, not on the original (i.e. 'historic') cost. Also, all contract work costs are included, including those specific to an enterprise, although these are normally regarded as variable costs in gross margin analysis.
The *average* composition of these costs is as follows: depreciation $37\frac{1}{2}$%, repairs $22\frac{1}{2}$%, fuel and oil $22\frac{1}{2}$%, contract work $12\frac{1}{2}$%, vehicle tax and insurance 5% (approx.).
Strictly speaking, fuel and repair costs are largely, if not entirely, variable costs in the gross margin sense; they are normally included with fixed costs, however, partly because of the difficulty of recording and allocating them, partly because they are not usually large enough items to affect the gross margin sufficiently, and also because their total cost per farm does not alter very much with small changes in the farm plan.
General Overheads include general farm maintenance and repairs, office expenses, insurance, fees, subscriptions, etc.

Labour, machinery and buildings are the main items of "fixed" costs subject to change with major alterations in farm policy. Each is the subject of a separate section in this book.

2. RENTS AND LAND PRICES

A. Rents

Average Rent per hectare (acre) of Crops, Grass and Rough Grazing.

October 1983 and estimated for **mid-1985**: calculated from actual October 1983 levels plus approx. 15·0%. The average annual increase was 10·4% in the period October 1982 to October 1983, compared with 11·5% in the period October 1981 to October 1982. The rate of increase is expected to continue to decline.

Region	Average Rent (all farms) Oct. 1983	Average Rent (all farms) Mid-1985 (est.)	New Rent Levels* Oct. 1983	New Rent Levels* Mid-1985 (est.)
	£	£	£	£
East Anglia	94·5 (38·3)	108·5 (44·0)	101·5 (41·1)	116·5 (47·0)
South East ...	92·3 (37·3)	106·0 (43·0)	101·4 (41·0)	116·5 (47·0)
East Midlands ...	91·9 (37·2)	105·5 (43·0)	105·6 (42·7)	121·5 (49·0)
West Midlands ...	87·8 (35·5)	101·0 (41·0)	98·3 (39·8)	113·0 (45·5)
North West ...	85·6 (34·6)	98·5 (40·0)	95·8 (38·8)	110·0 (44·5)
South West ...	78·3 (31·7)	90·0 (36·5)	88·3 (35·7)	101·5 (41·0)
Yorks. and Humberside ...	68·0 (27·5)	78·0 (31·5)	79·5 (32·2)	91·5 (37·0)
Northern ...	43·2 (17·5)	49·5 (20·0)	49·7 (20·1)	57·0 (23·0)
Wales ...	40·8 (16·5)	47·0 (19·0)	52·9 (21·4)	61·0 (24·5)
England ...	79·7 (32·1)	91·5 (37·0)	89·6 (36·3)	103·0 (41·5)
England and Wales ...	76·1 (30·8)	87·5 (35·5)	86·2 (34·9)	99·0 (40·0)

*Where rents have been raised in previous 12 months.

N.B. Farms which had a rent change during the year previous to October 1983 (33 per cent) had an average increase of 29 per cent, to a level averaging 13 per cent above the average rent on all farms.

Source: Agricultural Development and Advisory Service, Booklet B2319(83).

Size Differences (England)

Area in ha	Average Rent Oct. 1983 £	Mid-1985 Rent (est.) £
less than 10	115·8 (46·9)	133·0 (54·0)
10-19·9	88·7 (35·9)	102·0 (41·5)
20-29·9	91·2 (36·9)	105·0 (42·5)
30-39·9	88·5 (35·8)	101·5 (41·0)
40-49·9	83·4 (33·7)	96·0 (39·0)
50-79·9	77·4 (31·3)	89·0 (36·0)
75-99·9	80·0 (32·4)	92·0 (37·5)
100-249·9	83·3 (33·7)	96·0 (39·0)
250 & over	68·6 (27·8)	79·0 (32·0)

Note. The above figures are derived from a very large sample, covering about 34 per cent of the tenanted land in the country. Rents on some farms are still at a fairly modest level. Most of the publicity on farm rents is aimed at the high levels occasionally, and exceptionally, achieved. Obviously the above *are* only averages, and the levels on, for example, largish arable farms on good soils, or well-equipped small dairy farms, will well exceed them, probably averaging about £125 per ha (£50 per acre), especially where the landlord is anxious to obtain a good rent. Furthermore, in the case of new lettings by tender the levels will well exceed even the latter figure, since there is a considerable scarcity value, 'key money' is included, and neighbouring successful farmers can afford to make very high bids for various well-known reasons; such bids for an average quality farm are unlikely to be successful at less than £160 per ha (£65 per acre) and those for top quality arable farms may even exceed £250 per ha (£100 per acre).

B. Sale Value of Farmland, England and Wales
£ per hectare (acre)

(1) *Auction Sales*
   (a) Oxford Institute series

| Size Group (hectares) | With Possession | | | | | | | Tenanted |
	2-20	20-40	40-60	60-120	Over 120	20 and over	All Farms	All Farms
1937-9	120	85	70	55	30	—	60	50
1946-8	400	210	165	130	110	—	170	90
1950-9	375	230	195	175	145	—	200	110
1960-1	500	335	290	260	265	—	305	155
1965	835	620	575	475	565	—	580	370
1969	1210	690	595	645	725	675	740	NA
1970	1115	600	505	605	565	575	605	NA
1971	1510	705	650	675	695	685	645	545
1972	2580	1370	1115	1480	1765	1505	1475	1315
1973	3705	2125	1960	1920	2270	2090	1870	1240
1974	—	—	—	—	—	—	1570	NA
1975	—	—	—	—	—	—	1330	NA
1976	—	—	—	—	—	—	1815	950
1977	—	—	—	—	—	—	2450	1210
1978	—	—	—	—	—	—	3280	2040
1979	—	—	—	—	—	—	4370	2725
1980	—	—	—	—	—	—	4265	NA
1981	—	—	—	—	—	—	4270	NA
1982	—	—	—	—	—	—	4555	NA
1983	—	—	—	—	—	—	5160 (2089)	NA

Source: A. H. Maunder, University of Oxford Institute of Agricultural Economics.

Figures based on auction sales reports published in the *Estates Gazette* except that, *after 1970*, "all farms" figures based on sales reports in both the *Estates Gazette* and the *Farmers Weekly*, plus some unpublished sales, with the minimum size included increased from 2 to 10 hectares, and weighting by region as well as by size.

NA—Insufficient sales reported.

(b) Farmland Market series

Size Group (hectares)	10-20	20-40	40-60	60-80	80-100	100-140	Over 140	All Farms
1972	1775	1370	1210	1285	1070	1260	1755	1370 (554)
1973	2530	2080	1815	1805	1885	1735	2100	1975 (799)
1974	2245	1745	1490	1565	1415	1335	1280	1685 (682)
1975	2115	1545	1340	1165	1200	1190	1090	1485 (601)
1976	2560	2015	1855	1830	1670	1610	1730	1965 (795)
1977	2825	2660	2365	2425	2230	2530	2325	2525 (1020)
1978	3970	3425	3125	3265	3180	3480	3595	3380 (1368)
1979	6280	4385	4220	3975	4330	4890	4315	4515 (1828)
1980	5585	4905	4270	4305	4405	4435	4130	4705 (1904)
1981	6135	4680	3880	4315	3760	4710	4355	4500 (1821)
1982	6455	4950	4465	4065	4705	4510	4325	4815 (1949)
1983	6825	5630	5160	5110	5095	5495	5130	5450 (2206) *

*Jan.-June 1984: 5545 (2245).

Source: The Farmland Market. Auction sales; with possession.

(2) *ADAS, AMC, CLA Combined Series (England)*

3 months ended				Vacant Possession			Tenanted
				Average Price (1)	Weighted Price (2)	Price Index (3)	
1980: March	...	...	...	3849	3758	193	2638
June	...	...	...	4410	4428	228	2239
September	...	...	...	3980	3925	202	2558
December	...	...	...	3541	3875	199	2190
1981: March	...	...	...	3763	3683	190	2391
June	...	...	...	3859	3807	196	2395
September	...	...	...	3988	4000	206	2535
December	...	...	...	4110	4100	211	2141
1982: March	...	...	...	3351	3855	198	3073
June	...	...	...	4407	4267	220	2521
September	...	...	...	3999	4180	215	2009
December	...	...	...	4404	4419	227	2163
1983: March	...	...	...	4393	4349	224	2453
June	...	...	...	4700	4716	243	2077
September	...	...	...	4700	4700	242	2295
December	...	...	...	4604	4750	244	2246
1984: March	...	...	...	4906	4994	257	N.A.
June	...	...	...	5161	5087	262	N.A.

(1) Total value of sales divided by total area sold. The most recent figures are provisional.

(2) Average price for each region × size-group category weighted by the area of land sold in that category in the three years 1976-78.

(3) Indexed based on weighted price; 1973 = 100 (£1,943).

By Regions (Vacant Possession only)

				1983	1982	1981	1980	1979
Northern	...	...	...	3548	2124	2554	2081	2916
Yorks/Humberside		...	...	4759	4081	3907	3819	3858
East Midland	...	...	...	5467	4598	4102	4341	4248
East Anglia	...	...	...	5196	4454	4661	4495	4956
South East	...	...	...	4501	4250	3975	4047	4169
South West	...	...	...	4332	3979	3631	3931	3966
West Midlands	...	...	...	5066	5117	4341	4471	4716
North West	...	...	...	4596	4597	4466	4683	4727
England	...	...	...	4631	4123	3941	3977	4138

By Size-Group (Vacant Possession only)

Size Group (ha)				1983	1982	1981	1980	1979
5—9	...	...	...	5710	5557	4886	5107	5062
10—19	...	...	...	5269	4933	4375	4415	4603
20—49	...	...	...	4856	4461	3968	4137	4078
50—99	...	...	...	4429	4162	3723	4030	4007
100 and over		...	...	4232	3399	3760	3539	3949
All	...	...	...	4631	4123	3941	3977	4138

By Land Classification (Vacant Possession only)

Land quality	(% of total area)	1983	1982	1981	1980	1979
1	(3·3)	7019	6600	5824	5385	5450
2	(16·7)	5627	4975	4739	4237	4798
3	(54·0)	4666	4199	4115	3774	4301
4	(15·7)	3341	2887	2520	2862	2711
5	(10·3)	1413	709	1183	614	1306

Notes:

Covers sales of 5 ha and above but excludes land sold for development or forestry, gifts, inheritances and compulsory purchases.
ADAS=Agricultural Development and Advisory Service.
AMC =Agricultural Mortgage Corporation.
CLA =Country Landowners Association.

Source: M.A.F.F. Press Notices.

(4) *Inland Revenue Returns* (England only)

The following figures are given for comparative purposes only. They are lower than the figures above, for the reasons explained below.

	Vacant Possession	Tenanted	All Sales
Oct. 1975-Sept. 1976	1205(488)	797(323)	1125(455)
Oct. 1976-Sept. 1977	1472(596)	1019(412)	1349(546)
Oct. 1977-Sept. 1978	1994(807)	1563(633)	1909(773)
Oct. 1978-Sept. 1979	2602(1053)	1687(683)	2434(985)
Oct. 1979-Sept. 1980	3227(1306)	2381(964)	3129(1266)
Oct. 1980-Sept. 1981	3470(1404)	2336(945)	3316(1342)
Oct. 1981-Sept. 1982	3418(1383)	2450(992)	3283(1329)
Oct. 1982-Sept. 1983	3669(1485)	2490(1008)	3535(1431)
Oct. 1983-Mar. 1984	3544(1434)	2371(960)	3373(1365)

These figures relate to all sales of agricultural properties of 5 ha (4 ha before Oct., 1978) and over except those for development and other non-agricultural purposes. They include any sales at prices below ruling open market value (as between members of a family), sales where the vendor retains certain (e.g. sporting) rights, and sales in which the farmhouse represents a substantial part of the total value. There is a delay between the dates when a price is agreed and when it is notified to the Inland Revenue and thus included in the above figures; this time-lag is thought to average between 6 and 9 months.

Source: M.A.F.F. Statistical Information.

3. BUILDINGS

A. Building Costs

Building costs are notoriously variable. Many factors influence a contractor's price, especially distance from his yard, size of contract, site access, site conditions and complexity of the work. This is true especially for small works in rural areas and this includes most farm buildings. The latter can be confused by the inclusion of large, specialist buildings and plant which are provided and erected by national firms, often employing labour on piece-work rates. Variable rates of inflation increase the problem of estimating costs. Furthermore, quoted prices for any single requirement at a particular time, but using different materials or contractors, can have a variable effect. Thus the guide costs given below must be treated with caution. However, one would normally hope for prices within 10-15% of those stated. They refer to new buildings, not conversions; erected by contractor, not farm labour; and *exclude any grant allowances* which may be available. Prices are based on average acceptable utility, and are forecasts for mid-1985.

References

National costs for urban buildings are published regularly within several architect and building journals. In addition, annual costs are published by Spons and Laxton and, rather more specifically for rural works, by Hutchins and by Griffiths. A Farm Building Cost Guide is published annually by the Scottish Farm Buildings Investigation Unit, and a cost of Farm Buildings Handbook is published and updated twice a year by the Land and Water Service (LAWS) of the Ministry of Agriculture, Fisheries and Food, which in fact forms the basis of most of the prices for the traditionally constructed operations included in this section.

I. Constituent Parts

Frame, Roof and Foundations

1. General-purpose portal frame building of steel, concrete or timber: including purlins, asbestos cement roof sheeting and gable peaks, concrete bases and compacted hardcore floor. No side cladding and erected on level site with good access. Eaves height 4·8 m.

	per m² floor area
7·62 m span	£47
9·14 m span	£45
13·72 m span	£43
Monopitch 5 m span	£36

2. Specialist, timber constructed frames with internal supports
   Otherwise as 1 above   £36
3. Materials and erection: breakdown average of total cost—

Materials:	Frame delivered	40%	
	Roofing	23%	63%
Erection:	Foundations	11%	
	Frame	15%	
	Roof cladding	11%	37%

Roof cladding

1. Natural asbestos cement sheets, 146 mm corrugations, fixed with drive screws onto (but excluding) purlins.

   Materials delivered (excluding profit)   £6·05 per m^2
   Materials plus erection   £9·00 per m^2
   Fixed as vertical cladding   £10·05 per m^2

2. Add to 1 above for "Thrutone" or plastic-coated steel:
       £1·95 per m^2

3. Add to 1 above for translucent sheets: £9·85 per m^2

4. Deduct from 1 above for 0·7 mm galvanised steel corrugated sheeting: £1·15 per m^2

5. Asbestos cement 150 mm half round gutters complete:
       £11·50 per m run

6. Asbestos cement 100 mm diameter rainwater pipe complete:
       £18·80 per m run

7. Asbestos cement ventilating ridge,   £20·00 per m run

Walls and Cladding

1. Hollow concrete blocks and erected with mortar joints to not above 2·5 m in height above ground.

   190 mm blockwork   £15·60 per m^2
   215 mm blockwork   £16·80 per m^2
   215 mm blockwork filled and reinforced   £25·30 per m^2

2. Wall element of 215 mm blockwork, complete with strip foundation with base 750 mm below ground level and with blockwork built up to 2·5 m above ground level.

   total cost erected   £53·50 per m run

3. Vertical space boarding of 150 mm boards with 19 mm gaps fixed with galvanised nails and including longitudinal rails all pressure impregnated   £16·80 per m^2

4. Weather boarding, otherwise as 3 above   £22·25 per m^2

5. Asbestos cement vertical cladding, all as before but including longitudinal rails   £13·65 per m^2

Floors   per m²
1. Concrete floor 100 mm thick, C20P mix, on
   150 mm hardcore, including excavation: £13·80

   Approximate breakdown:
   a) Excavate and level and compact   £1·05
   b) Hardcore   £1·55
   c) Blinding   £1·30
   d) Polythene membrane   £0·65
   e) Premix concrete spread and levelled   £7·80
   f) Float finish   £1·45

2. Extra to above for
   a) 150 mm concrete in lieu of 100 mm   £3·25
   b) Laying concrete to falls   £0·65
   c) Broom or textured finish   £0·95
   d) Carborundum dust   £2·30
   e) 50 mm insulation slabs set in floor   £6·30

3. Cattle bedded areas, including 300 mm excavation,
   100 mm rolled hardcore and 150 mm rolled chalk
   or marl variable to location, minimum   £5·35

4. R.C. slatted floors for cattle 125 mm wide with
   40 mm gaps and 3 m long   £47·50

5. R.C. slatted floors for pigs 75 mm wide with
   12 mm gaps and 0·9 m long   £31·00

6. Insulating floor with 40 mm screed over 25 mm
   expanded polystyrene sheet on 100 mm concrete
   on membrane and hardcore (excluding site
   excavation)   £21·00

7. Cubicle heelstones, mass concrete or bolted
   sleepers, 250 mm high × 100 mm wide   £7·60 per m run

8. Forming channel in concrete   £1·30 per m run

9. Excavating for and casting mass concrete
   bases for stanchions approximately 1 m³
   including grouting   £54 each

Services and Fittings
1. Drainage: 100 mm pitchfibre laid and jointed including excavation
   and backfill   £7·50 per m run

   Approximate breakdown:
   a) Excavate by machine 600 mm deep   £2·25 per m run
   b) 100 mm pitchfibre laid and jointed   £5·30 per m run
   c) Extra to a) above if 1,000 mm deep   £1·50 per m run
   d) Extra to b) above for 150 mm pitchfibre £5·60 per m run

2. Broken brick or stone soakaway 2 m³   £31·00 each

3. Trapped stoneware gulley with 150 × 100 mm cast iron grating set in concrete £24 each

4. Yard gulley 400 × 350 mm heavy duty grating and 450 mm deep below outlet rendered blockwork and concrete base £140

5. Inspection chamber with 228 mm brick rendered walls 900 mm deep on 100 mm thick concrete with 600 × 450 mm opening and cast iron cover £220

6. Above ground storage tanks, coated galvanised steel, inclusive of concrete base, complete excluding machinery, pumps etc., 4·16 m high × 17·06 m diameter £16,400

7. Reception pit to above, 20 m³ capacity including grid £2,700

8. Gantry and ladder £550

9. Slurry pit 3 m wide × 2 m deep, in reinforced blockwork and concrete base ready to receive slats, including draw off points

£320 per m run

10. Lighting: 1,200 mm single fluorescent £37·50 each
Extra for 1500 mm single fluorescent £4·50 each
Extra for conduit £13·25 each
Power: Per 13 amp outlet in conduit £45 each

11. Mangers: Single portable softwood £22 per m run
With hayrack over £46 per m run
300 mm glazed trough including
haunching in concrete £24 per m run

12. Cubicle Divisions: Galvanised, wall fixed,
set in concrete £55 each

13. Fencing: 3 rail timber with posts,
pressure impregnated £11 per m run

14. Cattle gate 3·00 × 1·14 m high of galvanised steel complete with steel posts set in concrete £145 each
Extra to above for 3·6 m gate £22 each

II. Complete Buildings

Fully Covered and Enclosed Barn

Portal frame, 14 m span × 4·8 m bays, asbestos cement roof and cladding, perimeter block walls to 2 m high with overall eaves height of 3·6 m. Sliding access doors each end, 150 mm concrete floor on hardcore and membrane, excluding services:
per m² covered £75

NB: There are wide variations in cost related to layout, construction and fittings. In general terms, the simplest kennels would cost £220 per cow place and cubicle houses £300 to £625. Covered strawed yards complete with walling and cladding and concrete floors at 4·5 m² per cow, would cost £310.

1. Cubicle House: 12·8 m span portal frame, asbestos cement roof with open ridge and roof lights: walling of 140 mm block taken 1·8 m above ground on strip foundation with 1·2 m high space boarding over to eaves, complete with gutters and storm drains; having four rows of 1·2 m cubicles on concrete floor and timber divisions and concrete kerb; with two 2·1 m wide concrete passageways between cubicles with cross passage and water troughs; complete with sliding doors and external aprons 9 m wide; per cow place   £300

2. Cubicle house with slatted passageways, over 1·2 m deep pits; otherwise as 1 above; per cow place   £400

3. Cubicle House, with feed area, 22·8 m span; as 1 above but with central tractor passage, tubular divisions and rails; per cow place   £625

4. Covered collecting yards: allowed as freestanding portal frame structure, 9·14 m span, with asbestos cement roof, walling of 190 mm block taken 1·8 m above ground on strip foundation with 1·20 m space boarding over to eaves, complete with gutters, storm drains, concrete floor and gates; per cow place   £85

5. Parlours: approx. £120 to £130 per m² excluding equipment, for traditional construction of block, trussed roof with asbestos cement and rooflights, rendered walls, grano finish to floors, pit and water supply.

   Parlour 10·46 × 9·00 m to take rotary, excluding equipment (18 places)   £11,000

   Parlour 8·60 × 7·00 m to take herringbone excluding equipment but including mangers (12 places)   £7,750

   Parlour 10·60 × 7·00 m to take herringbone, as above (16 places)   £9,000

6. Parlour equipment:

12 place: 12 point static herringbone	£1,350 per point
12 place: 6 point static herringbone	£1,850 per point
16 place: 16 point static herringbone	£1,325 per point
16 place: 8 point static herringbone	£1,700 per point
20 place: 20 point abreast rotary	£1,950 per point

   Extra to above for automatic cluster removal (A.C.R.)
       £435 per point

   Feed conveyor equipment   £270 per point

7. Dairy: with hygienic surfaces and insulated ceiling taken as free standing and varying between 26 and 52 m² £150 per m²
Bulk tanks extra: installed at approximately £3·65 per litre stored inclusive of all fittings.
8. Loose box: with rendered walls 15·5 m² in area £140 per m²
9. Bull pen and open run £8,000
10. Cattle crush and 20 m run of race, excluding cover £3,300

Pig Housing
1. *Rearing* *per piglet*
   a) Prefabricated flat deck housing complete with all base work, plumbing, heating and electricity £40

   per sow and litter
   b) Outdoor: simple huts with wire fenced run in paddocks
   £230
   c) Insulated huts with fittings and small compound timber fenced £600
   d) Solari-type range of farrowing pens, insulated roof, all rails and external runnel £800
   e) Farrowing pens each 2·36 × 1·8 m with crate and side creeps, prefabricated superstructure and including all basework, insulated floor and slatted channels. Structure 6·2 m span
   £840
   Individual bolt down farrowing crate £125

2. *Fattening* *per baconer*
   a) Zig zag finishing house 10·8 m span with kennels 3 × 2·4 m; insulated concrete floor, asbestos cement roof over blockwork and space boarding £150
   b) Finishing house 11 m span with sleep feed areas and central feed passage, including all base work, with slatted dung channels and prefabricated superstructure for but excluding mechanical ventilation £90
   c) Trobridge finishing house 4·68 m span with sleep feed areas and external passages, including all base work, with slatted dung channel and prefabricated superstructure £57
   d) Suffolk finishing house 9·9 m span with feeding/dunging area and kennels with insulated covers, asbestos cement roof over insulated blockwork and hinged gapped boarding; natural ventilation £145

3. *Dry Sows, etc.*   *per sow*
    a) Loose housed in covered yards, pitched roof over block
        walls and space boarding including feeders and concrete
        floor   £550
    b) Individual bolt down sow feeding crate   £80

    c) *Dry sow house with in situ* crates, bowls, part slatted areas over
        channels, feed and access panels, fully insulated and with
        ventilation hoppers and fan extraction chimney shafts £340
    d) Boar pens: as part of 3c above   £815

4. *Total Pig Unit*

    Costs calculated on the basis of a three week weaning system with
    sows farrowing 2·26 times per year and rearing 19·2 piglets per sow
    per year to bacon. Excludes slurry storage outside building and
    handling/weighing facilities.
    a) Naturally ventilated system   £1,325 (£850)
    b) Fan ventilated system   £1,400 (£900)
        (The figures in brackets denote rearing only.)

Poultry

The following figures are based on units of between 10,000 and
20,000 for laying birds and 10,000 for broilers (including all
equipment):

    a) Laying birds: Battery cages (five birds to 500 mm wide
                        cage)   £7·85 per bird
                        Deep litter (50% litter, 50% raised slatted or
                        wire floor: stocking density on overall area
                        0·14 m² per bird)   £9·50 per bird
    b) Broilers: 0·05 m² per bird   £3·40 per bird

Grain Storage and Drying   per tonne stored
    a) Bins within existing building, nests with central tunnel,
        catwalk, etc., with work area and intake pit, including handling
        and drying equipment   £110
    b) As above installed in new structure   £160
    c) Floor storage portal framed structure, 10·5 m span, under floor
        ducts, fan chamber and ventilating equipment   £120
    d) Drying equipment for bulk bins   £10
    e) Ventilating equipment for on-the-floor storage   £26
    f) Handling equipment for bulk bins   £21
    g) Hermetically sealed towers not over 11 m high, with unloading
        equipment   £82·50

Potato Storage

a) Pallet storage, portal framed insulated structure, 12 m span, overhead ducting and ventilating equipment   £102

b) Bulk on-the-floor storage, portal framed insulated structure, 13·7 m span, under floor ducts, fan chamber and ventilating equipment   £125

c) Ventilating equipment and ducting for pallet storage   £18

d) Ventilating equipment and main ducting for on-the-floor storage   £25

e) One tonne pallet box   £38

B. Standard Costs

The following are examples of *estimated* approximate standard costs as calculated for a number of M.A.F.F. grant schemes (forecast forward for mid 1985) where the farmer chooses this basis instead of actual costs. They are based on the cost of farm labour and new materials only, excluding overheads and profit. The latter are variable, but on average building firms would add about one-third to cover them. In addition several of the items embraced in this section have counterparts under section 3A. Comparing with contract costs, disparities are the result of varied specification or operational content.

Totally enclosed general purpose
building, excluding floor:

traditional construction
(the range is 2·4-3·6 m to
4·2 m to eaves)

100 m²	£76·25 to £100·25 per m²
300 m²	£62·50 to £76·25 per m²
500 m²	£56·75 to £67·25 per m²

framed construction
(2·4-3·6 m to 4·8 m to eaves)

100 m²	£68·25 to £92·25 per m²
300 m²	£52·50 to £61·75 per m²
500 m²	£46·50 to £55·25 per m²

Open fronted building (traditional
construction, excluding floor)

100 m²	£55·50 per m²
200 m²	£49·25 per m²
300 m²	£47·25 per m²

Dutch Barn type building, or covered cattle yard, or implement shed (framed construction, excluding floor)	£27·05 to £33·10 per m²
Concrete foundations for stanchions, excluding excavation	£33·00 per foundation
Excavations: up to 200 m³	£4·65 per m³
thereafter	£1·60 per m³
Hardcore filling	£8·00 per m³
Concreting, including formwork	
75 to 99 mm thick	£5·30 per m²
100 to 149 mm thick	£6·40 per m²
150 mm plus thick	£9·70 per m²
Waterproof membrane	£0·37 per m²
Floor insulation	£6·60 per m²
Roof insulation	£2·40 per m²
Walling: includes allowance for excavation, foundations and damp proof course	
Brick 100 to 199 mm thick	£13·35 per m²
200 to 324 mm thick	£25·40 per m²
325 mm plus thick	£34·40 per m²
Concrete block 100 to 139 mm thick	£11·75 per m²
140 to 189 mm thick	£15·60 per m²
190 mm plus thick	£23·25 per m²
Rendering walls (two coat work)	£3·50 per m²
Cladding, including supports	£6·75 to £10·75 per m²
Store or loose box: first 15 m²	£130 per m²
next 85 m²	£74·00 per m²
Milking Parlour (including stalls):	
Abreast or Herringbone	£155 per m²
Tandem	£195 per m²
Chute	£212 per m²
Dairy	£144 per m²
Cowshed	£106 to £122 per m² (according to size)
Manger front/feed barrier	£12·75 per m
Slatted floors for cattle	£33·50 per m²
Cubicle divisions: timber	£25·25 per division
steel or concrete	£28·00 per division
Heelstones	£4·10 per m
Pig fattening house	
enclosed building	
max. 12 m internal width	£113 per m²
over 12 m internal width	£91 per m²
Open yards	£38 per m²

Roads of broken stone or ungraded
  materials

New road	£2·70 per m²
Improvement of existing road	£1·65 per m²
Cattle grid, including pit	£395 each
Strained wire fence, 3 line	£0·75 to £1·55 per m
Woven wire fence (max. includes 2 line wire)	£1·30 to £2·60 per m
Wooden post and rail (nailed) fence: 3 rails	£5·70 per m
4 rails	£6·75 per m
Gate: wooden	£4·80 per 300 mm
steel, painted/galvanised	£4·80/£7·35 per 300 mm
Gate post	£18·50 each

Acknowledgement. The whole of the above section on Building Costs was completely revised by C. Cresser, MBE, FRICS, of ADAS in mid-1982 for 1983. For 1985 approximately 10 per cent has been added by the author to cover cost increases in the following two years.

C. Storage Requirements

Baled barley straw: 11·2 m³ per tonne

Baled oat straw: 10·5 m³ per tonne

Baled hay straw: 6·0 m³ per tonne

Silage, forage harvested, well consolidated: 1·25 m³ per tonne (800 kg per m³)

Silage, buckraked, cut late: 1·55 m³ per tonne (640 kg per m³)

Haylage: approx. 240 kg dry matter per m³, or 1·55 to 1·77 m³ per tonne (560 to 640 kg per m³) at 45-50 per cent dry matter

Grain in bulk:
  Wheat: 1·27 m³ per tonne (785 kg per m³)
  Barley: 1·41 m³ per tonne (705 kg per m³)
  Oats: 1·4 m³ per tonne (510 kg per m³)
  Beans: 1·19 m³ per tonne (835 kg per m³)

Potatoes in bulk: 1·55 m³ per tonne

Feedingstuffs, stacked 2 bags high, 1 tonne requires 1·7 m² floor space.

Fertilizer, 6 bags (1·1 m) high, 1 tonne requires 1·1 m² floor space.

Fertilizer, 10 bags (1·8 m) high, 1 tonne requires 0·7 m² floor space.

For comprehensive data on dimensions of farm buildings, see Farm Buildings Pocketbook and the Equipment of the Farm leaflets, both produced by M.A.F.F. (H.M.S.O.).

4. CAPITAL

(i) *Tenant's Capital* consists of:

(a) *Machinery.* Costs of new machinery are given on pages 88-92. Written-down values in 1985 are likely to be averaging about £450 per hectare taking all farm types together—based on current (*i.e.* replacement) costs.

(b) *Breeding Livestock.* Over all types of farm the 1985 average is estimated to be about £475 per hectare, but the figure can vary from zero to well over £1,000 for grazing livestock alone. Approximate average market values (£) of various categories of breeding livestock (of mixed ages in the case of adult stock) are as follows (actual value will vary according to average age and weight, quality and breed):

Friesian Dairy Cows (inc. dry cows): 550.
Channel Island Dairy Cows (inc. dry cows): 325.
Other Dairy Cows (inc. dry cows): 410.
Beef Cows: 500.

Other Cattle:	Dairy Followers		Beef Cattle
	Friesians	Ayrshires and C.I. Breeds	
In-calf heifers	500	300	425
Stores over 2 years	375	225	375
Stores 1-2 years	325	200	325
Stores 6-12 months	250	160	265
Calves under 6 months ...	150	90	170

Ewes: 50.

Sows and In-pig Gilts: 110.

(c) *Working Capital.* This is the capital needed to finance the production cycle, the length of which varies considerably between different crop and livestock enterprises and different combinations of these enterprises. Because of this, no generalizations are possible, but it can include the cost of purchased fattening stock, feed, seed, fertilizers, regular labour, machinery running costs, general overhead costs, rent and living expenses. This capital may be only a few pounds per hectare on an all-dairying farm but £500 or more per hectare on an all-cereals farm where the crop is stored until the spring. The average is likely to be about £275 per hectare in 1985.

(ii) *Return on Capital*

(a) *Tenant's Capital.* For all lowland farms (excluding intensive pig and poultry units, fruit and glasshouse production), this will probably average about £1,200 per hectare (£485 per acre) in 1985, with the (written-down) machinery valuations based on current ('replacement') costs. On the same basis, the average U.K. management and investment per hectare (acre) was in the order of £115 (£47·50) in 1982/83 (considered to be a relatively good year), compared with about £85 (£35) the year before. The 1983/84 figure looks like being about £100 (£40), and subsequent years will see the effects of E.E.C. quotas and price cuts. If an average of £100 (£40) is still however achieved, through cost economies and greater efficiency in general, the average return on tenant's capital would be approximately 8·5 per cent. 'Premium' levels (the average of the top 50 per cent of farms) would be likely to be about 50 per cent higher, with the levels achieved for cash cropping on the very best soils at least double the average. Note that no charge has been included for management.

(b) *Landlord's Capital* (*i.e.* land, buildings, roads, etc.). The recently imposed dairy quotas and proposed future price cuts (especially in cereals) could cause land prices to fall; (they have already fallen in real terms by more than a quarter between 1979 and mid-1984). With land averaging, say, £4,800 per hectare (£1940 per acre), with vacant possession, an average lowland rent of say, £100 per hectare (£40 per acre) (see p. 108), and assuming ownership expenses at £40 per hectare (£16 per acre), the (net) return averages 1·25 per cent (ignoring capital gains and amenity values). If land is taken at its tenanted value (say £2,500 per hectare, or £1,000 per acre), the return rises to about 2·4 per cent. If 'tender' rents are paid the return will average about 2·8 per cent with land at the vacant possession price assumed and 5·4 per cent with land at the tenanted value assumed. Above average quality farms will acquire higher rents but will also obviously command higher prices than the average levels quoted above.

(c) *Total Owner-Occupier's Capital* (*i.e.* land plus 'tenant's' capital). The combined (net) return (£160 per hectare, or £64 per acre) on total capital, (£6,000 per hectare, or £2,425 per acre), with land at its vacant possession value, averages 2·7 per cent. This increases to 4·3 per cent if land is taken at its tenanted value. If higher rent levels are assumed (given the same farming return), the overall return remains the same, the distribution simply being reallocated in favour of the landownership share at the expense of the farming share. 'Premium' farming returns (as defined above), assuming the same capital requirements, raise the returns to 3·5 per cent with land at the vacant possession price and 5·7 per cent with tenanted land values. (To repeat, the above figures all assume that machinery depreciation and valuation are based on its current cost.)

(iii) *Average Tenant's Capital per hectare* (per acre in brackets) for Different Farm Types , as estimated for 1985 (based on 1982/83 levels plus 10 per cent), are as follows, for farms in South-East England:

Farm Type Group	Average No. Hectares	Livestock £	Crops, Cultivns., Stores £	Machinery and Equipment* £	Total Tenant's Capital £ £
Mainly Dairying:					
under 60 ha ...	37·5	1015	185	545	1745 (705)
60 to 120 ha ...	90	785	190	575	1550 (625)
Over 120 ha ...	250	735	255	480	1470 (595)
Mainly Arable:					
under 100 ha ...	65	90	520	445	1055 (425)
100 to 200 ha ...	150	160	365	430	955 (385)
over 200 ha ...	375	175	485	415	1085 (440)
Diary and Arable:					
under 200 ha ...	130	515	280	660	1455 (590)
over 200 ha ...	320	415	365	425	1205 (490)
Mainly Sheep/Cattle:					
under 100 ha ...	65	455	75	320	850 (345)
over 100 ha ...	165	405	100	345	850 (345)
Sheep/Cattle and Arable:					
under 100 ha ...	65	330	180	350	860 (350)
over 100 ha ...	195	350	275	345	970 (395)
Dairy, Sheep/Cattle and Arable: ...	260	470	250	510	1230 (500)
Mixed, with Pigs/Poultry ...	135	700	280	600	1580 (640)
Intensive Arable:					
Fruit	70	50	2110	720	2880 (1165)
Vegetables... ...	55	0	430	695	1125 (455)

* Based on current (*i.e.* replacement) costs.

(iv) *Return on Capital to Individual Enterprises* on a mixed farm is virtually impossible to ascertain, except perhaps for a full-time pig or poultry enterprise, nor would it be of very much use even if it could be determined. It would require the arbitrary allocation both of costs and capital inputs that are common to several, in some cases all, of the enterprises on the farm.

What is relevant and important is the extra (net) return from an enterprise either to be introduced or expanded, as calculated by a partial budget, related to the extra (net) capital needed. The "net" in brackets relates, as regards return, to the addition to gross margins less any addition to (or plus any reduction in) "fixed" costs, bearing in mind that another enterprise may have to be deleted or reduced in size; and, as regards capital, to the fact that deletion or reduction of another enterprise may release capital.

In most cases of "marginal" substitution, it is differences in the value of breeding livestock and differences in variable costs that are particularly relevant, but the timing of both inputs and sales are also obviously very important.

(v) *"Marginal" Capital Requirements* for small changes in crop areas or livestock numbers can be estimated as follows:

Crops: variable costs till sale.

Dairy Cows and Egg Production: value of the cow (1) (2) or hens, plus one month's food.

Other Breeding Livestock: average value of stock (1) (2), plus variable costs to sale of the progeny (e.g. lambs)—or their transfer to another enterprise (e.g. weaners to the pig fattening enterprise).

Rearing Breeding Livestock (e.g. heifers, tegs, gilts, pullets): cost of the calf, lamb, weaner or chick (2), plus variable costs till they produce their first progeny/eggs.

Fattening Livestock and Production of Stores: cost of stock (2), plus variable costs till sale.

Notes

1. Value of breeding stock, including dairy cows: either the average value over their entire breeding or milk producing life (see table on page 122) or their value when they first produce progeny can be taken. The latter will give the lower return on (marginal) capital and is thus the severer test.

2. Home-reared stock: where stock to be used for milk or egg production, breeding or fattening are home-reared, there are two possibilities:

   (i) either they can be valued at variable costs of production when they are transferred from the rearing to the "productive" enterprise; in this case the return on (marginal) capital will be estimated over the combined rearing and "productive" enterprise.

   (ii) or they can be valued at market value at point of transfer. This is the procedure if one wishes to work out a return on (marginal) capital for the rearing and the "productive" enterprises separately.

(vi) **Return on "Marginal" Capital.** This is usually expressed as the gross margin of the enterprise expanded as a percentage of the "marginal", or extra, capital. Clearly, the resulting figure will often be a very high one, e.g. one hectare of winter wheat: £540 (gross margin) as a percentage of £200 (variable costs) is 270 per cent. Two points have to be remembered.

(i) If another enterprise has had to be reduced in size to enable the enterprise under consideration to be expanded, the capital released and the gross margin forfeited by reducing the size of the first enterprise must be brought into the calculation in estimating the net result of the change.

(ii) All the above statements on "marginal" capital refer to small changes. If the change is large enough to cause changes in labour, machinery or building requirements the capital changes brought about may be considerably greater.

(vii) *Return on Investments in Medium-Term and Long-Term Capital. Rate of Return and the Discounted Yield.*
Example: If £5,000 investment results in an annual net return of £500 (after deducting depreciation, but ignoring interest payments):

$$Rate\ of\ Return\ on\ Initial\ Capital = \frac{500}{5,000} \times 100 = 10\%$$

$$Rate\ of\ Return\ on\ Average\ Capital = \frac{500}{2,500} \times 100 = 20\%$$

It is more accurate to calculate the *"Discounted Yield"*, which is the discount rate that brings the present value of the net cash flows (which means ignoring depreciation) to the value of the investment.
The tables on pages 128 and 129 may be used.

"Short-Cut" Estimates of the Discounted Yield on depreciating assets
The Discounted Yield falls between the simple Rates of Return on Initial and Average Capital. In fact, for investments lasting 5 to 15 years, when the Rate of Return on Initial Capital is 10 per cent and on Average Capital 20 per cent, the Discounted Yield will be almost exactly halfway between, i.e. about 15 per cent. However, this is only so providing the anticipated annual net cash earnings are fairly constant—or fluctuate unpredictably around a fairly constant level.

There are three circumstances when the Discounted Yield will get closer to the Rate of Return on Initial Capital (i.e. the lower per cent return) and further from the Rate of Return on Average Capital:
(a) The longer the life of the investment.
(b) The higher the Rate of Return.
(c) The higher the net cash flow is in the later years of the investment compared with the earlier years.
When the opposite circumstances obtain, the Discounted Yield will be closer to the Rate of Return on Average Capital (i.e. the higher per cent return).
Granted that there are inevitably varying degrees of estimation and uncertainty in calculating future net annual earnings of investments, the following short-cuts might reasonably be used where the annual net cash earnings are expected to be fairly constant—or fluctuate unpredictably

(e.g. through weather effects on yields) around a fairly constant level. (W.O. period = write-off period; R.R.I.C. = rate of return on initial capital).

1. Where (i) the W.O. period is 5 years or less,

(ii) the W.O. period is 6 to 10 years and the R.R.I.C. is 15 per cent or less,

(iii) the W.O. period is 11 to 20 years and the R.R.I.C. is 10 per cent or less,

calculate the Return on Capital as being approximately midway between the Rates of Return on Initial and Average Capital, i.e. by calculating the Rate of Return on $\frac{2}{3}$ of the original investment.

For example, following the earlier example (page 126):

$$\frac{500}{3,333} \times 100 = 15\%.$$

2. Where (i) the W.O. period is 6 to 10 years and the R.R.I.C. exceeds 15 per cent,

(ii) the W.O. period is 11 to 20 years and the R.R.I.C. is between 10 per cent and 25 per cent,

(iii) the W.O. period exceeds 20 years and the R.R.I.C. is 10 per cent or less,

calculate the Return on Capital on 80 per cent of the original investment.

For example, again following the earlier example:

$$\frac{500}{4,000} \times 100 = 12\frac{1}{2}\%.$$

3. Where (i) the W.O. period is 11 to 20 years and the R.R.I.C. exceeds 25 per cent,

(ii) the W.O. period exceeds 20 years and the R.R.I.C. exceeds 10 per cent,

take the Return on Capital to be the R.R.I.C.

In borderline cases, use method 1 rather than 2, or 2 rather than 3 if there is a tendency for the cash flow to be higher in the earlier years, e.g. because of tax allowances on machinery. Take 2 rather than 1, and 3 rather than 2 if the likelihood is that the cash flow will be lower in earlier years and increase in later years.

However, where the annual cash flow is expected to vary (apart from unpredictable fluctuations) it is safer to make the full D.C.F. calculation. This is particularly so where the variation is both up and down and where further periodic investments are to be made during the life of the project.

Discounting Table A

Discount Factors for Calculating the Present Value of Future (irregular) Cash Flows.

Percentage

Year	5%	6%	7%	8%	9%	10%	11%	12%	13%	14%	15%	16%	18%	20%	25%	30%
1	0·952	0·943	0·935	0·926	0·917	0·909	0·901	0·893	0·885	0·877	0·870	0·862	0·847	0·833	0·800	0·769
2	0·907	0·890	0·873	0·857	0·842	0·826	0·812	0·797	0·783	0·769	0·756	0·743	0·718	0·694	0·640	0·592
3	0·864	0·840	0·816	0·794	0·772	0·751	0·731	0·712	0·693	0·675	0·658	0·641	0·609	0·579	0·512	0·455
4	0·823	0·792	0·763	0·735	0·708	0·683	0·659	0·636	0·613	0·592	0·572	0·552	0·516	0·482	0·410	0·350
5	0·784	0·747	0·713	0·681	0·650	0·621	0·593	0·567	0·543	0·519	0·497	0·476	0·437	0·402	0·328	0·269
6	0·746	0·705	0·666	0·630	0·596	0·564	0·535	0·507	0·480	0·456	0·432	0·410	0·370	0·335	0·262	0·207
7	0·711	0·665	0·623	0·583	0·547	0·513	0·482	0·452	0·425	0·400	0·376	0·354	0·314	0·279	0·210	0·159
8	0·677	0·627	0·582	0·540	0·502	0·467	0·434	0·404	0·376	0·351	0·327	0·305	0·266	0·233	0·168	0·123
9	0·645	0·592	0·544	0·500	0·460	0·424	0·391	0·361	0·333	0·308	0·284	0·263	0·225	0·194	0·134	0·094
10	0·614	0·558	0·508	0·463	0·422	0·386	0·352	0·322	0·295	0·270	0·247	0·227	0·191	0·162	0·107	0·073
11	0·585	0·527	0·475	0·429	0·388	0·350	0·317	0·287	0·261	0·237	0·215	0·195	0·162	0·135	0·086	0·056
12	0·557	0·497	0·444	0·397	0·356	0·319	0·286	0·257	0·231	0·208	0·187	0·168	0·137	0·112	0·069	0·043
13	0·530	0·469	0·415	0·368	0·326	0·290	0·258	0·229	0·204	0·182	0·163	0·145	0·116	0·093	0·055	0·033
14	0·505	0·442	0·388	0·340	0·299	0·263	0·232	0·205	0·181	0·160	0·141	0·125	0·098	0·078	0·044	0·025
15	0·481	0·417	0·362	0·315	0·275	0·239	0·209	0·183	0·160	0·140	0·123	0·108	0·084	0·065	0·035	0·020
20	0·377	0·312	0·258	0·215	0·178	0·149	0·124	0·104	0·087	0·073	0·061	0·051	0·037	0·026	0·012	0·005
25	0·295	0·233	0·184	0·146	0·116	0·092	0·074	0·059	0·047	0·038	0·030	0·024	0·016	0·010	0·004	0·001
30	0·231	0·174	0·131	0·099	0·075	0·057	0·044	0·033	0·026	0·020	0·015	0·012	0·007	0·004	0·001	—

Example: The Present Value of £500 received 10 years from now, at 12 per cent discount rate of interest = 500 × 0·322 = £161. Conversely, £161 invested now, at 12 per cent compound interest, will be worth £500 in 10 years' time.

Discounting Table B

Discount Factors for Calculating the Present Value of a Future Annuity (i.e. Constant Annual Cash Flow) Receivable in Years 1 to n inclusive.

Year	Percentage															
---	5%	6%	7%	8%	9%	10%	11%	12%	13%	14%	15%	16%	18%	20%	25%	30%
1	0·952	0·943	0·935	0·926	0·917	0·909	0·901	0·893	0·885	0·877	0·870	0·862	0·847	0·833	0·800	0·769
2	1·859	1·833	1·808	1·783	1·759	1·736	1·713	1·690	1·668	1·647	1·626	1·605	1·566	1·528	1·440	1·361
3	2·723	2·673	2·624	2·577	2·531	2·487	2·444	2·402	2·361	2·322	2·283	2·246	2·174	2·106	1·952	1·816
4	3·546	3·465	3·387	3·312	3·240	3·170	3·102	3·037	2·974	2·914	2·855	2·798	2·690	2·589	2·362	2·166
5	4·329	4·212	4·100	3·993	3·890	3·791	3·696	3·605	3·517	3·433	3·352	3·274	3·127	2·991	2·689	2·436
6	5·076	4·917	4·767	4·623	4·486	4·355	4·231	4·111	3·998	3·889	3·784	3·685	3·498	3·326	2·951	2·643
7	5·786	5·582	5·389	5·206	5·033	4·868	4·712	4·564	4·423	4·288	4·160	4·039	3·812	3·605	3·161	2·802
8	6·463	6·210	5·971	5·747	5·535	5·335	5·146	4·968	4·799	4·639	4·487	4·344	4·078	3·837	3·329	2·925
9	7·108	6·802	6·515	6·247	5·995	5·759	5·537	5·328	5·132	4·946	4·772	4·607	4·303	4·031	3·463	3·019
10	7·722	7·360	7·024	6·710	6·418	6·145	5·889	5·650	5·426	5·216	5·019	4·833	4·494	4·192	3·570	3·092
11	8·306	7·887	7·499	7·139	6·805	6·495	6·207	5·938	5·687	5·453	5·234	5·029	4·656	4·327	3·656	3·147
12	8·863	8·384	7·943	7·536	7·161	6·814	6·492	6·194	5·918	5·660	5·421	5·197	4·793	4·439	3·725	3·190
13	9·394	8·853	8·358	7·904	7·487	7·103	6·750	6·424	6·122	5·842	5·583	5·342	4·910	4·533	3·780	3·223
14	9·899	9·295	8·745	8·244	7·786	7·367	6·982	6·628	6·302	6·002	5·724	5·468	5·008	4·611	3·824	3·249
15	10·380	9·712	9·108	8·559	8·061	7·606	7·191	6·811	6·462	6·142	5·847	5·575	5·092	4·675	3·859	3·268
20	12·462	11·470	10·594	9·818	9·129	8·514	7·963	7·469	7·025	6·623	6·259	5·929	5·353	4·870	3·954	3·316
25	14·094	12·783	11·654	10·675	9·823	9·077	8·422	7·843	7·330	6·873	6·464	6·097	5·467	4·948	3·985	3·329
30	15·372	13·765	12·409	11·258	10·274	9·427	8·694	8·055	7·496	7·003	6·566	6·177	5·517	4·979	3·995	3·332

Example: The Present Value of £500 a year for the next 10 years, at 12 per cent discount rate of interest = 500 × 5·650 = £2,825. This is the same answer that would be obtained by multiplying 500 by each discount factor (at 12 per cent) in Table A for each year from 1 to 10, and adding together the ten resulting figures.

To obtain the Discounted Yield of a constant annual net cash flow, divide this into the original investment and look up the resulting figure in the table above, against the number of years. *Example:* an investment of £1,000 is estimated to produce £80 a year additional profit over 10 years (before charging interest). Add £100 depreciation a year = £180 annual net cash flow. 1000 ÷ 180 = 5·56. This equals just over 12 per cent (the 10 years/12 per cent figure being 5·650).

Compounding Table A
The Future Money Value of £1 after n Years

Year									Rate of Interest								
	5%	6%	7%	8%	9%	10%	11%	12%	13%	14%	15%	16%	18%	20%	25%	30%
1	1·05	1·06	1·07	1·08	1·09	1·10	1·11	1·12	1·13	1·14	1·15	1·16	1·18	1·20	1·25	1·30
2	1·10	1·12	1·14	1·17	1·19	1·21	1·23	1·25	1·28	1·30	1·32	1·35	1·39	1·44	1·56	1·69
3	1·16	1·19	1·23	1·26	1·30	1·33	1·37	1·40	1·44	1·48	1·52	1·56	1·64	1·73	1·95	2·20
4	1·22	1·26	1·31	1·36	1·41	1·46	1·52	1·57	1·63	1·69	1·75	1·81	1·94	2·07	2·44	2·86
5	1·28	1·34	1·40	1·47	1·54	1·61	1·69	1·76	1·84	1·93	2·01	2·10	2·29	2·49	3·05	3·71
6	1·34	1·42	1·50	1·59	1·68	1·77	1·87	1·97	2·08	2·19	2·31	2·44	2·70	2·99	3·81	4·83
7	1·41	1·50	1·61	1·71	1·83	1·95	2·08	2·21	2·35	2·50	2·66	2·83	3·19	3·58	4·77	6·27
8	1·48	1·59	1·72	1·85	1·99	2·14	2·30	2·48	2·66	2·85	3·06	3·28	3·76	4·30	5·96	8·16
9	1·55	1·69	1·84	2·00	2·17	2·36	2·56	2·77	3·00	3·25	3·52	3·80	4·44	5·16	7·45	10·60
10	1·63	1·79	1·97	2·16	2·37	2·59	2·84	3·11	3·39	3·71	4·05	4·41	5·23	6·19	9·31	13·79
11	1·71	1·90	2·10	2·33	2·58	2·85	3·15	3·48	3·84	4·23	4·65	5·12	6·18	7·43	11·64	17·92
12	1·80	2·01	2·25	2·52	2·81	3·14	3·50	3·90	4·33	4·82	5·35	5·94	7·29	8·92	14·55	23·30
13	1·89	2·13	2·41	2·72	3·07	3·45	3·88	4·36	4·90	5·49	6·15	6·89	8·60	10·70	18·19	30·29
14	1·98	2·26	2·58	2·94	3·34	3·80	4·31	4·89	5·53	6·26	7·08	7·99	10·15	12·84	22·74	39·37
15	2·08	2·40	2·76	3·17	3·64	4·18	4·78	5·47	6·25	7·14	8·14	9·27	11·97	15·41	28·42	51·19
20	2·65	3·21	3·87	4·66	5·60	6·73	8·06	9·65	11·52	13·74	16·37	19·46	27·39	38·34	86·74	190·0
25	3·39	4·29	5·43	6·85	8·62	10·83	13·59	17·00	21·23	26·46	32·92	40·87	62·67	95·40	264·7	705·6
30	4·32	5·74	7·61	10·06	13·27	17·45	22·89	29·96	39·12	50·95	66·21	85·85	143·4	237·4	807·8	2620·

Compounding Table B

The Future Money Value of £1 per annum after n Years

Year								Rate of Interest									
	5%	6%	7%	8%	9%	10%	11%	12%	13%	14%	15%	16%	18%	20%	25%	30%
1	1·05	1·06	1·07	1·08	1·09	1·10	1·11	1·12	1·13	1·14	1·15	1·16	1·18	1·20	1·25	1·30
2	2·15	2·18	2·21	2·25	2·28	2·31	2·34	2·37	2·41	2·44	2·47	2·51	2·57	2·64	2·81	2·99
3	3·31	3·37	3·44	3·51	3·57	3·64	3·71	3·78	3·85	3·92	3·99	4·07	4·22	4·37	4·77	5·19
4	4·53	4·64	4·75	4·87	4·98	5·11	5·23	5·35	5·48	5·61	5·74	5·88	6·15	6·44	7·21	8·04
5	5·80	5·98	6·15	6·34	6·52	6·72	6·91	7·12	7·32	7·54	7·75	7·98	8·44	8·93	10·26	11·76
6	7·14	7·39	7·65	7·92	8·20	8·49	8·78	9·09	9·40	9·73	10·07	10·41	11·14	11·92	14·07	16·58
7	8·55	8·90	9·26	9·64	10·03	10·44	10·86	11·30	11·76	12·23	12·73	13·24	14·33	15·50	18·84	22·86
8	10·03	10·49	10·98	11·49	12·02	12·58	13·16	13·78	14·42	15·09	15·79	16·52	18·09	19·80	24·80	31·01
9	11·58	12·18	12·82	13·49	14·19	14·94	15·72	16·55	17·42	18·34	19·30	20·32	22·52	24·96	32·25	41·62
10	13·21	13·97	14·78	15·65	16·56	17·53	18·56	19·65	20·81	22·04	23·35	24·73	27·76	31·15	41·57	55·41
11	14·92	15·87	16·89	17·98	19·14	20·38	21·71	23·13	24·65	26·27	28·00	29·85	33·93	38·58	53·21	73·33
12	16·71	17·88	19·14	20·50	21·95	23·52	25·21	27·03	28·98	31·09	33·35	35·79	41·22	47·50	67·76	96·63
13	18·60	20·02	21·55	23·21	25·02	26·97	29·09	31·39	33·88	36·58	39·50	42·67	49·82	58·20	85·95	126·9
14	20·58	22·28	24·13	26·15	28·36	30·77	33·41	36·28	39·42	42·84	46·58	50·66	59·97	71·04	108·7	166·3
15	22·66	24·67	26·89	29·32	32·00	34·95	38·19	41·75	45·67	49·98	54·72	59·93	71·94	86·44	137·1	217·5
20	34·72	38·99	43·87	49·42	55·76	63·00	71·27	80·70	91·47	103·8	117·8	133·8	173·0	224·0	428·7	819·2
25	50·11	58·16	67·68	78·95	92·32	108·2	127·0	149·3	175·8	207·3	244·7	289·1	404·3	566·4	1318	3053
30	69·76	83·80	101·1	122·3	148·6	180·9	226·9	270·3	331·3	406·7	500·0	615·2	933·3	1418	4034	11349

(viii) *Repayments of Capital and Interest*
Amortization Table
Annual charge to write off £1,000.

Write-off Period (Years)	Rate of Interest												
	8%	10%	11%	12%	13%	14%	15%	16%	17%	18%	19%	20%	25%
5	251	264	271	278	284	291	299	305	313	320	327	334	373
6	216	230	237	243	250	257	265	271	279	286	293	301	339
7	192	206	212	219	226	233	240	248	255	262	270	278	316
8	174	188	194	202	208	216	223	230	238	245	253	261	301
10	149	163	170	177	184	192	200	207	215	223	231	239	280
12	133	147	154	162	169	177	185	192	201	209	217	226	269
15	117	132	139	147	155	163	171	179	188	196	205	214	260
20	102	117	126	134	142	151	160	168	178	187	196	205	253
25	94	110	119	128	136	146	155	164	173	183	193	202	252
30	89	106	113	124	133	143	153	161	172	181	191	202	251
40	84	102	111	121	131	141	150	160	170	180	190	200	250

Example: £3,000 is borrowed to erect a building. The annual charge to service interest and capital repayment on the £3,000, repayable over 10 years at 12%, is 3 × £177 = £531. Where the write-off period of the building (10 years) is equal to the repayment period of the loan, then the average annual depreciation and interest will also equal £531.

Agricultural Mortgage Corporation
The following are the annual payments per £1,000 borrowed on annuity type loans, at four different rates of interest.

Term of Years	Gross Payment per annum	Average Capital Repayment per annum	Average Interest Payment per annum
10 per cent	£	£	£
40	102·06	25·00	77·06
30	105·66	33·33	72·33
25	109·56	40·00	69·56
20	116·56	50·00	66·56
15	130·12	66·67	63·45
10	160·50	100·00	60·50
12 per cent			
40	121·15	25·00	96·15
30	123·76	33·33	90·43
25	126·90	40·00	86·90
20	132·94	50·00	82·94
15	145·30	66·67	78·63
10	174·38	100·00	74·38

Term of Years	Gross Payment per annum	Average Capital Repayment per annum	Average Interest Payment per annum
14 per cent			
40	140·63	25·00	115·63
30	142·46	33·33	109·13
25	144·92	40·00	104·92
20	150·02	50·00	100·02
15	161·18	66·67	94·51
10	188·80	100·00	88·80
16 per cent			
40	160·34	25·00	135·34
30	161·60	33·33	128·27
25	163·50	40·00	123·50
20	167·74	50·00	117·74
15	177·66	66·67	110·99
10	203·72	100·00	103·72
18 per cent			
40	180·18	25·00	155·18
30	181·03	33·33	147·70
25	182·45	40·00	142·45
20	185·92	50·00	135·92
15	194·67	66·67	128·00
10	219·09	100·00	119·09
20 per cent			
40	200·10	25·00	175·10
30	200·66	33·33	167·33
25	201·72	40·00	161·72
20	204·52	50·00	154·52
15	212·16	66·67	145·49
10	234·92	100·00	134·92

In the earlier years, payments consist mainly of interest; the proportion of the gross annual repayment represented by capital repayment increases as the period progresses—see tables on pages 135-7.

(ix) *Rate of Interest on Bank Loans.* Typically 2% above Base Rate. Main range is 1½% above to 2½% above. Extremes are likely to be 1% above (minimum) and 3½% above (maximum).

(x) *Annual Percentage Rate (APR).* This is the effective rate of interest calculated on an annual basis and should be used when seeking to make a true comparison between interest charges on money borrowed from different sources. The *APR* allows for the fact that when interest is applied to accounts at half yearly, quarterly or monthly intervals an element of compounding will arise. For example, £100 borrowed for one year at a quoted annual *nominal* interest rate of 12% (*e.g.* 2% over base rate of 10%) with interest charged quarterly, will lead to an accumulated interest charge of £12·55 (*i.e.*, giving an APR of just under 12·6%). The higher the annual nominal interest rate and the more frequently the interest charges are applied to the account, the more pronounced the compounding element becomes. For example, an annual nominal interest rate of 20% produces an APR of 21% with half yearly charging, 21·6% with quarterly charging and 21·9% with monthly charging.

In the case of some loans and hire purchase agreements, interest charges may be quoted as a *flat rate* on the original amount borrowed. The APR will be considerably greater than the flat rate if the loan is repaid by equal periodic instalments, comprising part capital and part interest, so that the borrowing is completely repaid by the end of the agreed term. For example, the APR for a loan at a flat rate of interest of 8% repaid by monthly instalments over 5 years will be 15%. The shorter the repayment period, and the more frequent the payments, the higher is the APR compared with the flat rate.

(xi) *The Real Rate of Interest.* When preparing simple profit and loss budgets to estimate the worthwhileness of an investment in a fixed asset (machinery, buildings, land), it is usual to price inputs and outputs at present-day values even when most costs and returns are expected to rise due to inflation over the life of the investment. Where this *real terms* approach is adopted a more realistic estimate of the effect on profitability can be gained by basing charges for capital on the *real rate of interest* rather than the APR. The real rate of interest is the APR adjusted for the annual rate at which prices relevant to the investment are expected to increase. A crude estimate of the real rate of interest can be obtained by simply subtracting the expected rate of price increase from the APR ; for example, if the APR were 11% and the expected rate of inflation 6%, the real rate of interest would be $11 - 6 = 5\%$.

MORTGAGE REPAYMENT DATA

Items per £1,000 invested where I = Interest, P = Principal repaid, L = Loan outstanding

Loan through 5 years	10%			12%			14%			16%			18%			20%		
	I	P	L	I	P	L	I	P	L	I	P	L	I	P	L	I	P	L
1	100	164	836	120	157	843	140	151	849	160	145	855	180	140	860	200	134	866
2	84	180	656	101	175	670	119	172	677	137	169	686	155	165	695	173	161	704
3	66	198	458	80	197	469	92	196	481	110	196	490	125	195	501	141	194	511
4	46	218	240	56	221	248	67	224	257	78	227	263	90	230	271	102	232	279
5	24	240	0	30	248	0	32	257	0	42	263	0	49	271	0	56	279	0
10 years																		
1	100	63	939	120	57	943	140	52	948	160	47	953	180	43	957	200	39	961
2	94	69	868	113	64	879	133	59	889	152	54	899	172	50	907	192	46	915
3	87	76	792	106	71	808	124	68	821	144	63	836	163	59	848	183	55	860
4	79	84	709	97	80	728	115	77	744	134	73	762	153	70	778	172	67	793
5	71	92	617	87	90	638	104	88	656	122	85	677	140	82	696	159	80	713
6	62	101	516	77	100	538	92	100	556	108	99	579	125	97	599	143	96	617
7	52	111	405	65	112	425	78	114	442	93	114	465	108	115	484	123	115	502
8	40	122	282	51	126	299	62	130	312	74	133	332	87	135	348	100	138	364
9	28	134	148	36	141	158	44	148	164	53	154	178	63	160	189	73	166	199
10	15	148	0	19	158	0	23	164	0	29	178	0	34	189	0	40	199	0

MORTGAGE REPAYMENT DATA (continued)

Loan through 20 years	10%			12%			14%			16%			18%			20%		
	I	P	L	I	P	L	I	P	L	I	P	L	I	P	L	I	P	L
1	100	17	983	120	14	986	140	11	989	160	9	991	180	7	993	200	5	995
5	92	26	893	112	22	912	132	19	927	153	16	940	174	13	951	194	11	960
10	76	41	722	95	38	756	115	36	788	136	33	815	157	30	840	178	28	861
15	51	66	445	66	68	483	82	69	518	99	69	552	118	69	584	137	69	614
20	11	107	0	14	120	0	19	132	0	23	145	0	28	158	0	34	171	0
30 years																		
1	100	6	994	120	4	996	140	3	997	160	2	998	180	1	999	200	1	999
5	97	9	963	118	7	974	138	5	986	158	3	987	179	2	991	199	2	994
10	92	14	903	113	11	927	134	9	951	155	7	960	176	6	970	196	4	978
15	83	23	807	104	20	846	126	17	890	147	15	903	168	13	923	190	11	939
20	69	37	652	88	36	701	108	35	751	130	32	782	152	29	815	174	27	842
25	46	60	402	61	63	488	83	60	494	95	66	530	114	67	567	134	67	601
30	10	96	0	13	111	0	16	127	0	22	140	0	28	154	0	33	167	0

MORTGAGE REPAYMENT DATA (continued)

Loan through 40 years	10%			12%			14%			16%			18%			20%		
	I	P	L	I	P	L	I	P	L	I	P	L	I	P	L	I	P	L
1	100	2	998	120	1	999	140	1	999	160	0	1000	180	0	1000	200	0	1000
5	99	3	986	119	2	992	139	2	995	160	1	997	180	0	998	200	0	999
10	97	5	964	118	4	977	138	3	989	159	2	991	179	1	994	199	1	996
15	94	9	928	115	6	951	136	5	973	157	3	978	178	2	985	198	2	990
20	88	14	871	110	11	906	130	11	942	153	7	951	175	6	965	196	4	975
25	80	22	778	102	20	826	123	18	874	145	15	894	167	13	918	189	11	936
30	66	36	628	86	35	685	109	32	742	129	31	775	151	29	810	173	27	839
35	45	58	388	60	61	437	85	56	487	95	66	525	113	67	564	133	67	599
40	9	93	0	13	108	0	18	123	0	22	138	0	27	153	0	33	167	0

Note—All figures rounded to nearest £.

137

5. TAXATION

1. *Individual Taxation*

(a) *Rates of Tax (1984-85)*

Slice of taxable income £	Rate per cent	Cumulative Tax (at top of slice) £
0-15,400	30	4,620
15,401-18,200	40	5,740
18,201-23,100	45	7,945
23,101-30,600	50	11,695
30,601-38,100	55	15,820
Over 38,100	60	—

(b) *Allowances and Reliefs (1984-85)*

(i) Personal Allowance. Married: £3,155, Single: £2,005

(ii) Wife's earned income: £2,005.

(iii) Retirement Annuities (self-employed persons and employees not in pensionable employment): full relief on premiums up to $17\frac{1}{2}$% of net relevant income (basically earned income) in any one year. Higher percentages of relief are available for those born before 1934.

(iv) Husband and wife can jointly elect (by 5th April, 1986) for the wife's earnings for 1984/85 to be taxed separately. This will normally be beneficial where joint income exceeds £23,794 and wife's earnings exceed £6,389.

2. *Private Company Taxation*

(i) Profits are chargeable to Corporation Tax at 50 per cent (1983-1984) except where profits are less than £100,000 and where there are no associated companies, when the rate is reduced to 30 per cent. There is also marginal relief between £100,000 and £500,000: within this band the marginal rate is 55%, the rate on the first £100,000 being 30%. It is intended that the rate of Corporation Tax will be reduced in future years as follows: to 45% in 1984-85, 40% in 1985-86, and 35% in 1986-87.

(ii) Chargeable Gains are subject to an effective rate of tax of 30 per cent.

(iii) Distributions, e.g. dividends are not deductible in arriving at the amount of Corporation Tax profit. An Advanced Payment of Corporation Tax is required at the rate of 30/70ths of distributions made between April 1984 and April 1985. The recipient of distributions will be credited with a tax payment of 30/70ths of distributions received.

3. Agricultural Businesses: Other Items.

(a) Livestock

Dairy cows or breeding livestock may be treated on the herd basis or on a trading stock basis.

Herd basis: valuation changes are not included in the trading account, nor are additions to the herd, but sales from the herd and replacements are. On the sale of all or most of the herd, no tax is paid on any profit over the original cost price, nor is there any relief for loss.

Trading stock basis: purchases, sales and valuation changes are all included in the trading account.

(b) Allowances for Capital Expenditure

Machinery and Plant (whether new or second hand). A first year allowance of 75 per cent is available in 1984-85 but need not be claimed in full. The balance of any unclaimed expenditure is added to a "pool" of expenditure in the year following purchase. The proceeds of sale of machinery and plant disposed of during the year are deducted from the "pool" figure. A writing down allowance of 25 per cent is available on the adjusted "pool" figure, with the balance being carried forward to the next year. The first year allowance will be reduced to 50 per cent on 1st April, 1985 and withdrawn altogether on 1st April, 1986. After 1st April, 1986 a 25 per cent annual writing down allowance will be available on a reducing balance basis. Motor-cars are excluded from the first year allowance and are included in a separate "pool" in the year of purchase, on which a 25 per cent writing down allowance is available. Special rules apply where a motor-car is only partly used for business purposes and relief is restricted where the car costs over £8,000.

Buildings. Farm buildings, fencing, drainage and other improvements (including one-third of farmhouses) qualify for a capital allowance of 10 per cent annually, given equally over 10 years. However, it is also possible to claim an initial allowance of up to 20 per cent in the first year as well as the 10 per cent writing down allowance (e.g. where the full 20 per cent initial allowance is claimed, total allowances will be 30 per cent in the first year and 10 per cent in the next seven years). The 20 per cent initial allowance will be withdrawn on 1st April, 1986 and the writing down allowance will be reduced from 10 per cent to 4 per cent per year.

(c) *Profit Averaging*

This relief is to enable farmers, other than companies, to average their taxable profits over two consecutive years; (but is not available for opening and closing years). Where the difference between the profits of two consecutive years is 30 per cent or more of the higher profits, the total profits for the two years are equally divided between the two years. Marginal relief is available where the difference is less than 30 per cent but more than 25 per cent of the higher profits. Profit for the purposes of tax averaging calculations will be before the deduction of capital allowances and stock relief.

4. *Capital Gains Tax*

Applies to capital gains by an individual since 6th April, 1965; (n.b. husband and wife are treated as one person for C.G. Tax purposes, although they can elect by 6th July following the end of a tax year to be treated separately). Capital gains accruing to companies are chargeable to Corporation Tax. A capital gain is the difference between the acquisition value and the sale price. In the case of agricultural property, allowance would be made for any capital expenditure undertaken to improve the property. For assets owned on 6th April, 1965 and disposed of subsequently, only the proportion of the gain attributable to the period after that date is taxable, i.e. the chargeable gain is the gain over the whole ownership time apportioned to the period after 6th April, 1965, or on the gain from a valuation at 6th April, 1965 to the date of disposal, at the taxpayer's option. Capital Gains Tax is chargeable only on the disposal (including gifts) of assets. From April, 1982 Capital Gains Tax will be payable on that part of the gain which exceeds the rise in the Retail Prices Index. This provision for indexing the value of assets does not cover periods of ownership prior to April, 1982 and it is only available where assets have been owned for more than one year.

The first £5,600 of capital gains realised by an individual in a year are free of tax. Capital gains in excess of £5,600 are chargeable at a rate of 30 per cent.

Capital Gains Tax is not payable on death. For persons of 65 or over, up to £100,000 is exempt on gains accruing from the disposal by sale or gift of a family business or shares or securities in the family trading company; this exemption reduces by £20,000 for each full year below the age of 65; it only applies where the business has been owned at least ten years and the person has been either the proprietor, a partner, or a full-time working director in a family company. C.G. Tax retirement relief is also available in part for those over the age of 60 who have held the assets for more than one year, increasing to full relief after ten years. Exempt assets include a principal private residence (e.g. farm house) if occupied as such, normal life assurance policies, animals and tangible movable property (i.e. chattels) disposed of for £3,000 or less. Compensation payments for assets damaged or destroyed are taxable (though personal compensation payments are exempt).

Payment of tax may be deferred on gains accruing from the sale of business assets if all the proceeds are spent on acquiring new assets liable to the tax. The tax is deferred by deducting the gain from the acquisition price of the new asset. Normally it can only be done if the new asset is acquired within 12 months before and 3 years after the disposal of the old assets. Disposal and acquisition dates for Capital Gains purposes are almost always contract, not completion, dates.

Payments of tax may also be deferred where disposal is by gift. The amount of the chargeable gain which would normally have accrued to the donor will be held over; the value at which the donee is deemed to acquire the asset will be its market value reduced by the amount of the donor's chargeable gain held over. The held over gain is netted down by any time apportionment or retirement relief available to the donor.

Should a transaction produce a loss, this may be set against any long term chargeable gains arising in the same year or, if these are insufficient, those accruing in subsequent years. Losses brought forward will be used only to the extent necessary to reduce gains for the year to £5,600.

5. Development Land Tax

From 1st August, 1976 any realised development gain on land (i.e. the excess of sale price less 115 per cent of current use value as agricultural land or acquisition cost, whichever is the higher) will be subject to Development Land Tax. Disposals on or after 12th June, 1979 will be chargeable at a single rate of 60 per cent. The first £75,000 of development gain realised in any one year will be exempt from D.L.T. for each individual land owner. The £75,000 exempt from D.L.T. is chargeable to Capital Gains Tax.

6. Capital Transfer Tax

This tax, which replaced Estate Duty, is charged on the cumulative total of life-time transfers (gifts) within the preceding ten years and transfers on death. Where life-time gifts are made more than three years before death lower rates of tax apply.

Slice of Cumulative Gross Chargeable Transfer	Lifetime transfers (gifts) Rate	Cumulative Total of CTT Payable*	Transfers on death (or within 3 years of death) Rate	Cumulative Total of CTT Payable*
£	per cent	£	per cent	£
0- 64,000	0	Nil	0	Nil
64,000- 85,000	15	3,150	30	6,300
85,000- 116,000	17·5	8,575	35	17,150
116,000- 148,000	20	14,975	40	29,950
148,000- 185,000	22·5	23,300	45	46,600
185,000- 232,000	25	35,050	50	70,100
232,000- 285,000	27·5	49,625	55	99,250
Over 285,000	30	—	60	—

*Cumulative total at top bracket

Exemptions include: transfers between husband and wife; the first £3,000 of gift made by a donor in the income tax year and separately up to £250 per year to any number of persons; gifts made out of income which form part of normal expenditure; marriage gifts within limits of £5,000 for a parent, £2,500 for a lineal ancestor and £1,000 for other donors.

Relief may be available for agricultural land. Subject to a general rule that the agricultural land must have been occupied by the transferor (or by his controlled company) for two years, or owned by the transferor for 7 years and occupied for agricultural purposes by someone else before any relief is granted, the relief is at two different rates. If the basis of valuation is vacant possession, the taxable value of the land is reduced by 50%. If the basis of valuation is tenanted value, the taxable value of the land is reduced by 30% of that tenanted value. Ownership and occupation periods normally include prior periods of ownership or occupation by husbands and wives. Where a transfer was entitled to 50% relief at 10th March 1981 under the old rules (including in some cases not occupying the land) the relief is continued at 50% irrespective of the basis of valuation, but with an upper limit of £250,000 or 1,000 acres (approx. 400 hectares), whichever is the greater.

Relief is also available in respect to "business property" transferred during lifetime or on death. The relief extends to the business assets of a proprietor and the interest of a partner or controlling shareholder of a company in the business capital. The value of such property, providing certain tests are satisfied (e.g. it has been owned by the transferor for two years preceding transfer), is reduced by 50 per cent. It applies to all farming assets including the balance of any owner-occupied land outside the limits for the 50 per cent agricultural relief. Where a partner or controlling shareholder owns assets (e.g. land) that the business uses the value will be reduced by 30 per cent. Minority shareholdings in unquoted companies are eligible for a 30 per cent reduction in market value.

In the case of the transfer of property eligible for Agricultural Relief the tax can be paid by annual instalments over ten years free of interest. This also applies to transfers eligible for Business Asset relief, though if the transfer is not, or is not connected with, the transfer of and interest in a business, the instalments will carry interest at 8% net (lifetime transfers) or 6% net (transfers on death).

7. *Stamp Duty*

Stamp Duty arises when the title to property changes hands. In the case of land the duty will usually be paid by the purchaser; the rate payable is 1 per cent on the full value where the consideration (purchase price) or value (in the case of a gift) is over £30,000. There is an exemption for land (including houses) where the consideration is below £30,000.

8. Value Added Tax

Agricultural businesses with an annual turnover of taxable goods and services in excess of £18,700 are required to register for VAT. Businesses with a turnover of less than £18,700 may apply for voluntary registration. Most agricultural products, with the exception of certain non-edible products such as wool, are zero rated for VAT purposes. VAT has to be paid on certain inputs. Registered businesses are eligible to reclaim the tax paid where the goods or services purchased have been used in the production of zero-rated supplies. Registered businesses are in effect collecting agencies for the tax.

9. National Insurance Contributions

	Employee	Employer*
Class 1. Employed		
Not contracted out, on up to £250 a week	9·00%	10·45%
Contracted out		
(i) on first £34 a week	9·00%	10·45%
(ii) on excess up to £250 a week	6·85%	6·35%
Married women and widows with certificates of reduced liability and who are eligible to pay reduced contributions	3·85%	as above
Men over 65 and women over 60	Nil	10·45%
Children under 16	Nil	Nil
Class 2. Self-employed flat rate (no liability if earnings below £1,850 a year)	£4·60 a week	
Class 3. Non-employed (voluntary) flat rate	£4.50 a week	
Class 4. Self-employed. On profits or gains between £3,950 and £13,000 a year	6·3%	

* A surcharge of 1% should be added to the employer's contribution for the period from 1st August, 1983 until 30th September, 1984.

GRANTS

1. Agriculture and Horticulture Grant Scheme (AHGS)

Rates of grants (%) are as follows (LFA = Less Favoured Areas):

	Standard	LFA	Hortic. Business
Provision of farm buildings, grain stores (where grain is for feeding on the farm), waste disposal systems, buildings for hortic. use (other than production); supply of gas and electricity	20	20	20
Replacement or reconditioning of hortic. production buildings; installation of insulation; watercress beds	—	—	20
Replacement or reconditioning of heated glasshouses	—	—	37·5
Water supply and storage; fencing; flood protection works	20	50	20
Field drainage	30	60	30
Roads	20	40	20
Walls and hedges	20	60	20
Orchard grubbing	20	20	20
Hops wirework	20	20	—
Shelter belts	—	60	20
Land reclamation and re-seeding of grassland	—	50	—
Replacement of apple and pear orchards grubbed up after November 1982	22·5	22·5	22·5
Provision of glasshouse heating systems; wirework for cane fruit; plant and equipment for the preparation for market of hortic. produce	—	—	15

N.B.—*Grant aid is limited* to a maximum of £49,108 of eligible expenditure per labour unit and an overall limit of £98,985 per business (£129,918 for heated glasshouses). Additionally, in the case of *dairying* aid is limited to that part of the investment needed to reach a herd size of 40 cows, and in the case of *pig production* to the investment needed to reach 550 fattening pig places per business.

2. *Agriculture and Horticulture Development Scheme (AHDS)*

Based on approved development plans (for up to six years) to enable business to provide incomes comparable with those in non-agricultural occupations.

	Standard	LFA	Hortic. Business
Rates of grant (%) are as follows:			
Provision of farm buildings, grain stores (where grain is for feeding on the farm), waste disposal systems, buildings for hortic. use (other than production); supply of gas and electricity	32·5	37·5	32·5
Replacement or reconditioning of buildings for hortic. production; installation of insulation; watercress beds	—	—	32·5
Provision or enlargement of buildings for hortic. production	—	—	5
Replacement or reconditioning of heated glasshouses	—	—	50
Roads; water supply and; storage; fencing; flood protection	32·5	50	32·5
Walls and hedges	32·5	60	32·5
Field drainage	50	70	50
Orchard grubbing; wirework for vineyards and hops	32·5	32·5	32·5
Wirework for cane fruit	20	20	20
Shelter belts	5	60	32·5
Purchase of livestock (not pigs, poultry or dairy cows)	5	10	—
Replacement of apple and pear orchards grubbed up after November 1982	32·5	32·5	32·5
Plant and equipment for the preparation for market of hortic. production	—	—	20
Provision of facilities for farming fresh water fish for food production	5	10	—
Claying; marling; soil mixing	5	10	5
Preparation of development plans	32·5	32·5	32·5

A special *Guidance Premium* can be claimed if a development plan provides for the breeding or keeping of cattle or sheep suitable for meat production so that when the plan is completed sales of cattle or sheep will account for more than half the net sales (i.e. sales less purchases of livestock). The premium, which is payable on the area necessary to support these livestock on completion of the plan, is spread over 3 years as follows:

Year 1: £30·56 per hectare up to a limit of £3,056 per holding
Year 2: £20·67 per hectare up to a limit of £2,067 per holding
Year 3: £10·52 per hectare up to a limit of £1,052 per holding

Applicants have to undertake to keep certain *accounts;* grants are paid as follows: Year 1, £205; years 2 to 4, £103 a year.

Grant aid is limited to a maximum of £49,108 of eligible expenditure per labour unit and an overall limit of £136,104 per business.

Grant aid for dairying is limited to that part of the investment needed to reach either: (i) a maximum of 40 cows per labour unit for businesses with up to 1·5 labour units (*i.e.,* up to 60 cows), or (ii) an increase in the number of dairy cows of not more than 15% for businesses with more than 1·5 labour units.

Grant aid for pig production is limited to the investment needed to reach 550 fattening pig places per business.

Detailed information on the AHGA and AHDS is given in leaflets AHS2 and AHS5, available from M.A.F.F.

3. *Farm Structure (Payment to Outgoers) Scheme 1976*
Under certain circumstances where an 'uneconomic' unit is amalgamated with other land or is used for afforestation or public use the outgoer may be eligible for a grant. If the outgoer is 55 years of age or over but less than 65 years old the grant is either:
(a) a lump sum of between £1,000 and £3,000; or
(b) an annuity of between £250 and £450 (until aged 65 years).
Outside this age range reduced lump sum grants may be paid up to a maximum of £1,000.

4. *Agricultural and Horticultural Co-operation Scheme*
Grants are available to assist the promotion, organisation and carrying out of approved co-operative activities.

Grant aid may also be available to assist groups and organisations set up for the following purposes:
(a) organisations of fruit and vegetable producers set up on the producers' own initiative and designed to sell their members' produce, to encourage the concentration of supplies and the stabilisation of prices.
(b) groups set up to integrate the production activities of their members such as sharing machinery and labour.
(c) forage groups in the 'less favoured areas'.

Note: For beef and sheep grants, other than the guidance premiums above, see page 53.

147

7. FERTILIZER PRICES
(for crops harvested in 1985)
A. Compounds

Compound Type					Analysis			Price per tonne*
					N.	P.	K.	£
1 : 1 : 1	...	...	...	...	17	17	17	159
,,	...	...	...	...	15	15	15	142
High N	...	...	...	...	20	14	14	162
,,	...	...	...	...	25	9	9	160
,,	...	...	...	...	22	11	11	157
,,	...	...	...	...	20	10	10	141
,,	...	...	...	...	15	10	10	112
,,	...	...	...	...	29	5	5	152
,,	...	...	...	...	27	5	5	147
,,	...	...	...	...	20	5	10	122
Low N	...	...	...	...	10	23	23	167
,,	...	...	...	...	10	20	20	148
,,	...	...	...	...	10	15	15	123
,,	...	...	...	...	9	24	24	164
,,	...	...	...	...	5	24	24	147
,,	...	...	...	...	5	20	20	128
,,	...	...	...	...	9	23	18	149
,,	...	...	...	...	8	20	16	132
No N	...	...	...	...	—	24	24	126
,,	...	...	...	...	—	20	20	111
High P	...	...	...	...	12	18	12	138
,,	...	...	...	...	10	25	15	157
,,	...	...	...	...	6	24	15	139
Low P	...	...	...	...	24	4	15	141
,,	...	...	...	...	20	8	14	138
,, (and High K)	...	...	...	16	8	24	139
No P	...	...	...	...	25	—	16	132
High K	...	...	...	...	15	15	21	153
,,	...	...	...	...	13	13	20	135
,,	...	...	...	...	10	10	18	112
,,	...	...	...	...	7	14	28	127
,,	...	...	...	...	8	16	32	146
No K (and High P)	...	...	...	12	24	0	135
No K (High N and P)	...	...	...	25	20	0	182

*These are *estimated* net cash prices per tonne, delivered to the farm, in 20 tonne lots, after deducting a 5 per cent discount for early payment and an average 5 per cent for early delivery (usually up to 10 per cent for delivery in previous June). Add approximately £2 for 10 tonne lots, £4 for 6-9 tonne lots, £6 for 4-5 tonne lots.

Type	Price per tonne*
	£
Nitram (34·5 N.)	133
Nitro top (33·5 N.)	130
Nitro-Chalk (26 N.)	103
Sulphate of Ammonia (21 N.)	73
Urea (46 N.)	140
Superphosphate (18 P.)	81
Triple Supers (46 P.)	148
Muriate of Potash (60 K.)	94
Sulphate of Potash (50 K.)	125

*See footnotes on page 148.

Average price (p) per kg: N : 39.
P : 45 (supers); 32 (triple supers).
K : 16 (muriate); 25 (sulphate).

8. MANURIAL VALUE OF SLURRY AND FARMYARD MANURE

1. *Composition* (% by weight)

	N.	P.	K.
Undiluted Slurry (faeces plus urine, or droppings):			
Cow	0·5	0·2	0·5
Pig	0·6	0·2	0·2
Poultry	1·7	1·4	0·7
Farmyard Manure:			
Cattle	0·5	0·4	0·6
Pig	0·6	0·6	0·4
Poultry	1·8	1·8	1·2

2. *Available Nutrients* (kg)

	N.	P.	K.
Undiluted Slurry (per 10m³*):			
Cow	35	11	58
Pig	42	11	23
Poultry	118	82	82

(* = 10 tonnes; 10,000 litres)

	N.	P.	K.
Farmyard Manure (per 10 tonnes):			
Cattle	17	20	46
Pig	20	31	31
Poultry	110	92	92

3. *Amount per head*

(faeces plus urine, or droppings)

	litres per day	kg per year (1) N.	P.	K.
1 dairy cow	40	51	16	84
1 pig (dry meal fed)	4·5	6·8	1·8	3·7
100 laying hens	13	55	39	39

(1) assuming housed all year and no losses.

9. AGROCHEMICAL COSTS (1984)

Application rates can vary and there are differences between the prices of various proprietary brands. Only the names of the active ingredients are given below, with their principal use.

Material	Main Use	Approx. Cost £ per ha
M.C.P.A.	Weeds in Cereals or Grassland	3·00-6·00
2,4-D	Weeds in Cereals (not Oats)	4·00-5·50
Mecoprop	Weeds in Cereals	6·50-10·00
Dicamba+Mecoprop+ M.C.P.A.	Weeds in Cereals	12·00-13·50
Ioxynil+Bromoxynil	Weeds in Cereals	6·70-19·00
Ioxynil & Bromoxynil + Mecoprop	Weeds in Cereals	11·50-20·00
M.C.P.A.+M.C.P.B.	Weeds in Undersown Cereals	11·50-14·50
Benazolin + 2,4-D.B. + M.C.P.A.	Weeds in Undersown Cereals	23·50
Chlortoluron	Blackgrass and Wild Oats in W. Wheat and W. Barley	23·00-30·00
Tri-allate	Blackgrass and Wild Oats in Wheat and Barley	21·00-23·50
Metoxuron	Blackgrass in W. Wheat and W. Barley	35·50
Isoproturon	Blackgrass in W. Wheat and W. Barley	30·00-35·00
Methabenzthiazuron	Blackgrass in W. Wheat and W. Barley	30·00
Difenzoquat	Wild Oats in Cereals	46·00
Chlormequat	Reduced Straw Length in Oats and Wheat	4·00-8·00
Ethirimol	Mildew Control on Spring Barley	6·75
Triademefon	Fungicide for Cereals	12·75
Benomyl	Fungicide for Cereals	5·20
Carbendazim	Fungicide for Cereals	5·00-5·50
Propiconazole	Fungicide for Cereals	15·00-19·00
Pirimicarb	Aphid control in Cereals	8·40
Glyphosate	Couch Grass, etc. in Stubbles	58·00
Paraquat	General Weed and Grass Killer Prior to Direct Drilling	9·00-24·00 18·00-42·00
Linuron	Pre-emergence Weed Control in Potatoes	15·00-23·00
Metribuzin	Pre- and Post-emergence Weed Control in Potatoes	19·50-39·00
Metalaxyl + Mancozeb	Potato Blight Control (per application)	15·50
Diquat	Potato Haulm Desiccation	28·00
Metamitron	Weeds in Sugar Beet: Low Dose (per application) Band	24·00 21·00-28·00
Chloridazon	Pre-emergence Herbicide for Sugar Beet: Overall Band	24·00-71·00 8·00-24·00
Phenmedipham	Weeds in Sugar Beet: Low Dose (per application) Band	30·00 24·00-29·00
Aldicarb	Insecticide for Sugar Beet	25·00-50·00
Simazine	Weeds in Beans	4·25-5·75
Cyanazine	Pre-emergence Weed Killer for Peas	18·50-31·00
Atrazine	Weeds in Maize	5·75-8·50
Desmetryne	Weeds in Brassicas	15·00-22·00
Propachlor	Weeds in Brassicas, Onions, Leeks	27·00-52·00
Trifluralin	Weeds in Brassicas	8·00-9·00
Triazophos	Insecticide for Winter Oil Seed Rape	8·50
H.C.H.	Control of Leatherjackets, etc.	19·50

10. FEEDINGSTUFF PRICES

		£ per tonne
1. *Cattle*	Dairy: Nuts	160-190
	Summer Grazing Nuts	130-155
	Concentrate	260-320
	Beef Fattener Nuts	135-170
	Concentrate	200-250
	Calf: Baby Calf Food	580-780
	Calf Weaner Pellets	175-195
	Calf Rearer Nuts	160-170
2. *Sheep*	Creep Feed Pellets	170-185
	Ewe and Lamb Nuts	145-160
	Sheep Nuts	135-155
3. *Pigs*	Baby Pig Pellets	450-600
	Creep Feed Pellets	240-300
	Sow Nuts	170-190
	Grower Feeds	210-220
	Finisher Feeds	185-205
	Sow Concentrate	245-275
	Grower Concentrate	255-285
4. *Poultry*	Breeder Feeds	190-195
	Chick Feeds	180-205
	Layer Feeds	175-195
	Broiler Feeds	200-235
	Turkey Feeds	190-250
	Rabbit Feeds	185-190
5. *Straight Feeds*	White Fish Meal (66%)	315-345
	Copra Cake (34%)	145-155
	Meat and Bone Meal (45-48%)	150-160
	Soya Bean Meal	150-180
	Rapeseed Meal (35/36%)	80-130
	Palm Kernel Cake (23%)	125-150
	Manioc	100-125
	Grass Meal (15/16%)	125
	Grass Cubes (bulk)	115-130
	Wheatfeed	85-120
	Maize Meal/Flaked Maize	180-190
	Molasses	90-100
	Dried Brewers' Grains	85-90
	Wet Brewers' Grains	15-40

The straight feed prices are approximate levels in mid-1984 (excl. delivery charges). The other prices are estimated averages for 1985. They are delivered prices on the farm and exclude any credit charges. For bulk delivery there would be a rebate of approximately £10 per tonne.

ME requirements for Friesian cows (590kg LW) (see page 152)

Liveweight Change (kg/day)	Maintenance	Milk yield (kg/day)			
		20	25	30	35
−0·5		147	172	196	221
0	62	161	186	210	235
+0·5		178	203	227	252

Source: Broster, W.H. and Alderman, G., Livestock Production Science, 4 (1977), pp. 263-275.

11. FEEDINGSTUFFS: NUTRITIVE VALUES

Type of Feed			Dry Matter Content g/kg	Metab-olizable Energy MJ/k DM	Digestible Crude Protein g/kg DM
Pasture, rotational close grazed (monthly)	...	...	200	11·2	130
Ryegrass, perennial post flowering	...	...	250	8·4	72
Hay—moderate digestibility grass	...	...	850	8·8	39
Silage—moderate digestibility grass	...	...	200	8·8	102
Pea Haulm and Pods (Canning) Silage	...	...	210	8·7	95
Barley (spring) Straw	...	...	860	7·3	9
Oat (spring) Straw	...	...	860	6·7	11
Threshed Ryegrass Hay (approximate)	...	...	850	7·0	38
Kale (marrow stem)	...	...	140	11·0	114
Mangels (white globe)	...	...	110	12·5	64
Swede Turnips	...	...	120	12·8	91
Turnips	...	...	90	11·2	73
Sugar Beet Tops	...	...	160	9·9	88
Rape	...	...	140	9·5	144
Potatoes	...	...	210	12·5	47
Brewers' Grains (barley)—fresh	...	...	220	10·0	149
Brewers' Grains (barley)—dried	...	...	900	10·3	145
Barley	...	...	860	13·7	82
Oats	...	...	860	11·5	84
Maize	...	...	860	14·2	78
Wheat	...	...	860	14·0	105
Flaked Maize	...	...	900	15·0	106
Dried Sugar Beet Pulp	...	...	900	12·7	59
Beans, field spring	...	...	860	12·8	248
Dec. Groundnut Cake	...	...	900	12·3	449
Dec. Cotton Cake	...	...	900	12·3	393

Source: M.A.F.F. Technical Bulletin 33, Energy Allowances and Feeding Systems for Ruminants.

Relative value of feeds
(based on their energy contents fed to dairy cows)

	Weight equivalent (1)	Relative Value (2)		Weight equivalent (1)	Relative Value (2)
Good hay	154	70	Fresh brewers' grains	589	18
Medium hay	165	65	Pressed sugar beet pulp	515	21
Dried grass	143	75	Dried distillers' gians	108	99·5
Swedes	767	14	Molassed dried beet pulp	107	100·5
Potatoes	449	24	Wheat middlings	113	95
Mangolds	857	12·5	Flaked maize	87	123·5
Cabbage	1030	10·5	Maize germ meal (14%)	88	122
Oats	119	90	Barley straw	218	49
Wheat	98	110	Oat straw	228	47
Sorghum	102	105	Wheat straw	245	44
Maize	97	111	Pea haulm straw	211	51
			Wheat bran	133	81

(1) equivalent to 100 of barley   (2) value (£) compared wth barley at £107·50 per tonne
Source: A.D.A.S. (D. Morgan)

12. GRAZING AND REARING CHARGES: CATTLE AND SHEEP

Grazing charges vary widely according to the quality of the pasture and local supply and demand. The following figures are typical charges (estimated for 1985):

Summer Grazing

Store Cattle and in-calf heifers over 21 months, dry cows, and fattening bullocks over 18 months	£2·50	per head per week
Heifers and Steers, 12-21 months	£1·95	,, ,, ,, ,,
6-12 months Cattle	£1·45	,, ,, ,, ,,
Cattle of mixed ages	£2·00	,, ,, ,, ,,
Ewes	26p	,, ,, ,, ,,

Winter Grazing

"Strong" Cattle	£1·45-£1·95	per head per week
Heifers	£1·15-£1·45	,, ,, ,, ,,
Sheep	26p	,, ,, ,, ,,

Grazing Charge per hectare

Whole Summer: £80-£225
Whole Year: £100-£250
These figures are highly variable, especially between one part of the country and another. The charge can be very high where the pasture is good, the supply scarce and the demand strong, e.g. in 1983 (a high price season) some grass keep was let at rents as high as £630 per ha (in Cumbria); however, even in 1983 the *average* even in the North-west was only £215 per ha, the lowest average region being the South-east: £110 per ha. (Source: 1983 Grass Keep Enquiry, Land Economics and Valuation Section, ADAS.)

Winter Keep (Cattle)

Grazing + 9 kg hay and some straw	£4·30	per head per week
Full winter keep in yards	£4·60-£6·00	,, ,, ,, ,,
Calf rearing for beef (0 to 12 weeks or 0 to 6 months)	£6·25	,, ,, ,, ,,

Heifer Rearing charges

Points to clarify in any arrangement are: who pays for transport, who pays the vet. and med. expenses, who bears the losses or pays for replacements, how often are payments made (monthly payments save the rearer interest compared with lump sum payments when the heifer is returned)?

Two possible arrangements are:

1. Farmer X sells calf to Rearer at agreed price; the calf is then Rearer's responsibility and he pays for all expenses and bears any losses. Farmer X has first option on heifers, which he buys back two months before calving. Approx. price: £475 above cost of calf for Friesians, £300 for Channel Islands. Rearer fetches calf; Farmer X supplies transport for heifer.

2. Farmer X retains ownership of calf. Approx. charges: £19 per month from 10 to 14 days old (£21 if two-year old calving), or £17 per month from 6 months old (£19·50 if two-year old calving), (£28 per month from 10 to 14 days to 6 months). As Rearer has no interest

on capital to bear, he supplies transport and pays for vet. and medical expenses. Rearer either refunds payments for losses or replaces calf (this means Farmer X and Rearer share a loss averaging approx. £14 each per heifer reared, assuming 10 per cent losses at average 6 months old). Receipts for culls go to Farmer X; he and Rearer share cost of replacement calf equally.

Calf and Heifer Rearing for Shorter Periods

Calf, 10 days to 3 months, £80 (for food, labour and housing) to £90 (all costs, and rearer bearing losses). Heifers, average from 3 months old to steaming up: approx. £9 per month in summer, £26 in winter.

13. STANDARD OUTPUTS, STANDARD GROSS MARGINS AND STANDARD MAN-DAYS

Crops (per hectare)

		S.O.	S.G.M.	S.M.D.
Winter Wheat	...	710	510	
Spring Wheat	...	510	350	
Winter Barley	...	575	400	2·5 (1)
Spring Barley	...	490	360	
Winter Oats	...	540	400	
Spring Oats	...	475	350	
Potatoes	...	2300	1150	22
Sugar Beet	...	1200	750	8
Vining Peas	...	800	650	3·5
Dried Peas	...	640	450	1·75
Field Beans	...	540	430	1·75
Oilseed Rape	...	870	650	1
Herbage Seeds	...	680	500	1·75
Hops	...	5500	4500	80
Mangolds	...	—	—	28
Turnips/Swedes:				
folded	...	—	—	5
lifted	...	—	—	10
Kale: cut	...	—	—	10
Kale: grazed	...	—	—	2
Hay/Silage: 1 cut	...	—	—	2·5
Hay/Silage: 2 cuts	...	—	—	4
Grazing only	...	—	—	1
Hay for sale	...	300	220	2·5
Keep let	...	175	150	1
Bare Fallow	...	—	—	1·5

Livestock (per head) (2)

		S.O.	S.G.M.	S.M.D.
Dairy Cows: parlour	...	800	400	5
Dairy Cows: cowshed	...			7
Bulls	...	—	—	3·5
Beef Cows (S.S. inc. Calf)	...	250	150	1·5
Barley Beef (0-12 months)	...	350	75	2·5
15-18 month Beef (6-15/18 months)		380	170	2·5
Other Cattle over 2 years	...	180	100	2·0
Other Cattle 1-2 years	...	180	100	1·5
Other Cattle ½-1 year (3)		90	50	0·75
Calves, M.S.-to 6 months (3) (add to S.S.)	...	120	40	0·75
Calves, Others, to 6 months (3):				
steers		150	65	1·5
heifers		125	55	1·5
Ewes (lowland)	...	47·5	27·5	0·5
Rams	...	—	—	0·5
Other Sheep over 6 months	...	20	12	0·3
Sows	...	500	100	4
Boars	...	—	—	2
Other Pigs over 2 months	...	120	15	0·5
Laying Birds (Intensive)		9	1·4	0·05
Pullets reared (3)	...	1·7	0·4	0·025
Broilers per 100(3)	...	110	2·8	0·25
Turkeys (3)	...	10	2	0·05

1. Including straw; 1·75 if straw burnt or ploughed in.
2. In calculating the Standard Outputs and Standard Gross Margins for livestock, herd depreciation or livestock (e.g. calf) purchases or the value of transfers in have been deducted.
3. For these livestock, S.O., S.G.M. and S.M.D. per annum should be based on numbers produced during the year. For all other livestock, average numbers during the year should be used (i.e. average of numbers at end of each month).

For number of Standard Man-Days per worker per year, see page 65.

The above figures are the author's estimates, for 1985.

14. FARM RECORDS

The following records should be kept for management purposes:

1. *Basic Whole Farm Financial Position*

   1. Cash Analysis Book, fully detailed.
   2. Petty Cash Book.
   3. Annual Valuation, including physical quantities, with crops in store and livestock at (near) market value, less any variable costs yet to be borne. Fertilizers, seeds, sprays, casual labour or contract work applied to growing crops should be recorded, but "cultivations" and manurial residues can be ignored for management purposes.
   4. Debtors and creditors at the end of the financial year.

2. *Other Financial and Physical Records*

   1. Output (quantities and value) of each Crop and Livestock Enterprise for the "Harvest Year" (or Production Cycle). It may be possible to get information of Sales from a fully detailed cash analysis book (although, for crops, the financial year figures will then have to be allocated between crops from the current harvest and those from the harvest in the previous financial year, in order to check on the accuracy of the opening valuation of crops in store; this is particularly a problem with Michaelmas ending accounts). The following records of Internal Transfers and Consumption will also be required:

      (a) Numbers and Market Value of livestock transferred from one livestock category to another, e.g. dairy calves to Dairy Followers or Beef Enterprise, or dairy heifers to Dairy Enterprise.

      (b) Quantity and Market Value of Cereals fed on farm and used for seed.

      (c) Quantity and Market Value of Milk and other produce consumed by the farmer or his employees, used on the farm (e.g. milk fed to calves), or sold direct.

2. A Monthly record of Livestock Numbers; preferably reconciled with the previous month according to births, purchases, deaths, sales and transfers.

3. Costs and Quantities of Concentrate Feed to each category of livestock, including Home-Grown Cereals fed on the farm.

4. Allocation of costs of seed, fertilizer, sprays, casual labour and contract work specific to an enterprise. This is in order to calculate gross margins, where required. It is less essential than the other records listed.

5. Breeding record for cows, including bulling dates, date(s) served, type of bull used, pregnancy testing, estimated calving date, actual calving date, and date when dried off.

6. For each crop, total output and yield per hectare, in both quantity and value. Include each field where the crop has been grown and its approximate yield, where this can be satisfactorily obtained.

7. For each field, keep one page to cover a period of say, ten years. Record on this, each year, crop grown, variety sown, fertilizer used, sprays used, date sown, date(s) harvested, approximate yield (if obtainable), and any other special notes that you feel may have significance for the future.

8. A rotation record. On a single page, if possible, list each field down the side and say, ten years along the top. Colour each field-year space according to the crop grown, e.g. barley yellow, potatoes red, etc.

15. DEFINITIONS OF FARM MANAGEMENT TERMS

Mainly abstracted from "Terms and Definitions used in Farm and Horticulture Management", M.A.F.F., 1970.

1. Valuations and Capital

Valuations. Valuation is essentially a process of estimation. Thus alternative bases are sometimes possible, according to the purpose intended. The basis should be consistent throughout the period of any series of figures.

(i) *Saleable crops in store.* At estimated market value (including deficiency payments when based on quantity produced) less costs still to be incurred, e.g. for storage and marketing. Both may be estimated either at the expected date of sale or at the date of valuation.

(ii) *Growing crops.* Preferably at variable costs to the date of valuation, although estimated total cost can alternatively be used.

(iii) *Saleable crops ready for harvesting* but still in the ground. Preferably valued as (i), less estimated harvesting costs, although they can alternatively be treated as (ii).

(iv) *Fodder stocks (home-grown).* Preferably at variable costs when calculating gross margins. Alternatively at estimated market value (based on hay-equivalent value according to quality). Fodder crops still in the ground, e.g. kale, treated as (ii).

(v) *Stocks of purchased materials (including fodder).* At cost net of discounts (where known) and subsidies.

(vi) *Machinery and equipment.* Original cost net of investment grants, less accumulated depreciation to date of valuation.

(vii) *Livestock.* At current market value, including deficiency payments less cost of marketing. Fluctuations in market value expected to be temporary should be ignored.

Tenant's Capital. The estimated total value of capital on the farm, other than land and fixed equipment. There is no easy way of determining this sum precisely and estimates are made in several ways depending on the information available and the purpose for which the estimate is required. One method is to take the average of the opening and closing valuations (at either market value or cost) of livestock, crops, machinery and stores (feed, seed, fertilizers). See also page 122.

Landlord's Capital. Value of the land and fixed equipment (including buildings).

2. Output Terms

Revenue (or Income). Receipts adjusted for debtors at the beginning and end of the accounting period. Items such as subsidies, grants, contract receipts and wayleaves are included.

Returns. Revenue adjusted for valuation changes (add closing, deduct opening, valuation).

Gross Output. Returns plus the value of produce consumed in the farmhouse or supplied to workers for which no payment is made, less purchases of livestock, livestock products and other produce bought for resale.

Enterprise Output. The total value of an enterprise, whether sold or retained on the farm. It therefore equals Gross Output of the enterprise plus the market value of any of the products kept on the farm (transfers out). Products transferred from another enterprise to be used in the production of the enterprise whose output is being calculated are deducted at market value (transfers in). Instead of the accounting year the "harvest year" can be used for crops; valuations are then not relevant.

(Enterprise) Output from Forage. Primarily the sum of the enterprise outputs of grazing livestock, but includes keep let and occasional sales, e.g. of surplus hay, together with an adjustment for changes in the valuation of stocks of home-grown fodder. However, fortuitous changes in stocks caused by yield variations due to the weather, the severity or length of the winter, or minor changes in livestock numbers or forage area can be either ignored (if small in relation to total annual usage) or included in miscellaneous output.

Adjusted Forage (Enterprise) Output is Output from Forage less rented keep and purchases of bulk fodder.

Net Output. Gross Output less the cost of purchased feed, livestock keep, seed, bulbs and plants.

Standard Output. The average enterprise output per hectare of a crop or per head of livestock calculated from either national or local average price and average yield data.

3. Input Terms

Expenditure. Payments adjusted for creditors at the beginning and end of the accounting period. Capital expenditure is not included.

Costs. Expenditure adjusted for valuation changes (add opening, deduct closing, valuation), with the following adjustments. Add: depreciation on capital expenditure including machinery, any loss made on machinery sales (add to depreciation) and the value of payments in kind to workers if not already included in their earnings. Deduct: purchases of livestock, livestock products and other produce bought for resale, any profit made on machinery (deduct from depreciation), allowance for private use of farm vehicles (deduct from machinery costs), the value of purchased stores used in the farmhouse (e.g. electricity) or sold off the farm (deduct from the relevant item), and fertilizer and lime subsidies.

Inputs. Costs with the following adjustments, made in order to put all farms on a similar basis for comparative purposes. Add: the value of unpaid family labour, including the manual labour of the farmer and his wife, and, in the case of owner-occupiers, an estimated rental value (based on average rents of similar farms in the area), less any cottage rents received. Deduct: any mortgage payments and other expenses of owner-occupation, interest payments and the cost of paid management. A proportion of the rental value of the farmhouse may also be deducted.

Fixed Costs. See page 106.

Variable Costs. See page 1.

4. Margin Terms

Management and Investment Income. Gross Output less Inputs. It represents the reward to management and the return on tenant's capital invested in the farm, whether borrowed or not. It is mainly used for comparative purposes, all farms having been put on a similar financial basis by the adjustments made to costs in calculating Inputs.

Net Farm Income. Management and Investment Income, less paid management, plus the value of the manual labour of the farmer and his wife.

Profit (or Loss). Gross Output less Costs. This represents the surplus or deficit before imputing any notional charges such as rental value or unpaid labour. In the accounts of owner-occupiers it includes any profit accruing from the ownership of land.

Gross Margin. See page 1.

Net Margin. A term sometimes used to denote Gross Margin less direct labour and machinery costs charged to an individual enterprise. This is not, however, nationally accepted terminology.

5. Area Terms

Total Hectares. All hectares comprising the farm.

Hectares. Total hectares less the area of woods, waste land, roads, buildings, etc.

Adjusted Hectares. Hectares reduced by the conversion of rough grazings into the equivalent hectares of average quality grassland. This is the figure often used for lowland farms when calculating "per hectare" results.

Forage Hectares. Total hectares of forage crops grown, less any hectares exclusively used by pigs or poultry and the area equivalent of any home-grown fodder fed to barley beef. Usually, too, the area of rough grazings is converted to its grassland equivalent (see Adjusted Hectares). Forage crops are all crops, grass and rough grazings grown specifically for grazing livestock, other than catch crops and crops harvested as grain and pulses.

Adjusted Forage Hectares. Forage hectares adjusted as follows. Add area equivalent of keep rented, deduct area equivalent of keep let; deduct the area equivalent of occasional sales of fodder, e.g. surplus hay, and seed cuts (note: hay and seed grown regularly for sale should be regarded as cash crops, not forage crops); add or deduct the area equivalent of planned changes in the valuation of stocks of home-grown fodder (fortuitous changes in stocks resulting from weather conditions may be ignored); convert rough grazings into their grassland equivalent if not already done. The following adjustments also may be made: add the area equivalent of catch crops and of grazing from cash crops of hay or seed: add the area equivalent of purchased fodder.

In calculations such as *Gross Margins per Forage Hectare*, Adjusted Forage Hectares are usually used. If the area equivalent of purchased fodder has been added the cost of purchased fodder must not be charged as a variable cost: this is probably the best calculation for comparative purposes. Alternatively, when considering all the grazing enterprises taken together, purchased fodder can be deducted as a variable cost and no addition made for its area equivalent.

16. AGRISTATS

Some basic agricultural statistics relating to U.K. agriculture.
(All figures are for the U.K. unless otherwise stated. Some 1983 figures
are provisional.)

1. *Agriculture's contribution to gross domestic*
   product: £5,308 million (1983)
   2·3% (1982)

2. (a) *Agriculture's proportion of total manpower* 2·7% (1983)

(b) *Numbers of Persons Engaged in Agriculture* (June)

	1978	1983
A. Employed:		
(i) Regular Whole-time:		
Hired: male	143,000	122,200
female	12,000	10,500
Family: male	34,000	30,000
female	7,000	5,000
Total male	(177,000)	(152,200)
Total female	(19,000)	(15,500)
Total	196,000	167,700
(ii) Regular Part-time:		
Hired: male	21,000	18,800
female	24,000	22,500
Family; male	15,000	12,500
female	9,000	6,800
Total male	(36,000)	(31,300)
Total female	(33,000)	(29,300)
Total	69,000	60,600
(iii) Seasonal or Casual:		
Total male	58,000	56,900
Total female	43,000	41,000
	101,000	97,900
(iv) Salaried managers*	8,000	7,800
Total Employed	374,000	334,000
B. Employers (farmers, partners, directors):**		
Whole-time	216,000	***202,800
Part-time	88,000	86,800
Total employers**	303,000	289,600
Wives/husbands of farmers, etc. doing farm work	80,000	75,700
Overall Total	757,000	699,300

* Great Britain only.
** Includes *non-principal* partners and directors for Great Britain only.
*** 159,900 are principal farmers and partners.

161

3. *Inputs and Outputs* (1983 forecast, £ million).

Inputs		Outputs		%
Feedingstuffs	2832	Cereals	2005	(17·3)
Seeds	285	Potatoes	504	(4·3)
Fertilizer and lime	826	Other farm crops	499	(4·3)
Livestock (imptd. & inter-fm.)	171	Vegetables	681	(5·9)
Labour:		Fruit and other hortic. ...	445	(3·8)
Hired 1265		Fat cattle and calves ...	1831	(15·8)
Family & partners 562	1827	Fat sheep and lambs ...	562	(4·9)
Machinery:		Fat pigs	911	(7·9)
Depreciation ... 869		Poultry	617	(5·3)
Repairs 387		Milk and milk products ...	2486	(21·4)
Fuel and oil ... 436		Eggs	501	(4·3)
Other 79	1771	Miscellaneous	521	(4·5)
Farm maintenance	233	Stocks: Volume change (+)	32	(0·3)
Deprec. on buildings				
and works	463	TOTAL GROSS OUTPUT	11595	(100)
Net rent	121			
Interest	492	Total Crops	3008	(26·0)
Miscellaneous	1010	Total Horticulture ...	1126	(9·7)
Stocks: Volume change (−)	28	Total Livestock ...	4015	(34·6)
		Total Livestock Products ...	3047	(26·3)
TOTAL INPUTS	10059	Other	399	(3·4)
FARMING INCOME	1536			
	11595	TOTAL GROSS OUTPUT	11595	(100)

4. *U.K. Farming Income, 1970-83*

Year	Farming Income (£ mill.)	Real Farming Income (in 1970 £) (£ mill.)	Index of Real Farming Income (1970 = 100)
1970	567	567	100
1971	640	584	103
1972	682	583	103
1973	952	744	131
1974	803	541	95
1975	1005	545	96
1976	1293	601	106
1977	1269	510	90
1978	1252	464	82
1979	1141	373	66
1980	1018	282	50
1981	1318	326	57
1982	1802	410	72
1983*	1536	334	59

*Forecast.

162

5. Net Farm Income per Farm in Real Terms by main Types of Farming, UK: Index Numbers (1977/78 = 100)

	Dairy	LFA Cattle and Sheep	Lowland Cattle and Sheep	Cereals	Other Cropping	Pigs and Poultry
1977/78 ...	100	100	100	100	100	100
1978/79 ...	106	109	107	126	188	134
1979/80 ...	66	50	48	92	181	94
1980/81 ...	65	58	57	97	109	84
1981/82 ...	81	101	66	93	157	96
1982/83 ...	93	85	53	147	165	67
1983/84 ... (forecast)	65	80	45	160	230	25

6. Crop Areas (two-year averages, in June)

	Area ('000 ha) 1977/78	Area ('000 ha) 1982/83	% Total Area 1982/83	% Crops and Grass (excl. R.G.) 1982/83
Wheat	1,166	1,679	9·0	13·9
Barley	2,374	2,183	11·6	18·1
Oats	188	118	0·6	1·0
Other Grain	30	16	0·1	0·1
Total Cereals	3,758	3,996	21·3	33·1
Potatoes	223	194	1·0	1·6
Sugar Beet	205	201	1·1	1·7
Oilseed Rape	60	198	1·0	1·6
Horticulture	295	239	1·3	2·0
Other Crops and Fallow ...	357	297	1·6	2·4
Total Tillage	4,898	5,125	27·3	42·4
Temporary Grass (under 5 years old)	2,096	1,853	9·9	15·4
Total Arable	6,994	6,978	37·2	57·8
Permanent Grass (5 years old and over)	5,002	5,102	27·2	42·2
(Total Grass (excluding R.G.)) ...	(7,098)	(6,955)	(37·1)	(57·6)
Total Crops and Grass (excl. R.G.)	11,996	12,080	64·4	100·0
Rough Grazing (R.G.)	6,388	6,168*	32·9	
Other Land	459	512**	2·7	
Total Agricultural Area***	18,843	18,760	100·0	

* Including an estimated 1,213,000 ha of common grazing
** All other land on agricultural holdings, including 289,000 ha of woodland.
*** Urbanised and other non-agricultural area (ha): approx. 3·5 million; forest approx. 2 million; total U.K. land area including inland waters: 24·1 million.

7. *Livestock Numbers* (two-year averages, in June; '000 head):

	1977/78	1982/83
Dairy cows	3,268	3,292
Beef cows	1,630	1,373
Heifers in calf		
—for dairying	} 842	688
—for beef		161
Other cattle and calves	7,995	7,753
Total cattle and calves	13,735	13,267
Ewes	11,330	13,110
Shearlings	2,602	2,902
Other sheep and lambs	14,963	17,556
Total sheep and lambs	28,895	33,568
Sows for breeding	724	745
Gilts in pig	111	116
Other pigs	6,887	7,237
Total pigs	7,722	8,098
Table fowls (incl. broilers)	56,236	59,481
Laying fowls	49,804	43,155
Growing pullets	16,807	13,422
Other poultry	12,961	15,754
Total poultry	135,808	131,812

8. *Size Structure*
Number and Size distribution of holdings, 1983

Crops and Grass area (ha)	No. of holdings ('000)	% of holdings	% of crops and grass area
Under 20	97·3	41·5	6·7
20- 50	65·4	27·9	} 42·5
50-100	41·4	17·6	
100 and over	30·6	13·0	50·8
Total	234·7	100·0	100·0

Average area of crops and grass per holding: 50·7 ha (total area = 71·6 ha).

Size of business* (SMD)	No. of holdings ('000)		% of holdings	
Under 250	124·0		51·0	
250-499	44·6	} 119·2	18·3	} 49·0
500-999	43·5		17·9	
1000 and over	31·1		12·8	
Total	243·3		100·0	

Average size over 250 SMD = 913 SMD, 119 ha (total area)
% output from holdings over 250 SMD = approx. 90·8

*Includes holdings with no crops and grass.

SMD = Standard Man-Days.

Number and Size distribution of holdings in England and Wales, 1983:

Size Groups (ha)	By Total Area				By Crops and Grass Area			
	Holdings		Hectares		Holdings		Hectares	
	'000	%	'000,000	%	'000	%	'000,000	%
1- 10	50·6	26·5	0·22	2·0	56·2(1)	29·5	0·21	2·2
10- 30	45·1	24·6	0·85	7·9	45·2	24·8	0·86	9·2
30- 50	27·5	15·0	1·08	10·0	27·9	15·2	1·09	11·7
50-100	33·4	18·1	2·36	21·7	31·8	17·2	2·24	23·7
100-200	19·2	10·4	2·65	24·2	16·9	9·1	2·32	24·6
200-300	5·4	2·9	1·29	11·7	4·5	2·4	1·07	11·1
300-500	3·2	1·7	1·20	11·0	2·5	1·3	0·92	9·7
500-700	0·9	0·4	0·51	4·5	0·6	0·3	0·35	3·7
700 and over	0·7	0·4	0·75	7·0	0·4	0·2	0·39	4·1
Total	186·0	100·0	10·91	100·0	186·0	100·0	9·46	100·0

1. Including 6·9 with nil crops and grass.

9. Average Size of Enterprises, 1983

	hectares		no.
Crops and Grass	50·7	Dairy cows	58
Cereals	41·1	Beef cows	18
Potatoes	4·7	Breeding sheep	191
Sugar Beet	16·8	Breeding pigs	41
Oilseed Rape	24·2	Fattening pigs	265
		Laying fowls	812
		Broilers	31,302

10. Tenure

The following figures are for England and Wales, 1983; the areas are '000 hectares (percentages in brackets).

	No. of holdings	Area owned	Area rented
Wholly owned	106,672(57·4)	4,496(41·2)	—
Mainly owned	24,285(13·1)	1,704(15·6)	437 (4·0)
Wholly rented	37,971(20·4)	—	2,657(24·4)
Mainly rented	17,065 (9·2)	368 (3·4)	1,249(11·4)
Total	185,993(100)	6,568(60·2)	4,344(39·8)

N.B. Mixed tenure holdings: mainly owned = over 50% owned; mainly rented = over 50% rented.
    Wholly or mainly owned, 70·5% of holdings; wholly or mainly rented, 29·6%

U.K. (1977): 59·2% owned; 40·8% land rented. (However, while this is the figure obtained from M.A.F.F. statistics, it is now widely believed that in fact only 35 per cent of our agricultural land is now tenanted; ref. Northfield Report, 1979.)

11. Self-Sufficiency

(a) Total production (1983 forecast)

Value of home production as percentage of U.K. food supplies: 60 per cent.

Value of home production as percentage of indigenous-type food supplies: 76 per cent.

(b) Individual Products (1983 forecast):

(Production as % of total new supply for use in the U.K.)

Wheat	101	Beef and veal	98
Barley	126	Mutton and lamb	71
Oats	96	Pork	104
Rye	75	Bacon and ham	45
Total Cereals	101	Poultry meat	98
		Total Meat	89
Oilseed rape	112	Liquid milk	100
Potatoes	87	Butter	66
Sugar	54	Cheese	70
Hops	99	Cream	79
Apples	44	Eggs	100
Pears	39		
Cauliflowers	84	Wool	43
Tomatoes	32		

12. Food Consumption

Expenditure on food as % of total household expenditure (1981): 21·7; alcoholic drink, 4·8.

Estimated Household Food Consumption per head per annum (kg, 1982)

Bread	45·7	Liquid milk (litres)	117
Flour	7·8	Other milk (litres)	13
Buns, cakes, biscuits, etc.	13·9	Cheese	5·6
Breakfast cereal and oatmeal	5·8	Butter	4·7
Sugar	15·2	Margarine	6·4
Beef and veal	10·4	Lard/cooking fat	2·6
Mutton and lamb	5·3	Eggs (no.)	183
Pork	5·9	Potatoes (unprocessed)	60·6
Bacon and ham	7·5	Fresh green vegetables	16·6
Poultry	10·1	Tomatoes, fresh	5·9
Other cooked and canned meats	3·7	Other fresh vegs. and frozen vegs.	24·9
Sausages, uncooked	4·9	Canned tomatoes, peas and beans	11·9
Offals	1·4	Fresh fruit	27·6
Other meat products	7·7	Canned fruit	3·9
Fish (all)	7·4	Dried fruit, and nuts	1·8

Sources: Annual Review of Agriculture 1983 (Items 1, 2, 3, 4 (part), 5, 6, 7, 8 (part), 9, 11).
Other M.A.A.F. Statistics (Items 8 (part), 10).
Annual Abstract of Statistics (Item 12).

17. RATE OF INFLATION; PRICE AND COST INDICES

1. *Retail Price Index* (all items; 1970 = 100)

	Index	% increase on year earlier	Value of £ (1970 = £1)
1970	100	—	£1
1971	109·5	9·5	91p
1972	117	7	85p
1973	128	9	78p
1974	148·5	16	67p
1975	184·5	24	54p
1976	215	16·5	47p
1977	249	16	40p
1978	270*	8·3	37p
1979	306*	13·4	33p
1980	361*	18	28p
1981	404*	11·9	25p
1982	439*	8·6	23p
1983	459*	4·6	22p
1984 (est.)	482*	5·1	21p

Index in 1965: 80.

„ „ 1962: 70.

* Imputed figures, as indices for 1978 onwards are now based on 1975=100.

Source: Economic Trends.

2. *Price and Cost Indices 1983* (1975 = 100)

(a) *Producer Prices*

Milling Wheat	218	Dessert Apples	202
Feed Wheat	222	All Fresh Fruit	188
Malting Barley	217	*All Farm & Hortic. Crops*	196
Feed Barley	210	Clean Cattle	252
Milling Oats	203	Lambs	271
Feed Oats	209	Wool	157
All Cereals	217	Pigs (excl. sows)	152
Early Potatoes	78	Poultry	185
Maincrop Potatoes	172	Milk	200
Sugar Beet	165	Eggs	157
Oilseed Rape	229	*All Animals/Animal Products*	203
Fresh Vegetables	188	*All Farm Produce*	200

(b) *Input Prices*

General Expenses	277	Straight Feedingstuffs	217
Seeds	187	Compound Feedingstuffs	213
Straight Fertilizers	237	All Feedingstuffs	214
Compound Fertilizers	193	Energy, Lubricants	360
All Fertilizers	210	Maintce./Repair of Plant	235
Plant Protection Products	206	Machinery & Other Equipt.	267
Animals for Rearing/Prodn.	294	Buildings	261

Source: M.A.F.F. Statistical Information (adapted by the author).

18. METRIC CONVERSION FACTORS
(approximate figures, with accurate figures in brackets)

Metric to Imperial		*Imperial to Metric*	
1 hectare (ha) = 2½ acres	(2·471)	1 acre = $\frac{2}{5}$ hectare	(0·405)
(1 hectare = 10,000 sq.m)			
1 kilogram (kg) = 2¼ lb.	(2·205)	1 lb. = ½ kilogram	(0·454)
1 kilogram = ·11 score	(0·110)	1 score = 9 kg	(9·07)
50 kilograms = 1 cwt.	(0·984)	1 cwt. = 50 kilograms	(50·80)
1000 kilograms	(0·984)	1000 kilograms	(1016)
1 tonne $\Big\} = 1$ ton	(2204·6 lb.)	1 tonne $\Big\} = 1$ ton	(1·016)
1 kilogram (fert.) = 2 units	(1·969)	1 unit (fert.) = ½ kilogram	(0·508)
£/cwt. = ½ × p/kg	(0·508)	pence/kg = 2 × £/cwt.	(1·967)
£/score = ·09 × p/kg	(0·091)	pence/kg = 11 × £/score	(11·02)
1 kg/ha = 0·9 lb./acre	(0·892)	1 lb./acre = 1 kg/ha	(1·121)
100kg (1 quintal) ha = $\frac{4}{5}$ cwt./acre		1 cwt./acre = 125 kg (1¼ quintals)/ha	
	(0·797)		(125·5)
1000 kg/ha = 8 cwt./acre	(7·95)	1 ton/acre = 2500 kg/ha	(2511)
1 tonne/ha = $\frac{2}{5}$ ton/acre	(0·398)	1 ton/acre = 2½ tonne/ha	(2·511)
1 kg (fert.)/ha = $\frac{4}{5}$ unit/acre	(0·797)	1 unit (fert.)/acre = 1¼ kg/ha	(1·255)
1 litre/ha = 0·1 gal./acre	(0·089)	1 gal./acre = 11 litres/ha	(11·24)
1 litre = $\frac{2}{9}$ gal.	(0·220)	1 gal. = 4½ litres (cu. decimetres)	
			(4·546)
1 litre = 1¾ pints	(1·760)	1 pint = $\frac{3}{5}$ litre	(0·568)
1 kg milk = $\frac{1}{5}$ gal.	(0·214)	1 gal. milk = 4¾ kg	(4·681)
1 kg milk = 1¾ pints	(1·712)		
1 litre milk = 1 kg	(1·030)		
1 millimetre (mm) = $\frac{1}{25}$ inch	(0·039)	1 inch = 25 mm	(25·4)
1 centimetre (cm) = $\frac{2}{5}$ inch	(0·394)	1 inch = 2½ cm	(2·54)
1 metre (m) = 3¼ feet	(3·279)	1 foot = $\frac{1}{3}$ metre	(0·305)
1 metre = 1·1 yard	(1·094)	1 yard = 0·9 metre	(0·914)
1 kilometre (km) = $\frac{5}{8}$ mile	(0·621)	1 mile = 1·6 kilometres	(1·609)
1 sq. metre (m²) = 1¼ sq. yards.			
	(1·196)	1 sq. yd. = 0·85 sq. metre	(0·836)
1 sq. metre = 11 sq feet	(10·764)	1 sq. ft. = $\frac{1}{10}$ sq. metre	(0·093)
1 cu. metre (m³) = 1¼ cu. yards	(1·31)	1 cu. yd. = $\frac{3}{4}$ cu. metre	(0·765)
1cu. metre = 35 cu. ft.	(35·31)	1 cu. ft. = 0·028 cu. metre	(0·028)
		(28 cu. decimetres)	(28·32)
1 kW = 1⅓ h.p.	(1·341)	1 h.p. = $\frac{3}{4}$ kW	(0·746)

19. USEFUL ADDRESSES AND TELEPHONE NUMBERS

1. GENERAL

Agricultural Central Trading Ltd.
1 White Hill, Chesham, Bucks. HP5 1AA — 0494 784931

Agricultural Credit Corporation Limited
Agriculture House, Knightsbridge, London SW1X 7NJ. — 01-235 6296

Agricultural Development and Advisory Service
Great Westminster House, Horseferry Road, London SW1P 2AE — 01-216 6311

Agricultural Engineers Association Limited
6 Buckingham Gate, London SW1E 6JU — 01-828 7973

Agricultural Mortgage Corporation Limited
Bucklersbury House, 3 Queen Victoria Street, London EC4N 8DU — 01-236 5252

Agricultural Training Board
Bourne House, 32-34 Beckenham Road, Beckenham, Kent BR3 4PB — 01-650 4890

Agricultural Wages Board,
Eagle House, 90-96 Cannon Street, London EC4N 6HUT — 01-623 4266

British Agricultural Export Council
35 Belgrave Square, London SW1X 8QN — 01-245 9819

British Agricultural and Garden Machinery Association Limited
14-16 Church Street, Rickmansworth, Herts WD3 1RQ — 09237 77241

British Agrochemicals Association Ltd.
Alembic House, 93 Albert Embankment, London SE1 7TU — 01-735 8471/2

British Institute of Agricultural Consultants
84 Wellingborough Road, Irthlingborough, Northamptonshire NN9 5RF — 0933 650615

British Grassland Society
c/o Grassland Research Institute, Hurley, Maidenhead, Berks. SL6 5LR — 062 882 3626

British Poultry Federation
High Holborn House, 52/54 High Holborn, London WC1V 6SX — 01-242 4683

British Sugar plc
PO Box 26, Oundle Road, Peterborough PE2 9QU — 0733 63171

British Wool Marketing Board
Oak Mills, Station Road, Clayton, Bradford,
West Yorkshire BD14 6JD — 0274 882091

Central Council for Agricultural and Horticultural Co-operation
Market Towers, New Covent Garden Market,
1 Nine Elms Lane, London SW8 5NQ — 01-720 2144

Commonwealth Agricultural Bureaux
Farnham House, Farnham Royal, Slough SL2 3BN — 02814 2662

Country Landowners Association
16 Belgrave Square, London SW1X 8PQ — 01-235 0511

Countryside Commission
John Dower House, Crescent Place, Cheltenham,
Gloucestershire, GL50 3RA — 0242 21381

Centre for Management in Agriculture
Management House, Cottingham Road, Corby, Northants NN17 1TT — 05363 4222

Dairy Trade Federation
19 Cornwall Terrace, London NW1 4QP — 01-486 7244

Department of Agriculture and Fisheries for Scotland
Chesser House, 500 Gorgie Road, Edinburgh EH11 3AW — 031-443 4020

Department of Agriculture, N. Ireland
Dundonald House, Upper Newtownards Road, Belfast BT4 3SB 0232 650111

Farmers Club
3 Whitehall Court, London SW1A 2EL 01-930 3557

Farmers Union of Wales
Llys Amaeth, Queens Square, Aberystwyth, Dyfed SY23 2EA 0970 612755

Farming and Wildlife Advisory Group
The Lodge, Sandy, Beds. SG19 2DL 0767 80551

Farming and Wildlife Trust Ltd.
Brentwood, Wragby Road, Sudbrooke, Lincoln LN2 2QU 0522 750006

Fatstock Marketing Corporation
19/23 Knightsbridge, London SW1X 7NF 01-235 5081

FEOGA
Great Westminster House, Horseferry Road, London SW1P 2AE 01-216 7399

The Fertilizer Manufacturers' Association Ltd.
Greenhill House, 90-93 Cowcross Street, London EC1M 6BH 01-251 6001/2

Food from Britain
301-304 Market Towers, New Covent Garden Market,
1 Nine Elms Lane, London SW8 5NQ 01-720 2144

Forestry Commission
231 Corstorphine Road, Edinburgh EH12 7AT 031-334 0303

Grain and Feed Trade Association Ltd.
24/28 St. Mary Axe, London EC3P 8EP 01-283 5146

Health and Safety Executive
HM Agricultural Inspectorate, Baynards House, 1 Chepstow Place,
London W2 4TF 01-229 3456

Home Grown Cereals Authority
Hamlyn House, Highgate Hill, London N19 5PR 01-263 3391
Price Information Service 01-263 3494

Hops Marketing Board
Hop Pocket Lane, Paddock Wood,
Tonbridge, Kent TN12 6BY 089 283 3415

Institute of Agricultural Secretaries
N.A.C., Stoneleigh, Kenilworth, Warwickshire CV8 2L2 0203 20623

Intervention Board for Agricultural Produce
Fountain House, 2 West Mall, Reading, Berkshire 0734 583626

Lands Improvement Company
1 Brewers Green, Buckingham Gate, London SW1H 0RB 01-222 5531

Meat and Livestock Commission
PO Box 44, Queensway House, Bletchley,
Milton Keynes MK2 2EF 0908 74941

Milk Marketing Board
Thames Ditton, Surrey KT7 0EL 01-398 4101

Ministry of Agriculture, Fisheries and Food
3 Whitehall Place, London SW1A 2HH 01-233 3000

National Agricultural Centre
Stoneleigh, Kenilworth, Coventry CV8 2LG 0203 56151

National Association of Agricultural Contractors
Huts Corner, Tilford Road, Hindhead, Surrey GU26 65F 042873 53600

National Cattle Breeders Association
Cholesbury, Nr. Tring, Herts. 024029 544

National Dairy Council
National Dairy Centre, 5-7 John Princes Street, London W1M 0AP 01-499 7822

National Farmers Union
Agriculture House, 25-31 Knightsbridge, London SW2X 7NJ   01-235 5077

National Farmers Union of Scotland
17 Grosvenor Crescent, Edinburgh EH12 5EH   031-337 4333/6

National Federation of Young Farmers Clubs
YFC Centre, NAC, Kenilworth CV8 2LG   0203 56131

National Pig Breeders Association
7 Rickmansworth Road, Watford WD1 7HE   0923 34377

National Seed Development Organisation Ltd.
Newton Hall, Newton, Cambridge   0223 871167

National Sheep Association
Cholesbury, Nr. Tring, Herts.   024029 544

National Union of Agricultural and Allied Workers
Headland House, 308 Gray's Inn Road, London WC1 8DS   01-278 7801

Potato Marketing Board
50 Hans Crescent, Knightsbridge, London SW1X 0NB   01-589 4874

Royal Agricultural Society of England
National Agricultural Centre, Stoneleigh, Kenilworth   0203 56151
London Office   01-235 5323

Royal Highland and Agricultural Society of Scotland
Ingliston, Newbridge, Midlothian EH28 8NF   031-333 2444

Royal Horticultural Society
Vincent Square, London SW1P 2PE   01-834 4333

Royal Institute of Chartered Surveyors
12 Great George Street, Parliament Square, London SW1   01-222 7000

Royal Welsh Agricultural Society Ltd.
Llanelwedd, Builth Wells   0982 55 3683

Tenant Farmers' Association
68a London Road, Reading, Berks. RG1 5AS   0734 874700

United Agricultural Merchants Ltd.
Springbank House, Basing View, Basingstoke, Hants. RG21 2 EQ   0256 67171

UK Agricultural Supply Trade Association Ltd.
3 Whitehall Court, London SW1A 2EQ   01-995 2829

2. UNIVERSITY AGRICULTURAL ECONOMISTS
(Farm Management Survey Work)

ENGLAND AND WALES

Northern: Department of Agricultural Economics,
University of Newcastle-upon-Tyne,
Newcastle-upon-Tyne NE1 7RU   0632 328511

North Eastern: Askham Bryan College of Agriculture and
Horticulture, Askham Bryan, York YO2 3PR   0904 702121

North Western: Department of Agricultural Economics,
The University, Manchester M13 9PL   061-273 7121

East Midland: Department of Agriculture and Horticulture,
University of Nottingham, School of Agriculture,
Sutton Bonington, Loughborough, Leics. LE12 5RD   0602 506101

Eastern: Agricultural Economics Unit, Department of
Land Economy, University of Cambridge,
Silver Street, Cambridge CB3 9EL   0223 355262

South Eastern: Farm Business Unit, School of Rural Economics,
Wye College (University of London),
Nr. Ashford, Kent TN25 5AH   0233 812401

Southern:	Department of Agricultural Economics and Management, University of Reading, Building No. 4, Earley Gate, Whiteknights Road, Reading, Berks. RG6 2AR	0734 875123
South Western:	Agricultural Economics Unit, University of Exeter, Lafrowda House, St. German's Road, Exeter, Devon EX4 6TL	0392 73025
Wales:	Department of Agricultural Economics, Institute of Rural Science, University College of Wales, Penglais, Aberystwyth, Dyfed SY23 3DD	0970 3111

SCOTLAND (Advisory Services also)

North:	North of Scotland College of Agriculture, School of Agriculture, 581 King Street, Aberdeen AB9 1UD	0224 40291
East:	University of Edinburgh and the East of Scotland College of Agriculture, West Mains Road, Edinburgh EH9 3JG	031-667 1041
West:	West of Scotland Agricultural College, Auchincruive, Ayr KA6 5HW	0292 520331

NORTHERN IRELAND (Advisory Services also)

	Dundonald House, Upper Newtownards Road, Belfast BT4 3SB	0232 650111

3. AGRICULTURAL DEVELOPMENT AND ADVISORY SERVICE (ADAS)

The following offices have **Regional Farm Management Advisers**

REGION

Northern:	Block 2, Government Buildings, Lawnswood, Leeds LS16 5PY	0532 674411
	Government Buildings, Kenton Bar, Newcastle-upon-Tyne NE1 2YA	0632 869811
Midland and Western:	Woodthorne, Wolverhampton WV6 8TQ	0902 754190
	Block 7, Chalfont Drive, Nottingham NG8 3SN	0602 291191
	Government Buildings, Cop Lane, Penwortham, Preston, Lancs. PR1 0SP	0772 44123
Eastern:	Block C, Government Buildings, Brooklands Avenue, Cambridge CB2 2DR	0223 58911
	Government Buildings, Willington Road, Kirton, Boston, Lincs. PE20 1EJ	0205 722391
South Eastern:	Block A, Government Buildings, Coley Park, Reading, Berks. RG1 6DT	0734 581222
South Western:	Block C, Government Buildings, Burghill Road, Westbury-on-Trym, Bristol BS10 6NJ	0272 500000
	Staplake Mount, Starcross, Exeter EX6 8PE	062 689481
Wales:	Trawsgoed, Aberystwyth, Dyfed SY23 4HT	0970 615022

4. COMMERCIAL BANKS: AGRICULTURAL DEPARTMENTS

Barclays Bank PLC
Agricultural Dept., Juxon House, 94 St. Paul's Churchyard,
London EC4M 8EH   01-248 9155

Lloyds Bank PLC
Advance Dept., P.O. Box 215, 71 Lombard Street,
London EC3P 3BS   01-626 1500

Midland Bank PLC
Agricultural Dept., Poultry, London EC2P 2BX   01-606 9911

National Westminster Bank PLC
Agricultural Office, 3rd Floor, 24 Broadgate, Coventry CV1 1NB   0203 553721

5. RESEARCH ORGANISATIONS

Animal Breeding Research Organisation
King's Building, West Mains Road, Edinburgh EH9 3JQ   031-667 6901

Agricultural and Food Research Council
160 Great Portland Street, London W1N 6DT   01-580 6655

Food Research Institute
Colney Lane, Norwich NR4 7UA   0603 56122

Hannah Research Institute
Ayr, Scotland KA6 5HL   0292 76013

Hill Farming Research Organisation
Bush Estate, Penicuik, Midlothian EH26 0PY   031-445 3401

Institute of Animal Physiology
Babraham, Cambridge CB2 4AT   0223 832312

Institute for Research on Animal Diseases
Compton, Newbury, Berks. RG16 0NN   063522 411

Meat Research Institute
Langford, Bristol BS18 7DY   0934 852661

National Institute of Agricultural Botany
Huntingdon Road, Cambridge CB3 0LE   0223 276381

National Institute of Agricultural Engineering
Wrest Park, Silsoe, Bedford MK45 4HS   0525 60000

National Institute for Research in Dairying
Shinfield, Reading, Berks. RG2 9AT   0734 883103

Poultry Research Centre
Roslin, Midlothian EH25 9PS   031-440 2726

Rowett Research Institute
Bucksburn, Aberdeen AB2 9SB   0224 712751

Weed Research Organisation
Begbroke Hill, Sandy Lane, Yarnton, Oxford OX5 1PF   08675 3761

6. NATIONAL AGRICULTURAL COLLEGES

Harper Adams Agricultural College
Newport, Salop   0952 811280

National College of Agricultural Engineering
Silsoe, Bedford MK 45 4DT   0525 60428

Royal Agricultural College
Cirencester, Glos.   0285 2531

Seale-Hayne College
Newton Abbot, Devon   0626 2323

Shuttleworth Agricultural College
Old Warden Park, Biggleswade, Beds. SG18 9DX   076727 441

Welsh Agricultural College
Llanbadarn Fawr, Aberystwyth SY23 3AL   0970 4471

Writtle Agricultural College
Chelmsford, Essex CM1 3RR   0245 420705

N.B. The Scottish Colleges are listed on page 172.

INDEX

OTHER PUBLICATIONS

Other Farm Business Unit publications include:

	Post Free
Farm Business Statistics for South-East England, 1984.	£2.50
The Outlook for the Glasshouse Tomato Industry.	£5.00
Wye Farm Management Game Manual.	£1.50
Calculating Machinery Depreciation on Farms During a Period of Inflation. F.B.U. Occasional Paper No. 2.	£1.20
Farm Planning Systems for Small Computers. F.B.U. Occasional Paper No. 3.	£5.00
Labour and Machinery Use on the Larger, mainly Arable Farm. F.B.U. Occasional Paper No. 4.	£2.00
Appraising the Profitability and Feasibility of an Agricultural Investment under Inflation. F.B.U. Occasional Paper No. 5.	£2.00
The Feasibility of Financing Investments Using Borrowed Money During a Period of Inflation and High Interest Rates. F.B.U. Occasional Paper No. 6.	£2.50
The Comparative Efficiency of Friesians and Holsteins for Milk and Beef Production. F.B.U. Occasional Paper No. 7.	£3.00
The Economic Potential for Deer Farming in the U.K. F.B.U. Occasional Paper No. 8.	£3.00
Crop Areas and Livestock Numbers, England and Kent, 1939 to 1982. F.B.U. Occasional Paper No. 9.	£3.00

Available from Publications, School of Rural Economics, Wye College, Ashford, Kent, TN25 5AH. (From which a full list of the School's publications is available).

Please send cheque (made out to Wye College) with order.

NOTES

NOTES

NOTES

NOTES

NOTES